can be exceptionally useful, whether in the boardroom or the home. In an era dominated by incessant broadcasting and attention-seeking behavior on social media, listening offers both a salve and a solution." —*Booklist*

"From communication researchers to general audiences, this informative and well-documented book will prod readers to reexamine the way they listen to others, individually and collectively, and to consider the many negative repercussions of not doing so." —*Library Journal*

"The premise of this book couldn't be more timely. . . . Inspiringly profound . . . Smart and playful . . . It feels like a reiteration of something essential. . . . Murphy is here to remind us—entertainingly and compellingly—exactly why it matters so much, especially right now. Hear, hear." —*The Observer*

YOU'RE
NOT
LISTENING

What You're Missing
and Why It Matters

KATE MURPHY

CELADON
BOOKS

NEW YORK

www.celadonbooks.com

Designed by Steven Seighman

The Library of Congress has cataloged the hardcover edition as follows:

Names: Murphy, Kate (Journalist), author.
Title: You're not listening : what you're missing and why it matters / Kate Murphy.
Description: First edition. | New York : Celadon Books, 2020. | Includes bibliographical references and index.
Identifiers: LCCN 2019034095 | ISBN 9781250297198 (hardcover) | ISBN 9781250760340 (international, sold outside the U.S., subject to rights availability) | ISBN 9781250297204 (ebook)
Subjects: LCSH: Listening. | Interpersonal communication.
Classification: LCC BF323.L5 M87 2020 | DDC 153.6/8—dc23
LC record available at https://lccn.loc.gov/2019034095

ISBN 978-1-250-77987-8 (trade paperback)

Our books may be purchased in bulk for promotional, educational, or business use. Please contact your local bookseller or the Macmillan Corporate and Premium Sales Department at 1-800-221-7945, extension 5442, or by email at MacmillanSpecialMarkets@macmillan.com.

First Celadon Books Paperback Edition: 2021

10 9 8 7 6 5

For anyone who has misunderstood or felt misunderstood

Contents

Introduction

When was the last time you listened to someone? *Really* listened, without thinking about what you wanted to say next, glancing down at your phone, or jumping in to offer your opinion? And when was the last time someone *really* listened to you? Was so attentive to what you were saying and whose response was so spot-on that you felt truly understood?

In modern life, we are encouraged to listen to our hearts, listen to our inner voices, and listen to our guts, but rarely are we encouraged to listen carefully and with intent to other people. Instead, we are engaged in a dialogue of the deaf, often talking over one another at cocktail parties, work meetings, and even family dinners; groomed as we are to lead the conversation rather than follow it. Online and in person, it's all about defining yourself, shaping the narrative, and staying on message. Value is placed on what you project, not what you absorb.

And yet, listening is arguably more valuable than speaking. Wars have been fought, fortunes lost, and friendships wrecked for lack of listening. Calvin Coolidge famously said, "No man ever listened himself out of a job." It is only by listening that we engage, understand, connect, empathize, and develop as human beings. It is fundamental to any successful relationship—personal, professional, and political. Indeed, the ancient Greek philosopher Epictetus said, "Nature hath given men one tongue but two ears, that we may hear from others twice as much as we speak."

So it's striking that high schools and colleges have debate teams and courses in rhetoric and persuasion but seldom, if ever, classes or activities that teach careful listening. You can get a doctorate in speech communication and join clubs like Toastmasters to perfect your public speaking, but there's no comparable degree or training that emphasizes and encourages the practice of listening. The very image of success and power today is someone miked up and prowling around a stage or orating from behind a podium. Giving a TED Talk or commencement speech is living the dream.

Social media has given everyone a virtual megaphone to broadcast every thought, along with the means to filter out any contrary view. People find phone calls intrusive and ignore voicemail, preferring text or wordless emoji. If people are listening to anything, it's likely through headphones or earbuds, where they are safe inside their own curated sound bubbles; the soundtracks to the movies that are their walled-off lives.

The result is a creeping sense of isolation and emptiness, which leads people to swipe, tap, and click all the more. Digital distraction keeps the mind occupied but does little to nurture it, much less cultivate depth of feeling, which requires the resonance of another's voice within our very bones and psyches. To really listen is to be moved physically, chemically, emotionally, and intellectually by another person's narrative.

This is a book in praise of listening and a lament that as a culture we seem to be losing our listening mojo. As a journalist, I've conducted countless interviews with everyone from Nobel laureates to homeless toddlers. I view myself as a professional listener, and yet, I, too, can fall short, which is why this book is also a guide to improving listening skills.

To write this book, I have spent the better part of two years delving into the academic research related to listening—the biomechanical and neurobiological processes as well as the psychological and emotional effects. There is a blinking external hard drive on my desk loaded with hundreds of hours of interviews with people from Boise to Beijing, who either study some aspect of listening or whose job, like mine, is listening intensive; including spies, priests, psychotherapists, bartenders, hostage negotiators, hairdressers, air traffic controllers, radio producers, and focus group moderators.

I also went back to some of the most accomplished and astute individuals I've profiled or interviewed over the years— entertainers, CEOs, politicians, scientists, economists, fashion designers, professional athletes, entrepreneurs, chefs, artists, authors, and religious leaders—to ask what listening means to them, when they are most inclined to listen, how it feels when someone listens to them, and how it feels when someone doesn't. And then there were all the people who happened to sit next to me on airplanes, buses, or trains or who perhaps encountered me at a restaurant, dinner party, baseball game, grocery store, or while I was out walking my dog. Some of my most valuable insights about listening came from listening to them.

Reading this book, you'll discover—as I did—that listening goes beyond just hearing what people say. It's also paying attention to how they say it and what they do while they are saying it, in what context, and how what they say resonates within you. It's not about simply holding your peace while someone else holds forth. Quite the opposite. A lot of listening has to do with how you respond—the degree to which you elicit clear expression of another person's thoughts and, in the process, crystallize your own. Done well and with deliberation, listening can transform your understanding of the people and the world around you, which inevitably enriches and elevates your experience and existence. It is how you develop wisdom and form meaningful relationships.

Listening is something you do or don't do every day. While you might take listening for granted, how well you listen, to whom, and under what circumstances determines your life's course—for good or ill. And, more broadly, our collective listening, or the lack thereof, profoundly affects us politically, societally, and culturally. We are, each of us, the sum of what we attend to in life. The soothing voice of a mother, the whisper of a lover, the guidance of a mentor, the admonishment of a supervisor, the rallying of a leader, the taunts of a rival are what form and shape us. And to listen poorly, selectively, or not at all is to limit your understanding of the world and deprive yourself of becoming the best you can be.

1

The Lost Art of Listening

I was sitting on the floor of my bedroom closet interviewing Oliver Sacks. Construction across the street from my apartment made the closet the quietest place I could go. So there I was, sitting cross-legged in the dark, pushing dangling dresses and pants legs away from the mic of my telephone headset while talking to the eminent neurologist and author, best known for his memoir *Awakenings,* which was made into a film starring Robin Williams and Robert De Niro.

The purpose of the interview was to talk about his favorite books and movies for a short column in the Sunday Review section of *The New York Times.* But we had left Baudelaire behind and plunged headlong into a discussion of hallucinations, waking dreams, and other phenomena that affect what Sacks poetically called the "climate of the mind." As my dog scratched at the closet door, Sacks described the climate of his own mind, which was at times clouded by an inability to recognize faces, including his own reflection. He also had no sense of direction, which made it hard for him to find his way home even after taking a short walk.

We were both pressed for time that day. In addition to the column, I had another story to turn in for *The Times,* and Sacks was squeezing me in between seeing patients, teaching, and lecturing. But we got immersed in our conversation, which, at one point, had us trading weather metaphors for states of mind: sunny outlook, hazy understanding, bolt of inspiration, drought of creativity, torrent of desire. I might have been sitting in a dark closet, but, listening to him, I experienced flashes of insight, recognition, creativity, humor, and empathy. Sacks died in 2015, a few years after we talked, but our conversation is alive in my memory.

As a frequent contributor to *The Times* and occasional correspondent for other news outlets, I have been privileged to listen to brilliant thinkers like Oliver Sacks as well as less well-known, but no less insightful, intellects, from couturiers to construction workers. Without exception, they have expanded my worldview and increased my understanding. Many have touched me deeply. People describe me as the type of person who can talk to anyone, but it's really that I can *listen* to anyone. It's worked for me as a journalist. My best story ideas often come from random conversations. Maybe with a guy running fiber-optic cable under the street, the hygienist at my dentist's office, or a financier turned cattle rancher I met at a sushi bar.

Many of the stories I have written for *The Times* have landed on the most-emailed and most-read lists, and not because I took down someone powerful or uncovered a scandal. It was because

I listened to people talk about what made them happy, sad, intrigued, annoyed, concerned, or confused and then tried my best to address and expand on what they said. It's really no different from what needs to happen before you can design a successful consumer product, provide first-rate customer service, hire and retain the best employees, or sell anything. It's the same thing that's required to be a good friend, romantic partner, or parent. It's all in the listening.

For every one of the hundreds of stories I have written in which you might see four or five quotes, I likely talked to ten or twenty people for corroboration, background information, or fact-checking. But as my closet conversation with Oliver Sacks suggests, the most memorable and meaningful interviews to me were not the ones that broke open or nailed the story but rather the ones that veered off topic and into the personal—maybe about a relationship, closely held belief, phobia, or formative event. The times when a person would say, "I've never told anyone that before," or "I didn't realize I felt that way until I just said it."

Sometimes the disclosures were so profoundly personal, I was the only other person who knew, and may still be. The person seemed as surprised as I was by what lay between us. Neither of us knew quite how we reached that moment, but it felt important, sacred, and inviolate. It was a shared epiphany wrapped in a shared confidence that touched and changed us both. Listening created the opportunity and served as catalyst.

Modern life is making such moments increasingly rare. People used to listen to one another while sitting on front porches and around campfires, but now we are too busy, or too distracted, to explore the depths of one another's thoughts and feelings. Charles Reagan Wilson, an emeritus professor of history and Southern studies at the University of Mississippi, recalled asking the short-story writer and novelist Eudora Welty why the South produced so many great writers. "Honey," she said, "we didn't have anything else to do but sit on the porch and talk, and some of us wrote it down."

Instead of front porches, today's homes more likely have front-facing garages that swallow up residents' cars at the end of a hectic day. Or people live compartmentalized in apartments and condominiums, ignoring one another in the elevator. Stroll through most residential neighborhoods these days and it's unlikely anyone will lean over the fence and wave you over for a word. The only sign of life is the blue glow of a computer or television screen in an upstairs window.

Whereas in the past, we caught up with friends and family individually and in person, now we are more likely to text, tweet, or post on social media. Today, you can simultaneously ping tens, hundreds, thousands, and even millions of people, and yet, how often do you have the time or inclination to delve into a deep, extended, in-person conversation with any one of them?

In social situations, we pass around a phone to look at pictures instead of describing what we've seen or experienced. Rather than finding shared humor in conversation, we show one another internet memes and YouTube videos. And if there is a difference of opinion, Google is the arbiter. If someone tells a story that takes longer than thirty seconds, heads bow, not in contemplation but to read texts, check sports scores, or see what's trending online. The ability to listen to anyone has been replaced by the capacity to shut out everyone, particularly those who disagree with us or don't get to the point fast enough.

When I interview people—whether it's a person on the street, CEO, or celebrity—I often get the sense that they are unaccustomed to having someone listen to them. When I respond with genuine interest to what they are saying and encourage them to tell me more, they seem surprised; as if it's a novel experience. They noticeably relax and become more thoughtful and thorough in their responses, assured I'm not going to rush them, interrupt, or glance at my phone. I suspect that is why so many end up sharing such tender things—unsolicited by me and wholly unrelated to the story I am writing. They find in me someone who will finally, at last, listen to them.

People get lonely for lack of listening. Psychology and sociology researchers have begun warning of an epidemic of loneliness in the United States. Experts are calling it a public health crisis, as feeling isolated and disconnected increases the risk of premature death as much as obesity and alcoholism combined. The negative health impact is worse than smoking fourteen cigarettes per day. Indeed, epidemiological studies have found links between loneliness and heart disease, stroke, dementia, and poor immune function.

Perhaps the canary in the coal mine for the current scourge of loneliness was an anonymous person who, back in 2004, just as the internet revolution was taking firm hold, posted,

"I am lonely will anyone speak to me" on a little-known online chat room. His cri de coeur went viral, accumulating a massive number of responses and media attention as the thread spawned similar threads still active on multiple online forums today.

Reading the posts, you'll notice that many people are lonely not because they are alone. "I'm surrounded by so many people every day but I feel strangely disconnected from them," one person wrote. Lonely people have no one with whom to share their thoughts and feelings, and, equally important, they have no one who shares thoughts and feelings with them. Note that the original post asked to be spoken to. He didn't want to talk to someone; he longed to listen to someone. Connectedness is necessarily a two-way street, each partner in the conversation listening and latching on to what the other said.

The number of people feeling isolated and alone has only accelerated since that 2004 post. In a 2018 survey of twenty thousand Americans, almost half said they did not have meaningful in-person social interactions, such as having an extended conversation with a friend, on a daily basis. About the same proportion said they often felt lonely and left out even when others were around. Compare that to the 1980s when similar studies found only 20 percent said they felt that way. Suicide rates today are at a thirty-year high in the United States, up 30 percent since 1999. American life expectancy is now declining due to suicide, opioid addiction, alcoholism, and other so-called diseases of distress often associated with loneliness.

It's not just in the United States. Loneliness is a worldwide phenomenon. The World Health Organization reports that in the last forty-five years, suicide rates are up 60 percent globally. The UK was moved in 2018 to appoint a "minister for loneliness" to help its 9 million citizens who often or always feel lonely, according to a 2017 government commissioned report. And in Japan, there's been a proliferation of companies such as Family Romance that hire out actors to pretend to be lonely people's friends, family members, or romantic partners. There's nothing sexual in the arrangements; customers are paying only for attention. For example, a mother might rent a son to visit her when she's estranged from her real son. A bachelor might rent a wife who will ask how his day went when he arrives home from work.

Loneliness does not discriminate. The latest research indicates no major differences between men and women or between races when it comes to feeling disconnected. However, it does show that those in generation Z, the first generation raised on screens, are the most likely to feel lonely and self-report that they are in worse health than other generations, including the elderly. The number of school-age children and adolescents hospitalized for suicidal thoughts or attempts has more than doubled since 2008.

Much has been written about how teenagers today are less likely to date, hang out with friends, get a driver's license, or even leave home without their parents. They are spending more time alone; blue in affect, as well as in appearance, thanks to the reflected glow of their devices. Studies indicate the greater the screen time, the greater the unhappiness. Eighth graders who are heavy users of social media increase their risk of clinical depression by 27 percent and are 56 percent more likely to say they are unhappy than their peers who spend less time on platforms like Facebook, Snapchat, and Instagram. Similarly, a meta-analysis of research on youths who habitually play video games showed they were more likely to suffer from anxiety and depression.

To combat loneliness, people are told to "Get out there!" Join a club, take up a sport, volunteer, invite people to dinner, get involved at church. In other words, get off Facebook and meet "face-to-face." But as mentioned previously, people often feel lonely in the presence of others. How do you connect with people once you're "out there" and "face-to-face"? You listen to them. It's not as simple as it sounds. Truly listening to someone is a skill many seem to have forgotten or perhaps never learned in the first place.

————

Bad listeners are not necessarily bad people. You likely have a dear friend, family member, or maybe a romantic partner who is a terrible listener. Perhaps you, yourself, are not the best listener. And you could be forgiven since, in many ways, you've been conditioned not to listen. Think back to when you were a little kid. If a parent said, "Listen to me!" (perhaps while holding you firmly by the shoulders), it's a good bet you weren't going to like what was coming next. When your teacher, Little League coach, or camp counselor beckoned, "Listen up!" what followed was usually a bunch of rules, instructions, and limits on your fun.

And certainly the virtues of listening are not reinforced by the media or in popular culture. News and Sunday talk shows are more often shouting matches or exercises in "gotcha" than respectful forums for exploring disparate views. Late-night talk shows are more about monologues and gags than listening to what guests have to say and encouraging elaboration to get beyond the trite and superficial. And on the morning and daytime shows, the interviews are typically so managed and choreographed by publicists and public relations consultants that host and guest are essentially speaking prepared lines rather than having an authentic exchange.

The dramatic portrayal of conversation on television and in the movies is likewise more often speechifying and monologues than the easy and expanding back-and-forth that listening allows. Screenwriter Aaron Sorkin, for example, is praised as a master of dialogue. Think of his characters' breathless banter and verbal jousting on *The West Wing, A Few Good Men,* and *The Social Network.* His walk-and-talk scenes and epic confrontations, of which there are endless compilations on YouTube, are fun to watch and full of great lines—"You can't handle the truth!" But instructive on how to listen so you have a mutually responsive and fulfilling conversation, they are not.

All this, of course, is in the grand tradition of conversational grandstanding that dates back to the Algonquin Round Table—a group of writers, critics, and actors in the 1920s who met daily for lunch at the Algonquin Hotel in Manhattan to trade wisecracks, wordplay, and witticisms. Their competitive and razor-sharp repartee, which was published in major newspapers at the time, captivated the country and arguably still defines clever conversation in the popular imagination.

And yet, many of the regular members of the Round Table were profoundly lonely and depressed people, despite being part of a lively group that met almost every day. For example, the writer Dorothy Parker made three suicide attempts, and theater critic Alexander Woollcott was so beset with self-loathing that shortly before he died of a heart attack, he said, "I never had anything to say." But then, this was not a group that listened to one another. They were not trying to truly connect with others around the table. They were just waiting for an opening, for someone to take a breath, so they could lob their verbal firecrackers.

In her more reflective later years, Dorothy Parker said, "The Round Table was just a lot of people telling jokes and telling each other how good they were. Just a bunch of loud-mouths showing off, saving their gags for days, waiting for a chance to spring them . . . There was no truth in anything they said. It was the terrible day of the wisecrack, so there didn't have to be any truth."

Our political leaders are not model listeners, either. Consider the spectacle of U.S. congressional hearings, which are not so much hearings as occasions for senators and representatives to pontificate, pander, chastise, berate, or otherwise cut off in mid-sentence whoever is unfortunate enough to appear before them. The most common feature of transcripts of congressional hearings is the all-caps insertion of the word CROSS-TALK, which indicates everyone is talking over one another, and the transcriber, or recorder, of the debate can't make sense of what anyone is saying.

Similarly, Prime Minister's Questions, the weekly questioning of the British prime minister by members of Parliament, is seen as less an exercise in listening than Kabuki theater. The showboating has gotten so extreme that many MPs no longer attend. During his tenure as Speaker of the House of Commons, John Bercow told the BBC, "I think it is a real problem. A number of seasoned parliamentarians, who are not shrinking violets, not delicate creatures at all, are saying, 'This is so bad that I am not going to take part, I am not going to come along, I feel embarrassed by it.'"

The blowhard factor is in part responsible for ongoing political upheaval and divisiveness both in the United States and abroad, as people feel increasingly disconnected from and unheard by those in power. Those feelings seem justified, as political leaders, the mainstream media, and the upper echelons of society were gobsmacked by the disaffection laid bare in election results, most notably the 2016 victory of President Donald J. Trump and the British vote to exit the European Union the same year. Voters did the equivalent of throwing an electoral grenade to get their leaders' attention. Few saw it coming.

Polling proved a poor substitute for actually listening to people in their communities and understanding the realities of their everyday lives and the values that drive their decisions. Had political forecasters listened more carefully, critically, and expansively, the election results would have come as little surprise. Data derived from unrepresentative samples (i.e., people who answer unknown numbers popping up on their caller ID and who honestly answer pollsters' questions when they do) was misleading. So, too, was media coverage that relied heavily on social media to gauge public sentiment.

And yet, social media activity and polling continues to be used as a proxy for what "real people" are thinking. Tempted by the ease and seemingly broad access, it's now common for print and television journalists and commentators to quote from Twitter and Facebook rather than going out and getting quotes that come from actual people's mouths. Seen as efficient and data driven, looking at what's trending on social media or conducting online surveys is largely how listening is done in the twenty-first century by the press, politicians, lobbyists, activists, and business interests.

But it's questionable that social media activity reflects society at large. Repeated investigations have shown that fake or bot accounts are responsible for much of the content. It's estimated that 15–60 percent of social media accounts do not belong to real people. One study showed 20 percent of tweets related to the 2016 U.S. election came from bots. Audits of the Twitter accounts of music celebrities, including Taylor Swift, Rihanna, Justin Bieber, and Katy Perry found that the majority of their tens of millions of followers were bots.

Perhaps even more pervasive are *lurkers** on social media. These are individuals who set up accounts to see what other people are posting but who rarely, if ever, post anything them-

---

* The pejorative term *lurkers* was coined by internet companies to describe non-revenue-generating users. Online platforms typically make their money by collecting personal data that users volunteer (likes, dislikes, comments, clicks, etc.) and selling it to advertisers.

selves. The 1 percent rule, or 90-9-1 rule, of internet culture holds that 90 percent of users of a given online platform (social media, blogs, wikis, news sites, etc.) just observe and do not participate, 9 percent comment or contribute sparingly, and a scant 1 percent create most of the content. While the number of users contributing may vary somewhat by platform, or perhaps when something in the news particularly stirs passions, the truth remains that the silent are the vast majority.

Moreover, the most active users of social media and commenters on websites tend to be a very particular—and not representative—personality type who a) believe the world is entitled to their opinion and b) have time to routinely express it. Of course, what generates the most interest and attention online is outrage, snark, and hyperbole. Posts that are neutral, earnest, or measured don't tend to go viral or get quoted in the media. This distorts dialogue and changes the tenor of conversations, casting doubt on how accurately the sentiments expressed track what people would say in the presence of a live, attentive listener.

To research this book, I interviewed people of all ages, races, and social strata, experts and nonexperts, about listening. Among the questions I asked was: "Who listens to you?" Almost without exception, what followed was a pause. Hesitation. The lucky ones could come up with one or two people, usually a spouse or maybe a parent, best friend, or sibling. But many said, if they were honest, they didn't feel like they had anyone who truly listened to them, even those who were married or claimed a vast network of friends and colleagues. Others said they talked to therapists, life coaches, hairdressers, and even astrologers—that is, they paid to be listened to. A few said they went to their pastor or rabbi, but only in a crisis.

It was extraordinary how many people told me they considered it burdensome to ask family or friends to listen to them—not just about their problems but about anything more meaningful than the usual social niceties or jokey banter. An energies trader in Dallas told me it was "rude" not to keep the conversation light; otherwise, you were demanding too much from the listener. A surgeon in Chicago said, "The more you're a role model, the more you lead, the less permission you have to unload or talk about your concerns."

When asked if they, themselves, were good listeners, many people I interviewed freely admitted that they were not. The executive director of a performing arts organization in Los Angeles told me, "If I really listened to the people in my life, I'd have to face the fact that I detest most of them." And she was, by far, not the only person who felt that way. Others said they were too busy to listen or just couldn't be bothered. Text or email was more efficient, they said, because they could pay only as much attention as they felt the message deserved, and they could ignore the message or delete the message if it was uninteresting or awkward. Face-to-face conversations were too fraught. Someone might tell them more than they wanted to know, or they might not know how to respond. Digital communication was more controllable.

So begets the familiar scene of twenty-first-century life—at cafés, restaurants, coffeehouses, and family dinner tables, rather than talking to one another, people look at their phones. Or if they are talking to one another, the phone is on the table as if a part of the place setting, taken up at intervals as casually as a knife or fork, implicitly signaling that the present company is not sufficiently engaging. As a consequence, people can feel achingly lonely, without quite knowing why.

And then there were the people who told me that they were good listeners, though their claims were often undercut by the fact that they were talking to me on their mobile phones while driving. "I'm a better listener than most people," said a trial lawyer in Houston returning my call in his car during rush-hour traffic. "Wait, hold on a second, I have another call." Also unconvincing were the people who said that they were good listeners and then immediately pivoted to a wholly unrelated topic, in the vein of *The New Yorker* cartoon where a guy holding a glass of wine at a cocktail party says, "Behold, as I guide our conversation to my narrow area of expertise." Other self-described good listeners repeated what I had just said as if it were an original thought.

Again, this is not to say that poor listeners are necessarily bad or boorish people. When they finish your sentences for you, they truly believe that they are being helpful. They may interrupt because they thought of something that you would really want to know or they thought of a joke that was too funny to wait. They are the ones who honestly think that letting you have your say is politely waiting for your lips to stop moving so they can talk. Maybe they nod very quickly to move you along, sneak glances at their watches or phones, lightly tap the table, or look over your shoulder to see if there is someone else they could be talking to. In a culture infused with existential angst and aggressive personal marketing, to be silent is to fall behind. To listen is to miss an opportunity to advance your brand and make your mark.

But think of what would have happened had I been preoccupied with my own agenda when interviewing Oliver Sacks. It was a short column, and all I needed were a few circumscribed answers from him. I didn't need to listen to him wax poetic about the climate of the mind or describe the challenge of living without a sense of direction. I could have interrupted and made him cut to the chase. Or, wanting to express myself and make an impression, I could have leapt in to share things about my life and experiences. But then I would have disrupted the natural flow of the conversation, halted the unfolding intimacy, and lost much of the joy of the interaction. I would not, to this day, carry his wisdom with me.

None of us are good listeners all the time. It's human nature to get distracted by what's going on in your own head. Listening takes effort. Like reading, you might choose to go over some things carefully while skimming others, depending on the situation. But the ability to listen carefully, like the ability to read carefully, degrades if you don't do it often enough. If you start listening to everyone as you would scan headlines on a celebrity gossip website, you won't discover the poetry and wisdom that is within people. And you withhold the gift that the people who love you, or could love you, most desire.

2

That Syncing Feeling

The Neuroscience of Listening

Facebook CEO Mark Zuckerberg gave himself a "personal challenge" in 2017 to "talk to more people about how they're living, working, and thinking about the future." But he wasn't going to engage with just anybody. He had an advance team fan out across the country to find just the right people in just the right locations for him to talk to. When Zuckerberg arrived, he was accompanied by an entourage of up to eight aides, including a photographer to capture him "listening." The images were posted on, no surprise, Facebook.

What Zuckerberg got right was listening is a challenge. What he got wrong—and made him the object of considerable mockery online and in the press—was thinking contrived listening was the same as actual listening. You've probably had experiences with people who made a show of listening. Maybe they went through the motions, nodding earnestly with knitted brows, but there was a strange vacancy behind their eyes, and the nods did not correspond with anything in particular that you said. They might have responded generically ("Uh-huh" or "I hear you") but conveyed no real understanding of the points you'd made. It likely felt patronizing—and you might have even wanted to punch them in the face.

If you're like most people, you get aggravated when people don't listen to you, and worse when they condescend to listen to you. But what does it mean to really listen to someone? Interestingly, people can more readily describe what makes someone a bad listener than what makes someone a good listener. The sad truth is people have more experience with what makes them feel ignored or misunderstood than what makes them feel gratifyingly heard. Among the most frequently cited bad listening behaviors are:

- Interrupting
- Responding vaguely or illogically to what was just said
- Looking at a phone, watch, around the room, or otherwise away from the speaker
- Fidgeting (tapping on the table, frequently shifting position, clicking a pen, etc.)

If you do these things, stop. But that alone is not going to make you a good listener. It will just make it less obvious that you're a bad listener. Listening is more of a mind-set than a check-list of dos and don'ts. It's a very particular skill that develops over time by interacting with all kinds of people—without agenda or having aides there to jump in if the conversation goes anywhere unexpected or untoward. For sure, listeners take on more risk by making themselves available when they don't know what they will hear, but the greater risk is remaining aloof and oblivious to the people and the world around you.

It's a fair question to ask why, in this technological era, you should bother cultivating your listening skills. Electronic communication is arguably more efficient and allows you to communicate when you want and how you want with vastly larger numbers of people. And it's true that many speakers don't get to the point quickly. People may bore you with self-aggrandizing stories or give you way too much detail about their colonoscopies. And sometimes, they say things that are hurtful or disturbing.

But listening, more than any other activity, plugs you into life. Listening helps you understand yourself as much as those speaking to you. It's why from the time we are babies, we are more alert to the human voice and exquisitely tuned to its nuances, harmonies, and discordances. Indeed, you begin to listen before you are even born. Fetuses respond to sound at just sixteen weeks' gestation and, during the last trimester of pregnancy, can clearly distinguish between language and other sounds. An unborn child can be soothed by a friendly voice and startled by an angry outburst. Hearing is also one of the last senses you lose before you die. Hunger and thirst are the first to go, then speech, followed by vision. Dying patients retain their senses of touch and hearing until the very end.

Research on deaf and hearing-impaired children has shown they can have difficulty recognizing emotions and developing empathy. There is also extensive research on the detrimental emotional, cognitive, and behavioral effects on those who lose their hearing later in life. Helen Keller said, "I am just as deaf as I am blind . . . Deafness is a much worse misfortune. For it means loss of the most vital stimulus—the sound of the voice that brings language, sets thoughts astir, and keeps us in the intellectual company of man."

But it's important to emphasize that hearing is not the same as listening, but rather its forerunner. Hearing is passive. Listening is active. The best listeners focus their attention and recruit other senses to the effort. Their brains work hard to process all that incoming information and find meaning, which opens the door to creativity, empathy, insight, and knowledge. Understanding is the goal of listening, and it takes effort.

Many of the great collaborations in history were between people who fully understood and internalized what the other was saying. The fathers of flight, Orville and Wilbur Wright; WWII leaders Winston Churchill and Franklin Roosevelt; James Watson and Francis Crick, who codiscovered the structure of DNA; and John Lennon and Paul McCartney of the Beatles were all partners known for spending uninterrupted hours in conversation before they made their marks on history.

Of course, they were all brilliant on their own, but it took a kind of mind meld to achieve what they did. This congruence happens to varying degrees between any two people who "click," whether friends, lovers, business associates, or even between stand-up comedians and their audiences. When you listen and really "get" what another person is saying, your brain waves and those of the speaker are literally in sync.

Neuroscientist Uri Hasson looked at fMRI scans and found that the greater the overlap between the speaker's brain activity and the listener's brain activity, the better the communication. In one experiment conducted in his lab at Princeton University, subjects listened to another subject describe a scene from the BBC television series *Sherlock*. During the recollection, the speaker's brain waves looked much the same as when the speaker was actually watching the show. Upon hearing the story, the listeners' brains began to show the same neural pattern as the speaker's. This coupling, or syncing, of brain waves is visible, measurable proof of the transmission of thoughts, feelings, and memories.

A subsequent study conducted by researchers at the University of California–Los Angeles and Dartmouth College showed that the brains of good friends react similarly when watching short video clips. In fact, the more in line the subjects' brain activity while watching the videos (of baby sloths, an unknown couple's wedding, and a debate over whether to ban college football), the closer the subjects were as friends. This is partly due to the fact that people with similar sensibilities gravitate toward one another. But if considered in conjunction with Hasson's findings, it also suggests who we listen to shapes how we think and react. Our brains not only sync up the moment someone tells us something, the resulting understanding and connection influences how we process subsequent information (even videos of baby sloths). The more you listen to someone, such as a close friend or a family member, and the more that person listens to you, the more likely you two will be of like minds.

Consider the synchrony that developed between psychologists Daniel Kahneman and Amos Tversky. Their work on judgment and decision-making represents some of the most influential scholarship in behavioral economics and is the basis of Kahneman's bestselling book, *Thinking, Fast and Slow*. The pair were very different personalities—Tversky was impulsive and brazen while Kahneman was more reticent and considered. But they clicked through many hours of conversation—arguing, laughing, and occasional shouting—leading to many eureka moments neither could have accomplished alone.

Kahneman and Tversky spent so much time together, their wives became jealous. "Their relationship was more intense than a marriage," said Tversky's wife, Barbara. "I think they were both turned on intellectually more than either had ever been before. It was as if they were both waiting for it." When they wrote their research papers, the two men would sit side by side at a single typewriter. "We were sharing a mind," said Kahneman, who was awarded the Nobel Prize in Economics in 2002, six years after Tversky's death.

———

Our desire to have our brains sync, or to connect, with another person is basic and starts at birth. We are all "waiting for it." It's how we find friends, create partnerships, advance ideas, and fall in love. But if that yearning is not satisfied, particularly when we're very young, it can profoundly affect our well-being. No psychological concept emphasizes this more than attachment theory. It's the idea that our ability to listen and connect with people as adults is shaped by how well our parents listened and connected with us as children.

By the end of our first year, we have imprinted on our baby brains a template of how we think relationships work, based on how attuned our parents or primary caregivers were to our needs. In other words, your ability to form attachments, or your attachment style, is determined by the degree to which your caregivers' brain waves synced with yours. Attentive and responsive caregivers set you up to have a secure attachment style, which is characterized by an ability to listen empathetically and thus, form functional, meaningful, and mutually supportive relationships.

On the other hand, children whose parents were not dependably attentive typically grow up to be adults with an insecure anxious attachment style, which means they tend to worry and obsess about relationships. They do not listen well because they are so concerned about losing people's attention and affection. This preoccupation can lead them to be overly dramatic, boastful, or clingy. They might also pester potential friends, colleagues, clients, or romantic interests instead of allowing people their space.

An insecure avoidant attachment style comes from growing up with caregivers who were mostly inattentive—or perhaps overly attentive, to the point of smothering. People raised this way are often bad listeners because they tend to shut down or leave relationships whenever things get too close. They resist listening because they don't want to be disappointed or overwhelmed.

Finally, people who have an insecure disorganized attachment style display both anxious and avoidant behaviors in an illogical and erratic manner. This is often the result of growing up with a caregiver who was threatening or abusive. It's really hard to listen if you have a disorganized attachment style because intimacy can feel scary or frightening. Of course, not everyone fits neatly into one of these categories. Most people land somewhere along a continuum from secure to insecure. And, if more on the insecure side, you're on a continuum from anxious to avoidant.

But history doesn't have to be destiny when it comes to attachment styles. People can change how they are in relationships when they learn to listen and be emotionally responsive to others. And just as important, they must allow people to listen and be emotionally responsive to them—that is, they must form secure attachments. More often, though, people spend their lives seeking or creating circumstances that reproduce what they knew in childhood. They selectively listen to people who sound like who they heard first and, thus, reinforce old neural pathways. They are trying to sync in a way that feels familiar—like following old ruts in a dirt road.

An example is the gregarious owner of a shipping business I met several years ago while on assignment in New Orleans.

Married multiple times, he talked entertainingly, if inces-santly, answering his own questions and interrupting anyone who tried to get a word in. He talked loudly, almost like a stage actor, further discouraging input or participation from anyone else. It emerged during a rare reflective moment that as a child, whenever he tried to talk to his father, particularly about anything bothering him, his father would shut him down with an abrupt, "That's enough of that." Talking about your feelings, he said, shrugging off one of my questions, is how you "lose your audience." And that was something he seemed desperate to avoid, having grown up deprived of one. He couldn't tolerate syncing on another wavelength.

Several programs have emerged in the last decade to address the lack of resonance, or syncing, between parent and child, which leads to a cycle of disconnectedness passed down from generation to generation. Intervention strategies like Circle of Security, Group Attachment-Based Intervention, and Attach-ment and Biobehavioral Catch-Up essentially teach parents of young children how to listen and respond to their babies and toddlers before dysfunctional neural patterns get grooved into their tiny developing brains—that is, before children develop lifelong anxious and/or avoidant approaches to relationships. While the programs focus on helping parents listen to their kids, participants report using the same strategies to improve their relationships with spouses, coworkers, and friends.

Our culture makes it hard for people to listen even in the best of circumstances. But it's even tougher for participants in some of these programs, many of whom experienced abuse or neglect when they were growing up. Given they expect criticism or insult, they've developed a resistance to listening, either by tuning out or talking over people, without realizing it—like the shipping magnate in New Orleans. And yet, these programs have had tremendous success. Their efficacy, measured by marked reductions in children's problem behaviors and parents' improved listening skills, has been validated in several published studies. But the real proof is the growing demand for these programs worldwide. Within the past ten years, Circle of Security alone has trained more than thirty thousand facilitators in twenty-two countries.

Many of the attachment-based programs incorporate video. In the moment, people are often too distracted by the demands of their everyday lives, or are too much in their own heads, to realize when they are being inattentive. But with video, human interactions can be paused, slowed down, and watched frame by frame. For training purposes, program facilitators, usually psychologists and social workers, watch videos of themselves and other clinicians working with parents and children to learn how to be more effective listeners. So, too, parents watch videos of themselves or other parents interacting with their children to recognize missed listening opportunities and the impact on family dynamics.

In a darkened and cramped seminar classroom at the New School in New York, I sat with several psychology graduate students who were watching videos of clinicians to learn the best practices of the Group Attachment-Based Intervention program, which is offered at six specially designed parent-child centers in New York City. Score sheets in hand, the graduate students were not only grading how well the clinicians in the videos listened but also how effective they were at getting parents to listen and attend to their children. The scoring system measured several dimensions of listening, including emotional awareness and body positioning.

In the first vignette, a clinician was seated with a mother and child at a low table in a roomful of squealing toddlers. One of the clinician's arms was resting comfortably on the table and the other was on a chair back, creating an imaginary bubble encompassing both parent and child. The child was playing with Play-Doh, the mother was looking elsewhere, sighing and, at one point, even calling her child "weird" for playing make-believe. "Look," the clinician said in a low voice, leaning closer toward the child and willing the child's mother to follow. "She has an idea." The mother suddenly looked at her toddler with interest. What was her little girl thinking?

When the lights went up, the grad students nodded at one another approvingly as if they had just watched an Olympic gymnast execute a difficult maneuver and land squarely on her feet. They gave the clinician in the video a near-perfect score and all but high-fived one another. It wasn't clear to me why she was so exceptional until I watched videos of other clinicians. By comparison, they appeared stiff, more self-conscious, and more easily distracted. And while they chatted amiably enough with mothers or maybe played with the children and encouraged mothers to join in, what the clinician who scored like Simone Biles did was markedly different. She was exemplary not only for her calm demeanor, inclusive posture, and intent focus on both mother and child but also her deceptively simple observation: "She has an idea." Which is another way of saying, "Let's figure out what's going on in your daughter's head."

It's subtle, but profound. And it's what listening is all about. Everybody has something going on in their heads, whether it's your child, your romantic partner, your coworker, a client, or whoever. To listen well is to figure out what's on someone's mind and demonstrate that you care enough to want to know. It's what we all crave; to be understood as a person with thoughts, emotions, and intentions that are unique and valuable and deserving of attention.

Listening is not about teaching, shaping, critiquing, appraising, or showing how it should be done ("Here, let me show you." "Don't be shy." "That's awesome!" "Smile for Daddy."). Listening is about the experience of being experienced. It's when someone takes an interest in who you are and what you are doing. The lack of being known and accepted in this way leads to feelings of inadequacy and emptiness. What makes us feel most lonely and isolated in life is less often the result of a devastating traumatic event than the accumulation of occasions when nothing happened but something profitably could have. It's the missed opportunity to connect when you weren't listening or someone wasn't really listening to you.

"What we're after is a snatch of magic in the parent-child

interaction, that moment of interest, attunement, and understanding, even if brief, that will stick in the minds of both parent and child, and might get them to notice and to listen later in another situation," said Miriam Steele, professor of psychology and codirector of the Center for Attachment Research at the New School in New York, who has published studies on the effectiveness of the Group Attachment-Based Intervention program.

Those "snatches of magic" are what make life meaningful and what you see concretely in Uri Hasson's fMRI scans of two brains in sync. It's the measurable moment when, by listening, you connect with someone. Steele gave the example of another mother in the Group Attachment-Based Intervention program who said she couldn't stand her baby's crying. A well-meaning person might have explained that humans are designed to react negatively to babies crying so we'll be moved to take care of them. Or maybe commiserated with the mother by saying, "Oh yeah, the sound of a baby crying can get to me, too." But those responses would have earned you a low score on the listening scale used by the New School's graduate students. The highest score, in fact, went to a clinician who didn't tell the mother anything. She paused and asked, "What is it about the crying that bothers you?"

Why was this better? Because the mother thought for a moment and said it reminded her of crying when she was little and no one doing anything. Her child's crying triggered a sort of post-traumatic stress. It made her fearful, resentful, and depressed. While the clinician and the young mother weren't hooked up to an fMRI at that moment, it's a good bet that if they had been, you would have seen their brain waves sync; that overlap of neural impulses that signals understanding and a significant relational shift. By listening first rather than jumping in prematurely to explain or reassure in a way that missed the point, the clinician was able to get on the mother's wavelength so they could connect on a deeper level. And having experienced being experienced, the mother will hopefully be able to extend a similar gift to her child. It's a model for how we could all listen better.

We are defined by our attachments in life, each relationship shaping how we are in the world and with one another. And these attachments come from listening to others, starting with our caregivers' coos to soothe our distress, continuing into adulthood, work, marriage, and everyday life. Talking without listening is like touching without being touched. More encompassing than touch, our entire self vibrates with the sounds that are the expressed thoughts and feelings of another. The human voice enters and moves us physically as well as emotionally. It's this resonance that allows us to understand and also to love. Evolution gave us eyelids so we can close our eyes but no corresponding structure to close off our ears. It suggests listening is essential to our survival.

3

Listening to Your Curiosity

What We Can Learn from Toddlers

Seated at a corner table in the bar at the Four Seasons Hotel in Washington, D.C., Barry McManus scanned the room, taking in and taking the measure of everyone there. It's a habit he developed during his twenty-six years working for the U.S. Central Intelligence Agency. A trim African American with almond eyes, McManus could pass himself off for any number of nationalities—and, in fact, has.

We sat together, hunkered down in leather club chairs and camouflaged by a potted palm, after a very spy-like rendezvous at the Lincoln Memorial. I was on foot when the headlights of his Mercedes SUV pierced the mist and fog. McManus slowed down just long enough for me to get in, and we sped to Georgetown, where he made a swift U-turn across several lanes of traffic to deftly slide into an open parking space that seemed to be waiting for us in front of the hotel. I'm not making this up.

As the CIA's chief interrogator and polygrapher, McManus worked in 140 countries interviewing terrorists, bomb makers, drug dealers, traitors, and other suspects. Lives depended on how well he listened. He retired in 2003 and now divides his time between teaching behavioral assessment at George Mason University in Fairfax, Virginia, and traveling the world doing security consulting. His clients are primarily foreign governments but also high-net-worth individuals who hire him to have what he calls "fireside chats" with prospective employees—particularly employees who will have close contact with the clients' families, such as domestic staff, private doctors and nurses, the pilots who fly their jets, and the crews on their yachts. "A background check will only tell you what this person got caught doing in the past," McManus said. "My job is to find out what the person didn't get caught doing or might do in the future."

While CIA agents are trained to be deceptive, manipulative, and even predatory in their quest for intelligence, what makes McManus effective is not some dark art. He simply gets a charge, almost a rush, out of listening to people who are different from him, even if (or maybe especially if) they have done very bad things. "Even if I don't get anything from them, I learn the mind-set, the stance, the beliefs. How does he look? What does he think? What does he think of the West? What does he think of a guy like me? It's a mind-blowing experience. It makes me better," McManus said. "It's your experiences in life that make you who you are. Even if you can't get through to the suicide bomber, it helps you maybe get through to the guy later on, who is on the fringe or who is on the fence. You can relate to him after meeting the guy who took that wrong turn."

McManus told me the CIA doesn't so much train agents to be good listeners as recruit good listeners to be agents. The very best listeners get routed into interrogation and espionage while others might get assigned to work as, say, analysts or cyber warriors. It's not surprising the agency would rather recruit than groom listeners because listening is more art than science. And the science that exists is pretty flimsy.

Listening is the neglected stepchild of communication research, pushed aside by investigations into effective elocution, rhetoric, argumentation, persuasion, and propaganda. Browse the three-volume, 2,048-page *International Encyclopedia of Interpersonal Communication* and you'll find only one entry specific to listening. And you won't even find *listening* in the index of *The SAGE Handbook of Interpersonal Communication*.

Much of what we think we know about listening comes from research on how students comprehend material taught in classrooms, which bears little resemblance to the listening we do in our everyday lives. Worse, scholars can't seem to agree on a definition of listening. They introduce a different jargony definition every few years. In 1988, it was "the process of receiving, attending to, and assigning meaning to aural stimuli." After several more iterations, in 2011, listening became "the acquisition, process, and retention of information in the interpersonal context." All fancy ways of saying you totally get what someone is trying to tell you.

And yet, there's lots of pat advice out there about how to

be a better listener. Most of it comes from business consultants and executive coaches who toss around the same ideas but use different (sometimes hilarious) terms and catchphrases like, *shared sonic worlds* and *co-contextualizing.* The advice typically boils down to showing that you are paying attention by making eye contact, nodding, and throwing in a "mmm-hmm" here and there. They instruct you not to interrupt, and when the speaker finishes, you are supposed to repeat or paraphrase back what the person said and then allow them to confirm or set you straight. Only at this point should you launch into what you want to say.

The premise is this: listen in a prescribed way to get what you want (i.e., get a date, make the sale, negotiate the best terms, or climb the corporate ladder). Listening may indeed and probably will help you accomplish your goals, but if that's your only motivation for listening, then you are just making a show of it. People will pick up on your inauthenticity. You don't need to act like you are paying attention if you are, in fact, paying attention.

Listening requires, more than anything, curiosity. McManus is almost compulsively curious. We all were at one point. When you were a little kid, everything was new, so you were curious about everything and everybody. Little kids will ask a million questions, sometimes embarrassingly personal questions, trying to figure you out. And they listen carefully to what you say, often repeating back what you least want them to—like an indiscreet comment or expletive you let slip.

"Everyone is born a scientist," said physicist Eric Betzig. "It's just unfortunate that with a lot of people, it gets beat out of them." He told me this in 2014 after learning he had won a Nobel Prize in Chemistry for his role in the development of a super high-resolution microscope that allows visualization of such minute biological processes as the transfer of DNA between cells. "I've been lucky to be able to maintain that kid-like curiosity and enthusiasm for experimenting and learning," he said.

Studies show that children and adults who are securely attached tend to be more curious and open to new information than people who are not. It's another tenet of attachment theory that if you have someone in your life who listens to you and who you feel connected to, then the safer you feel stepping out in the world and interacting with others. You know you will be okay if you hear something or find out things that upset you because you have someone, somewhere, you can confide in and who will relieve your distress. It's called having a *secure base,* and it's a bulwark against loneliness.

Pulitzer Prize–winning author and historian Studs Terkel made a career out of his curiosity. His landmark book *Working* was a collection of his interviews with people from all segments of society talking about their jobs—from garbage collectors and gravediggers to surgeons and industrial designers. Using their own words, Terkel demonstrated that we have something to learn from everybody. "The obvious tool of my trade is the tape recorder," said Terkel, who died at ninety-six in 2008. "But I suppose the real tool is curiosity."

It was a curiosity that developed during his childhood. His parents owned a boardinghouse in Chicago, and he grew up fascinated by the intrigues, arguments, and assignations he overheard. The boarders, while transient, took up permanent residence in his imagination and enlivened his later work—people like Harry Michaelson, the tippling tool and die maker; Prince Arthur Quinn, the local precinct captain in his leprechaun green fedora; and Myrd Llyndgyn, the Welsh scavenger, whom Terkel said was not only penniless, "he didn't have a vowel to his name."

The most valuable lesson I've learned as a journalist is that everybody is interesting if you ask the right questions. If someone is dull or uninteresting, it's on you. Researchers at the University of Utah found that when talking to inattentive listeners, speakers remembered less information and were less articulate in the information they conveyed. Conversely, they found that attentive listeners elicited more information, relevant detail, and elaboration from speakers, even when the listeners didn't ask any questions. So if you're barely listening to someone because you think that person is boring or not worth your time, you will actually make it so.

Think about a time when you were trying to tell a story to someone who was obviously uninterested; maybe they were sighing or their eyes were roaming around the room. What happened? Your pacing faltered, you left out details, or maybe you started babbling irrelevant information or overshared in an effort to regain their attention. Eventually, you probably trailed off while the other person smiled blandly or nodded absently. You also probably walked away from the encounter with a distinct dislike for that person.

In *How to Win Friends and Influence People,* Dale Carnegie wrote, "You can make more friends in two months by becoming interested in other people than you can in two years by trying to get other people interested in you." To listen is to be interested, and the result is more interesting conversations. The goal is to leave the exchange having learned something. You already know about you. You don't know about the person with whom you are speaking or what you can learn from that person's experience.

Ingvar Kamprad, founder of the international furniture retailer IKEA, knew this. While he reportedly lived mostly in seclusion, he would show up at IKEA locations around the world and anonymously stroll the floor, sometimes posing as a customer questioning employees, and other times approaching customers as if he were an employee. "I see my task as serving the majority of people," he told an interviewer several years before his death in 2018. "The question is, how do you find out what they want, how best to serve them? My answer is to stay close to ordinary people, because at heart I am one of them."

Kamprad's approach demonstrates not only good business sense but also a genuine curiosity about other people's thoughts and feelings. It's an eagerness to understand someone else's worldview and an expectation that you will be surprised by what you hear and will learn from the experience. Put another way, it's a lack of presumption that you already know what someone will say, much less that you know better.

———

Thinking you already know how a conversation will go down kills curiosity and subverts listening, as does anxiety about the interaction. It's why every day, strangers completely ignore one another in crowded public spaces like trains, buses, elevators, and waiting rooms. But what if you weren't allowed to keep to yourself? Behavioral science researchers at the University of Chicago ran a series of experiments involving hundreds of bus and train commuters whom they assigned to one of three conditions: 1) sit in solitude, 2) engage with a stranger, or 3) act as they normally would on their commutes.

While the study participants for the most part expected to be least happy and least productive if they had to engage with a stranger, the researchers found the opposite was true. The people who talked to strangers were the happiest following their commutes and didn't feel like it prevented them from doing work they would have otherwise done. And whereas the study participants were convinced other people wouldn't want to talk to them and the exchange would be uncomfortable, *none of them* reported being rebuffed or insulted.

Human beings detest uncertainty in general, and in social situations in particular. It's a survival mechanism residing in our primitive brains that whispers, "Keep doing what you've been doing because it hasn't killed you yet." It's why at parties you might gravitate toward someone annoying whom you know, rather than introducing yourself to a stranger. McDonald's and Starbucks are testaments to how much humans crave sameness. Their success relies largely on the fact that you can go into any location, anywhere in the world, and get an identical Big Mac or Frappuccino.

We love our daily routines and detailed calendars that tell

us exactly what to expect. Occasionally, we might inject a little novelty into our lives, but more typically, we walk or jog the same routes, sit in the same seats in class or during work meetings, shop aisles in the same order at the grocery store, stake out the same spots in yoga class, return to the same vacation places, go to dinner with the same people, and have pretty much the same conversations.

But paradoxically, it's uncertainty that makes us feel most alive. Think of events that shake you out of your rote existence: maybe attending a family wedding, making a big presentation, or going somewhere you've never been. It's on those occasions that time seems to slow down a little and you feel more fully engaged. The same holds true if the experience is risky, like mountain climbing or parasailing. Your senses are sharper. You notice more. Thanks to the release of a feel-good chemical in the brain called *dopamine,* you get a greater surge of pleasure from chance encounters with people than planned meetings. Good news, financial rewards, and gifts are more enjoyable if they are surprises. It's why the most popular television shows and movies are the ones with unexpected plot twists and astonishing endings.

And nothing is more surprising than what comes out of people's mouths, even people you think you know well. Indeed, you've likely sometimes been surprised by things that came out of your own mouth. People are fascinating because they are so unpredictable. The only certainty you achieve by not listening to people is that you will be bored and you will be boring because you won't learn anything new.

During our clandestine meeting at the Four Seasons, McManus told me, "I feel like there's very little I haven't heard at this point, but still, I will walk out of a room and think, 'I can't believe that guy just told me that.'" Like when a doctor he was vetting for a wealthy client volunteered she had a drug habit or a yacht captain who admitted to habitually cutting himself. McManus scanned the bar again, which made me do the same. "But that's the point," he said, slowly returning his gaze to me. "That's how you know you're at the top of your game."

While McManus's title at the CIA was chief interrogator, he said interrogation was his least preferred and least effective tactic. "I've never been big on interrogation. Trust me, I know what it is. If I berate the hell out of you, you're going to give me something. But is it credible and reliable?" He shook his head and continued, "I've got to take the time and be patient enough and be a good listener to get information that is going to be useful." His approach was to ask suspects to tell him their stories, not bully them to fess up.

As an example, McManus told me about getting Pakistani nuclear scientist Sultan Bashir-ud-Din Mahmud to admit that he met with Osama bin Laden. This was shortly after 9/11 when the intelligence community was scrambling to hunt down the mastermind of the attacks. Rather than be adversarial, McManus built an odd rapport with Bashir by having a surprisingly long and illuminating conversation with him about the African American experience. "I'm just listening to him as he told me all about the civil rights movement and the travails of black people in America. He knew more about

American history than I did," McManus said. "After all that, I asked him wouldn't he rather tell his story to someone like me than someone like 'them.' I wasn't sure who 'them' was. I wanted him to create a picture in his mind of 'them.'" The scientist said he'd rather tell McManus his story.

Listening for things you have in common and gradually building rapport is the way to engage with anyone. Interrogation doesn't work with terrorists, so why would it work when you meet someone at a social gathering? Peppering people with appraising and personal questions like "What do you do for a living?" or "What part of town do you live in?" or "What school did you go to?" or "Are you married?" is interrogating. You're not trying to get to know them. You're sizing them up. It makes people reflexively defensive and will likely shift the conversation into a superficial and less-than-illuminating résumé recitation or self-promoting elevator pitch.

In the Chicago commuter study, the participants who engaged with strangers were told to try to make a connection. They were instructed to find out something interesting about the other person and to share something about themselves. It was a give-and-take. Had they aggressively started asking personal questions about the person's employment, education, and family, it wouldn't have gone so well. Instead, they might have started out by talking about the commute or maybe noticing someone's Chicago Cubs ball cap, asking if the person ever goes to games—listening and letting the conversation build organically. By being genuinely curious, courteous, and attentive, the study's participants discovered how correspondingly gracious—and ultimately, interesting—their fellow commuters could be.

Curious people are those who will sit at the airport with a book in their lap but never open it or who forget about their phones when they are out and about. They are fascinated by, rather than fearful of, the unpredictability of others. They listen well because they want to understand and connect and grow. Even people who you would think had heard it all— CIA agents, priests, bartenders, criminal investigators, psychotherapists, emergency room intake nurses—will tell you they are continually amazed, entertained, and even appalled by what people tell them. It's what makes their lives interesting, and it's what makes them interesting to others.

4

I Know What You're Going to Say

Assumptions as Earplugs

"You're not listening!"
"Let me finish!"
"That's not what I said!"

After "I love you," these are among the most common re-
frains in close relationships. While you might think you'd be
more likely to listen to a loved one than a stranger, in fact, the
opposite is often true. It's a phenomenon psychologist Judith
Coche knows all too well. She is widely recognized as an au-
thority on couples' group therapy, and her success at saving
seemingly hopeless marriages was documented in the book
The Husbands and Wives Club by Laurie Abraham.

When I met Coche in her downtown Philadelphia office
late one evening, the sofa and chairs were still warm and the
throw pillows twisted and disheveled from the couples' group

that had just left. I was there to find out why people so often feel unheard and misunderstood by their partners. Coche's answer was pretty simple: people in long-term relationships tend to lose their curiosity for each other. Not necessarily in an unkind way; they just become convinced they know each other better than they do. They don't listen because they think they already know what the other person will say.

Coche gave the example of spouses who answer questions or make decisions for each other. They might also give gifts that miss the mark, resulting in disappointment and hurt feelings. Parents can make the same sorts of mistakes, assuming they know what their children like or don't like and what they would or would not do. We actually all tend to make assumptions when it comes to those we love. It's called the *closeness-communication bias*. As wonderful as intimacy and familiarity are, they make us complacent, leading us to overestimate our ability to read those closest to us.

This was demonstrated by researchers at Williams College and the University of Chicago who, in an experimental setup similar to a parlor game, had two married couples, who didn't know each other, sit in chairs arranged in a circle facing away from each other. Each participant, in turn, was instructed to say phrases used in everyday conversation that could have multiple meanings. The participants' spouses said what they thought their partners meant, and then the strangers gave their best guesses. A sample statement was something like "You look different today," which could mean "You look terrible," or "See, I do notice your looks," or "Hey, I like the new look!"

or "Hmm, I feel like something is different, but I can't put my finger on it." While participants were convinced their spouses would understand them better than strangers, they did no better than strangers, and sometimes worse.

In a similar experiment, the researchers showed that close friends also overestimated how well they grasped each other's meaning. Pairing subjects with a close friend and then a stranger, the researchers had the subjects direct one another to take items from a large box divided into grid-like compartments in which there were various objects with the same names—for example, a computer mouse and stuffed furry mouse. Some of the cubbies were visible to only one person while others were visible to both. The friends' intimacy created an illusion of like-mindedness, making them more likely to assume their friends could see the same things they did. They were less likely to make that mistake with strangers—that is, they were more likely to immediately reach for the correct mouse, the one visible to both people, when directed by the stranger.

"The understanding, 'What I know is different from what you know,' is essential for effective communication to occur," said Kenneth Savitsky, professor of psychology at Williams College and lead author of the study. "It is necessary for giving directions, for teaching a class, or for ordinary conversation. But that insight can be elusive when the 'you' in question is a close friend or spouse."

It's as if once you feel a connection with someone, you assume it will always be so. The sum of daily interactions and activities continually shapes us and adds nuance to our understanding of the world so that no one is the same as yesterday nor will today's self be identical to tomorrow's. Opinions, attitudes, and beliefs change. So it doesn't matter how long you have known or how well you think you know people; if you stop listening, you will eventually lose your grasp of who they are and how to relate to them.

Relying on the past to understand someone in the present is doomed to failure. The French writer André Maurois wrote, "A happy marriage is a long conversation that always seems too short." How long would you want to stay with someone who insisted on treating you as if you were the same person you were the day you two met? This is true not just in romantic relationships but in all relationships. Even toddlers object to being treated like the infants they were just months earlier. Offer a two-year-old a helping hand with something they've already learned how to do and you'll likely get an exasperated, "I do it!" Listening is how we stay connected to one another as the pages turn in our lives.

One of the most widely cited researchers on the topic of human relations is British anthropologist and evolutionary psychologist Robin Dunbar. He told me a primary way we maintain friendships is through "everyday talk." That means asking, "How are you?" and actually listening to the answer. Dunbar is known for "Dunbar's Number," which is the cognitive limit to the number of people you can realistically manage in a social network. He pegs it at around 150. This is the number of people you are capable of knowing well enough to comfortably join for a drink if you bumped into any one of them at a bar. You don't have the mental or emotional capacity to maintain meaningful connections with more people than that.

But among those 150 people, Dunbar stressed that there are hierarchical "layers of friendship" determined by how much time you spend with the person. It's kind of like a wedding cake where the topmost layer consists of only one or two people—say, a spouse and best friend—with whom you are most intimate and interact daily. The next layer can accommodate at most four people for whom you have great affinity, affection, and concern. Friendships at this level require weekly attention to maintain. Out from there, the tiers contain more casual friends who you see less often and thus, your ties are more tenuous. Without consistent contact, they easily fall into the realm of acquaintance. At this point, you are friendly, but not really friends, because you've lost touch with who they are, which is always evolving. You could easily have a beer with them, but you wouldn't miss them terribly, or even notice right away, if they moved out of town. Nor would they miss you.

An exception might be friends with whom you feel like you can pick up right where you left off even though you haven't talked to them for ages. According to Dunbar, these are usually friendships forged through extensive and deep listening at some point in your life, usually during an emotionally wrought time, like during college or early adulthood, or maybe during a personal crisis like an illness or divorce. It's almost as if you have banked a lot of listening that you can draw on later to help you understand and relate to that person even after significant time apart. Put another way, having listened well and often to someone in the past makes it easier to get back on the same wavelength when you get out of sync, perhaps due to physical separation or following a time of emotional distance caused by an argument.

Sitting among the crumpled throw pillows in Judith Coche's office, I learned that reconnecting, at least for the couples in her groups, is not a quick or easy process. She requires that they commit to a full year of attending monthly, four-hour-long group sessions plus one weekend retreat. Moreover, Coche carefully vets couples before allowing them to join. She said she needs to make sure they are "ready and able to do this kind of work." And by that, she meant ready to listen, not only to their spouses but also to the others in the group.

The couples who seek Coche's help tend to suffer from closeness-communication bias in the extreme. Having once felt totally in sync, now they feel hopelessly disconnected. Both sides feel unheard by the other, leaving them out of touch, often physically as well as emotionally. They come to the group effectively deaf to each other's wants and needs. But an interesting thing happens as the couples air their grievances to the group, Coche told me. The other couples are listening even if the person's spouse is not, which elicits a clearer expression of problems. As mentioned earlier, an attentive listener changes the quality of the conversation.

You've probably experienced the phenomenon when someone close to you (maybe your spouse, child, parent, friend, etc.) revealed something that you didn't know when the two of you were talking to someone else. You might have even said,

"I didn't know that!" This likely occurred because the other person was listening differently than you previously had. Maybe that person showed more interest, asked the right questions, was less judging, or was less apt to interrupt.

Think of how you, yourself, might tell different people different things. It doesn't necessarily have to do with the type of relationship you have with them or degree of closeness. You might have once told a stranger something you hadn't told anyone else. What you tell, and how much you tell, depends on how you perceive the listener at that moment. And if someone is listening superficially, listening to find fault, or only listening to jump in with an opinion, then you're unlikely to make any kind of meaningful disclosure and vice versa.

In an in-depth study of a cohort of thirty-eight graduate students and confirmed in a larger online survey of two thousand people representative of all Americans, Harvard sociologist Mario Luis Small found that slightly more than half the time, people confided their most pressing and worrisome concerns to people with whom they had weaker ties, even people they encountered by chance, rather than to those they had previously said were closest to them—like a spouse, family member, or dear friend. In some cases, the subjects actively avoided telling the people in their innermost circle because they feared unkindness, judgment, blowback, or drama. It raises questions of why we choose the listeners we do.

"Some people are much better at listening than others, but it can be refined, it can be augmented, and can be turned into an art form," said Coche, whose couples' therapy groups are what you might call master classes in listening. Coche, whose default facial expression is one of wide-eyed solicitude, runs her group therapy sessions like a conductor, by turns eliciting more or less input from group members as if they were musicians in an orchestra. The conversational flow can falter and seem off-key in the initial sessions, but eventually things begin to fall into a more comfortable rhythm as trust builds and the couples become attuned to one another's cues and missed cues, which inevitably leads to breakthroughs. "These people get to mean a tremendous amount to each other because they are listening to how each other feels," said Coche. "If a partner isn't listening, the others are, and they will learn."

Group participants even start to call one another out for not listening to their spouses. "What happens is a new norm is established of what is good coupling," Coche told me, gesturing around the room at the ghosts of struggling couples who seemed to still animate the space. "You see people break out of these bad habits they developed because that's how they grew up and they never knew how to listen any better."

An example is a man whom Coche described as a typical "mansplainer." His conversational style was to lecture and correct, and as a result, he didn't know how to be close to anyone. "To suddenly watch his face as he can finally listen and can paraphrase what his wife is saying, though perhaps somewhat awkwardly, it is like, 'Oooh . . . now I see,'" said Coche. "For this man, it is a turning point, as it is for his partner. She will tear up. It's a not knowing how to listen. Growing up, his family didn't teach it or value it. It's not purposeful on his part."

But no matter how well we try to listen, or how close we feel to another person, it's important to remember we can never really know another person's mind. And prying is the quickest way to lose someone's confidence. In *Notes from Underground,* Fyodor Dostoyevsky wrote, "Every man has some reminiscences which he would not tell to everyone, but only to his friends. He has others which he would not reveal even to his friends, but only to himself, and that in secret. But finally there are still others which a man is even afraid to tell himself, and every decent man has a considerable number of such things stored away."

It recalls a story told to me by Daniel Flores, bishop of the Roman Catholic Diocese of Brownsville, Texas, which encompasses 4,226 square miles in the southernmost tip of the state. Like Coche, he sees a lot of struggling couples. They always make Flores think of his grandparents, who were married for sixty-five years. He remembers sitting at the dinner table as a child and hearing his grandmother say about his grandfather, "I will never understand that man." That moment has stayed with him. "Here was my grandmother who loved this man, they'd been together through good times and bad, but still, there was this element of the inconceivable between them," he said.

Bishop Flores believes that expecting complete understanding is the root of many troubled relationships. "We all long to express ourselves to another, but if we think there will be the perfect person who will be able to receive it all, we will be disappointed," he said. "Not that we shouldn't always try to

communicate and to give each other the gift of listening, for
that is love, even if we aren't always able to understand."

————

Listening to people who are not close to us brings a different set of biases, but they, too, are rooted in false assumptions.
Most notably, confirmation bias and expectancy bias, which
are caused by our craving for order and consistency. To make
sense of a large and complex world, we unconsciously create
file folders in our heads into which we drop people, usually
before they even start talking. The categories can be broad
stereotypes influenced by our culture or more individualistic
based on experience. They can be helpful and accurate in some
instances. But if we're not careful, our rush to categorize and
classify can diminish our understanding and distort reality. It's
the "Yeah, yeah, I got it" syndrome that makes us jump to
conclusions about people before we know who they really are.

What happens is we meet someone who fits into one of our
mental rubrics—maybe it has to do with gender, race, sexual
preference, religion, profession, or appearance—and we immediately think we know them or at least certain aspects of
them. Say I told you I'm a native Texan. Did that change how
you think of me? Probably. Depending on your mental picture of a Texan, it might have raised or lowered me in your
esteem. Same goes if you learn I'm covered with tattoos. It's a
reflexive mental tendency that gives you the illusion of understanding and, hence, lessens your curiosity and motivation to
listen. Without realizing it, you start listening selectively, hear-

ing only what fits your preconceived notions. Or you might even behave in ways that get me to confirm your expectations. Kidding about the tattoos, by the way.

Most people think other people are influenced by stereotypes but are oblivious to how often they, themselves, make knee-jerk assumptions. Research shows we all harbor prejudices because of our unconscious drive to categorize and the inherent difficulty of imagining realities we have not experienced ourselves. None of us is "woke," or fully awake, to the realities of people who are unlike us. At the same time, none of us can claim to share the same mind-set or values as people who we think are like us. When people say things such as, "Speaking as a white man," or "Speaking as a woman of color," that's impossible. One can only speak for one's self.

A white man, a woman of color, an evangelical, an atheist, a homeless person, a billionaire, a straight person, a gay person, a boomer, a millennial—each has a singular experience that separates them from everyone else who shares that label. Making assumptions of uniformity or solidarity based on age, gender, skin color, economic status, religious background, political party, or sexual preference reduces and diminishes us all. By listening, you might find comfort in shared values and similar experiences, but you'll also find many points where you diverge, and it's by acknowledging and accepting those differences that you learn and develop understanding. Our listening suffers from broadly applied and collective ideas of identity, which discourages discovery of what makes us and other people unique.

This relates to social signaling theory and social identity theory, which are two different but related theories dating back to at least the 1970s, which focus on how human beings indirectly communicate status and values. In more primitive times, social signaling might have been chest beating or hanging a large number of animal pelts outside the family cave. Social identification might have been affiliation with a certain tribe. Today, we gauge social status based on signals like the cars people drive, clothes they wear, schools they attended, or, as is increasingly the case, we judge people by their identification with an ideological faction such as alt-right, liberal, conservative, democratic socialist, evangelical, environmentalist, feminist, and so on.

There is an inverse relationship between signaling and listening. Say you see someone wearing a VEGANS MAKE BETTER LOVERS T-shirt or driving a truck with an NRA bumper sticker. You may feel that's all you need to know about either person. It's also fair to say that they may be so invested in those identities that it does tell you a lot. But it's important to remember that what you know is a persona and not a person, and there's a big difference. There's more than you can imagine below the surface.

In the past, it was more likely insecure teenagers who would resort to in-your-face signaling to establish identity and group affiliation (think goths, preps, jocks, stoners, geeks, slackers, gangstas, and punks). But today, it's a more widespread phenomenon. In our increasingly disconnected society, people have gotten notably more conspicuous and vocal about their affiliations—particularly their political and ideological affiliations—in an effort to quickly establish loyalties and rapport. These affiliations provide a sense of belonging and also the kind of guiding principles once provided by organized religions, which have correspondingly been losing adherents. Moreover, when people feel insecure or isolated, they tend to overdramatize and espouse more extreme views to get attention.

Of course, social media is custom-made for signaling. Showing that you follow certain individuals or organizations or retweeting or liking messages or images signals values and cool factor. Who needs to listen to people when you can just Google them? A Facebook page, Instagram feed, or LinkedIn profile, the thinking goes, tells you all you need to know. And yet, this is precisely why people may be reluctant to give their surnames upon meeting someone new, fearing that person will do the digital equivalent of going through their dresser drawers instead of getting to know them more organically. In dating situations, divulging your last name is now seen as a significant turning point in the relationship. The delay reflects a yearning to be known more deeply and individually first; to not be judged by posts, tweets, and other signals—which, after all, are not really accurate portrayals.

In T. S. Eliot's 1915 poem "The Love Song of J. Alfred Prufrock," he laments the need to "prepare a face to meet the faces that you meet." Listening is how you discover the person behind the "face" (or Facebook profile). It allows you to get beyond the superficial signaling and learn more about who the person really is—their simple pleasures and what keeps them up at night. By inquiring and listening, you show you are interested in the people you meet as well as demonstrate to those you care about that they retain your interest and concern as they inevitably evolve and change.

"Staying in touch" or "keeping up" with someone is nothing more than listening to what's on that person's mind—the frequency with which you check in determining the strength and longevity of the relationship. It's all too easy to get complacent about how well you know those closest to you, just as it's hard not to make assumptions about strangers based on stereotypes, particularly when reinforced by that person's own overt social signaling. But listening keeps you from falling into those traps. Listening will overturn your expectations.

5

The Tone-Deaf Response

Why People Would Rather Talk to Their Dog

Say a friend tells you that he just lost his job, which he says is okay because he never really liked his boss and the commute has been a killer and just today it took him an hour and a half to drive twenty miles to the office. He was always getting home late and eating dinner standing up in the kitchen because his wife eats with the kids and never waits for him. He chokes up when he says he doesn't know how he's going to tell his family he lost his job. And anyway, he says, clearing his throat, he has this big fishing vacation in Mexico planned and now he'll probably have to cancel.

Of course, it depends on how well you know the guy and the circumstances, but, generally, responses like "I'm sorry you lost your job" or "You'll find another job soon" come off as trite and dismissive. "You're better off not having that crummy job" also misses the point. And saying, "You think that's bad?

When I got laid off . . ." makes it all about you. But a good listener, noticing when the guy's voice caught and sensitive to what might be troubling him the most at that moment, might say something more along the lines of: "So now you have to break the news to your family? That's rough. How do you think they are going to react?"

Research by Graham Bodie, a professor of integrated marketing communication at the University of Mississippi, shows that people are more likely to feel understood if a listener responds not by nodding, parroting, or paraphrasing but by giving descriptive and evaluative information. Contrary to the idea that effective listening is some sort of passive exercise, Bodie's work reveals it requires interpretation and interplay. Your dog can "listen" to you. Siri or Alexa can "listen" to you. But ultimately, talking to your dog, Siri, or Alexa will prove unsatisfying because they won't respond in a thoughtful, feeling way, which is the measure of a good listener.

"People want the sense you get why they are telling you the story, what it means to them, not so much that you know the details of the story," Bodie told me. Trouble is, he and his colleagues have consistently found that most people are really bad at this. Their data suggests that listeners' responses are emotionally attuned to what speakers are saying less than 5 percent of the time, making your dog look pretty good by comparison.

So it's not that your friend lost his job that's significant but how it's impacting him emotionally. Sleuthing that out is the art of listening, particularly when people tend to bombard you with a lot of ancillary information (the commute, the fishing trip, and the detail about his wife). You are the detective, always asking, "Why is this person telling me this?" understanding that speakers sometimes may not know the answer themselves. Good listeners help speakers figure that out by asking questions and encouraging elaboration. You know you've succeeded as a listener when, after you respond, the other person says something like "Yes, exactly!" or "You totally get it!"

Carl Rogers, one of the most influential psychologists of the twentieth century, called this *active listening*. Perhaps because active listening sounds so appealingly dynamic, the term has been widely adopted in the business world but without much understanding of its meaning. Indeed, the definition of active listening in the employee handbook of a Fortune 500 consumer products company (given to me by a management trainee who was told during his performance review that he needed to work on his active listening) said nothing about interpreting feelings but focused instead on things like not appearing arrogant and keeping your lips pressed together while someone else is talking so you don't give the impression that you're about to cut in. The emphasis was on what an active listener looks like rather than what an active listener actually does.

Rogers described himself while active listening this way: "I hear the words, the thoughts, the feeling tones, the personal meaning, even the meaning that is below the conscious intent of the speaker." For him, active listening was more about being in a receptive mode than outward mannerisms. The idea is to go beyond "just the facts, ma'am," which is usually only a fraction of what's being conveyed. In conversation, people rarely tell you something unless it means something to them. It comes to mind and out of their mouths because it has valence, begging for a reaction. And it's in understanding the intent and meaning beneath the words that you relate to that person.

What if a coworker tells you her office is moving to another floor? The facts are her office will no longer be down the hall but on another floor. But did she say it with a subtle sigh or breathy excitement? Did she massage her temples, roll her eyes, or raise her eyebrows? Did she say she was moving to another "damn floor"? What does moving to another floor mean to her? Why is she letting you know?

Depending on how she said it, she could be aggravated that she has to pack up her things on top of all the other work she has to do, or she could be excited because she thinks the new office is in recognition of her importance to the organization. She might be anxious that the new office is on a higher floor because she's afraid of heights, or she could be sad that she'll be farther from your office because she has a mad crush on you. If you aren't actively listening as Rogers described, you'll miss the meaning beneath the message and be compromised, or clueless, in your future dealings with her.

When someone says something to you, it's as if they are tossing you a ball. Not listening or half listening is like keeping your arms pinned to your sides or looking away so the ball sails right past or bounces clumsily off you. In any of the possible scenarios suggested above, saying to your colleague, "Oh, okay," or "I've got some boxes if you want them," would be missing the ball. A good listener, by picking up on tonal and nonverbal cues and asking a clarifying question or two, can respond more sensitively and specifically, such as offering to reschedule a meeting you had planned if she's stressed or, picking up on her romantic interest, telling her you're bummed you won't see her as much—or not, if the feeling isn't mutual.

The world is easier to navigate if you remember that people are governed by emotions, acting more often out of jealousy, pride, shame, desire, fear, or vanity than dispassionate logic. We act and react because we feel something. To discount this and listen superficially—or not at all—is to operate at a serious disadvantage. If people seem simple and devoid of feeling, that only means you don't know them well enough. J. Pierpont Morgan said, "A man always has two reasons for what he does—a good one, and the real one." Listening helps you understand people's mind-sets and motivations, which is essential in building cooperative and productive relationships as well as knowing which relationships you're better off avoiding.

———

Gary Noesner retired from the U.S. Federal Bureau of Investigation in 2003 after a thirty-year career. For ten of those years, he was the bureau's lead hostage negotiator, which he told me really meant he was the "lead listener." Now an international risk consultant helping clients manage overseas kidnappings, Noesner likes to think of people's stories as two concentric circles—like a doughnut—where the facts of what happened are on the inside and surrounding that are the more important feelings and emotions. "It's not really what happens to us in life but how we feel about it," he said. "From television, people think hostage negotiation is Jedi mind tricks that makes the guy magically put down the gun or that you just present this really great argument that persuades him to surrender. But it's really the negotiator listening to try to understand the guy's point of view."

Noesner gave the scenario of a man holding his ex-girlfriend at gunpoint. "I say, 'Tell me what happened.' And I listen, and then I respond to what he's telling me like, 'Sounds to me like what she said really hurt you,'" Noesner said. "I'm sympathetic, taking time to listen to what he has to say, which he probably wasn't getting from his friends and family. If they were, maybe he wouldn't be there. It's simple stuff, but we often don't do it enough in our everyday lives."

When there is a mass shooting or terrorist attack, it's not un-common for people who knew the perpetrator to say he "kept to himself." Family members often say they had lost touch or had no idea what the person was up to. In the documentary *Bowling for Columbine,* heavy metal musician Marilyn Manson was asked what he would say to the kids and to the people in the community where the school shooting took place, an act some said was inspired by his music. "I wouldn't say a single word to them. I would listen to what they have to say," he said. "And that's what no one did."

Criminologists have found that mass shooters are typically not psychotic but depressed and lonely, motivated most often by a desire for revenge. *The Trace*, a journalism nonprofit dedicated to tracking gun violence, found that a striking commonality among mass murderers is a profound alienation from society. This was true whether the assailant was a disgruntled employee, estranged spouse, troubled teenager, failed business owner, jihadist, or traumatized veteran. They shared a sense that no one listened to or understood them, and they in turn ceased to listen to anyone, moved only by the often warped things they told themselves.

For Noesner, listening is not just a crisis negotiation tactic but authentic to who he is. Talking to him, you get the sense that you are his only focus, that there is nowhere else he needs to be, which makes him incredibly, if not irresistibly, likable. Dozens of perpetrators who surrendered to him reported that they didn't know what he said but they liked the way he said it. He actually said very little. But when he did respond, he was spot-on about what they were feeling.

When Noesner travels for work, he makes a habit of having dinner at the hotel bar in the evenings. "I look at others at the bar and tell myself, 'I'm going to engage this person and find out their story,'" he said. "It's amazing what you can learn when you are totally focused on someone." For example, a salesman he met whose hobby was tightrope walking. "That was a frigging fascinating conversation," Noesner said, recalling that the guy said he practiced walking on a wire strung between two trees in his backyard and that he overcame his fear of falling by starting out with elaborate padding and harnesses.

Much like the commuters in the University of Chicago

study who were not rebuffed when they tried to engage with strangers, Noesner doesn't recall anyone who wasn't eager to talk to him. In fact, he usually returns to his hotel room without the other person knowing they were talking to the former lead hostage negotiator for the FBI. They didn't stop talking long enough to ask.

It brings to mind an often-told story about the late Dick Bass, son of a Texas oil baron. He was known for going on ambitious mountain-climbing expeditions and talking about them, at length, to anyone within earshot, including a man who happened to be seated next to him on an airplane. For the duration of the cross-country flight, Bass went on about the treacherous peaks of McKinley and Everest and about the time he almost died in the Himalayas and his plan to climb Everest again. As they were about to land, Bass realized he hadn't properly introduced himself. "That's okay," the man said, extending his hand. "I'm Neil Armstrong. Nice to meet you."

You miss out on opportunities (and can look like an idiot) when you don't take a breath and listen. Talking about yourself doesn't add anything to your knowledge base. Again, you already know about you. When you leave a conversation, ask yourself, *What did I just learn about that person? What was most concerning to that person today? How did that person feel about what we were talking about?* If you can't answer those questions, you probably need to work on your listening. "If you go into every situation thinking you already know everything, it limits your ability to grow, learn, connect, and evolve," Noesner said. "I think a good listener is someone who is open to hearing someone else's experiences and ideas and acknowledges their point of view."

While being open and curious about someone else is a state of mind, the ability to acknowledge someone's point of view with a sensitive response that encourages trust and elaboration is a developed skill. Noesner is a good listener because he's a practiced listener. It takes awareness, focus, and experience to unearth and understand what is really being communicated. Good listeners are not born that way, they become that way.

6

Talking Like a Tortoise, Thinking Like a Hare

The Speech-Thought Differential

Have you ever been talking to someone and got so distracted by your own thoughts that it was like you put the other person on mute? The other person's lips were moving, and yet you heard nothing until a stray word or a phrase like *sex, stock tip,* or *borrow your car* snapped you back to attention—"Wait, what?"

Your brief exit from the conversation was caused by the *speech-thought differential,* which refers to the fact that we can think a lot faster than someone can talk. The average person talks at around 120–150 words per minute, which takes up a tiny fraction of our mental bandwidth powered by some eighty-six billion brain cells. So we wander in our excess cognitive capacity, thinking about a multitude of other things, which keeps us from focusing on the speaker's narrative.

When someone else talks, we take mental side trips. We check out momentarily to wonder if we have spinach in our teeth. We remind ourselves to get milk on the way home or worry about how much time is left on the parking meter. We get sidetracked by things like the speaker's hair, clothing, body type, or maybe a large mole. Of course, the biggest distraction is thinking about what urbane, witty, or, in contentious situations, devastating thing we want to say next.

Inevitably, we get too absorbed in our musings, diverting our attention just a little too long, only to return to the conversation somewhat behind. Having missed parts of the narrative, we unconsciously (and often incorrectly) fill in the gaps. In *Tender Is the Night,* F. Scott Fitzgerald captured it well: "Intermittently she caught the gist of his sentences and supplied the rest from her subconscious, as one picks up the striking of a clock in the middle with only the rhythm of the first uncounted strokes lingering in the mind." As a result, what the person is saying makes less sense. Rather than admit we're lost, we depart once again into our reveries.

The idea that higher intelligence makes you better able to avoid these mental side trips is false. In fact, smart people are often worse listeners because they come up with more alternative things to think about and are more likely to assume that they already know what the person is going to say. People with higher IQs also tend to be more neurotic and self-conscious, which means worry and anxiety are more likely to hijack their attention.

Introverts, because they are quieter, are often thought to

be better listeners. But this, too, is false. Listening can be particularly challenging for introverts because they have so much busyness going on in their own heads that it's hard to make room for additional input. Because they tend to be sensitive, they may also reach saturation sooner. Listening can feel like an onslaught, making it difficult to continue listening, particularly when the speech-thought differential gives their minds occasion to drift.

"The use, or misuse, of this spare thinking time holds the answer to how well a person can concentrate on the spoken word," wrote Ralph Nichols, a professor of rhetoric at the University of Minnesota, who is regarded by many as the father of listening research. He started his career as a high school speech teacher and debate coach and noticed that students who worked on their listening skills became more persuasive debaters. The realization sparked his interest and led him to author and co-author scores of articles and books on listening before his death in 2005.

According to Nichols, to be a good listener means using your available bandwidth not to take mental side trips but rather to double down on your efforts to understand and intuit what someone is saying. He said listening well is a matter of continually asking yourself if people's messages are valid and what their motivations are for telling you whatever they are telling you.

It seems straightforward, but lacking awareness, intent, and more than a little practice, few people are able to do it for the duration of even the briefest conversation. In studying several thousand students and businesspeople, Nichols found that immediately following a short talk, most people missed at least half of what was said, no matter how well they thought they were listening. Two months later, most people had retained only 25 percent. To beat those averages, it's helpful to think of listening as similar to meditation. You make yourself aware of and acknowledge distractions, then return to focus. But instead of focusing on your breathing or an image, you return your attention to the speaker.

Perhaps the greatest barrier to keeping our minds on track and following someone's narrative is the nagging concern about what we're going to say when it's our turn. It's easier to dispatch more mundane thoughts (what you need to pick up at the grocery store), but it's much harder to stop mentally preparing your rejoinder. Whether it's a crucial or casual conversation in your professional or personal life, everyone fears fumbling for words or, worse, saying the wrong thing.

The stakes seem higher in our increasingly polarized society where people seem ready to pounce on, and perhaps post online, any perceived insensitivity or imagined slight. Thanks to the unpitying Greek chorus on social media, it's legitimate to fear personal humiliation and professional ruin for a rhetorical slip or ill-considered opinion. Words must be chosen carefully, which leads us to weigh our options while our conversational partners are still talking.

The dancer and choreographer Monica Bill Barnes is known for her strong and confident performances. She's a study in power onstage with her head held high and body moving with seeming ease and certainty. But she told me that listening with her "whole self" made her feel vulnerable. "I think it's an issue of trusting that you can be imperfect in the conversation," she said. "Listening is a matter of you deciding you don't need to worry what to say next," which then allows "someone else's opinions and ideas to get past your border defenses."

The irony is that by remaining defensive and not listening fully, you actually increase your chances of responding inappropriately or insensitively. The more you think about the right thing to say, the more you miss, and the more likely it is that you'll say the wrong thing when it's your turn. Just as Nichols's debate students were more persuasive when they listened, a better response will come to you when you have taken in all that the other person has to say. Then, pause if you need to after the other person concludes to think about what you want to say. While we fear silences almost as much as saying the wrong thing (more about that later), a pause following someone's comments can actually work to your advantage, as it's a sign of attentiveness.

A career diplomat in Washington, D.C., told me he married his wife because "she actually pauses a couple of beats after I say something. I can tell she's thinking about what I said." He then added, "This wife is my second go-round. The first one didn't take because there wasn't much listening going on." It's also worth pointing out that it's okay to say, "I don't know what to say," when you don't. You can also say, "I'd like to think about that," which conveys that you honor what the other person said by taking time to think about it, while, at the same time, honoring that part of you that is uncertain and needs time to process.

Always having a ready bon mot may not be the best way to connect with people anyway. In fact, according to the tenets of self-psychology, committing a faux pas creates an opportunity to fix it, which strengthens your tie to the other person. First advanced by Austrian psychoanalyst Heinz Kohut in the 1960s but more widely embraced in the past ten years, self-psychology holds that repaired rifts are the fabric of relationships rather than patches on them. Indeed, if you think about the people whom you trust and feel closest to in your life, they are undoubtedly the ones who have come back after a flub and made it right.

The upshot is that worrying about what to say next works against you. Your responses will be better, your connections will be stronger, and you'll be more at ease if you free up your mind to listen. It also makes conversations that much more interesting because you are able to take in more information. Not only are you listening to the words, but you're also using your leftover brainpower to notice the speaker's body language and inflection as well as to consider the context and motivation.

Take first introductions. We often miss what people are saying—including their names—because we are distracted sizing them up, thinking about how we are coming across and what we are going to say. Not so when you meet a dog, which is why you can more easily remember a dog's name than its owner's. But if you marshal your mental resources so you fully listen to someone's opening gambit and nonverbal presentation, it's enormously interesting and can quickly clue you in to that person's insecurities and values. And you will be more likely to remember names.

Say you meet two women separately at a party. One woman lets you know straightaway that she went to an Ivy League school, and the other immediately begins talking about her husband who couldn't join her that evening. What are they really conveying? Perhaps it's "I'm smart. Respect me" in the first instance and "I'm not alone in the world. Someone loves me" in the second.

It's kind of like the scene in *Annie Hall* where the characters played by Woody Allen and Diane Keaton are awkwardly talking on a rooftop terrace. Subtitles run at the bottom, translating what they are really saying. Good listeners, rather than getting mired in their own thoughts, insecurities, and superficial judgments, pick up on the subtext of what people say as well as subtle nonverbal details like the clenched jaw of the Ivy League alum or the solo wife twisting her wedding ring around and around her finger. Good listeners use their excess brain capacity to notice these things, gathering more than just words.

You've probably had an experience when you became so engrossed in a conversation that you forgot yourself and lost track of the passage of time. There's no reason all conversations can't be like that. Recognizing and resisting mental side trips is what frees you to inhabit someone else's story. Such listening experiences not only enthrall us in the moment, they accumulate within us and form our characters. Even when you don't like someone and hope you never have to listen to that person again, this strategy can help.

A few years ago, I interviewed a famous poet. Despite his sensitive and accessible verse, he was prickly in person. "Don't you know anything?" he asked when I said I wasn't familiar with a writer he admired. In situations like that, the work of Nichols and other communication experts shows that people generally stop listening. They become understandably consumed with thinking about how the speaker is a jerk and how they can get back at, or get away from, this person.

In the case of the prickly poet, I had a job to do and was forced to continue listening. As a result, I realized how eager he was to impress by the way he crowbarred into the conversation celebrities he knew and awards he had received. His disdain for me seemed preemptive, lest I disapprove of him first. As he talked more about his life and interests, what came through was a melancholy and an insecurity that he was worthy of his acclaim. Had I been distracted, ruminating on his rudeness, I would have missed this. The conversation consisted of him repeatedly opening the door to his interior world a tiny crack and then slamming it in my face with a backhanded remark. While I can't say I ended up liking him, I was able to develop a degree of understanding and even sympathy.

7

Listening to Opposing Views

Why It Feels Like Being Chased by a Bear

.

In Gillien Todd's course on negotiation at Harvard Law School, she tells her students to always be mindful of their internal stances, or attitudes, while listening. She tells them that if they believe the other person has nothing to offer, is not worth their time, or is the enemy or inferior or dull, then no matter how much they nod, paraphrase, or look someone in the eye, it will come off as false, and their negotiations will be unsuccessful. "Your internal stance should be one of curiosity," Todd instructs her students. Which means they must ask questions out of curiosity as opposed to questioning to prove a point, set a trap, change someone's mind, or to make the other person look foolish.

It's a hard sell for her students. Most have advanced in their academic careers by arguing their points and positions clearly and forcefully. What if opening themselves up to hear another person's opinion makes them less firm in their own? "My students articulate that fear very clearly," Todd told me between classes. "They worry that if they really pay attention or really understand the other side's point of view, they will lose sight of what matters to them."

It's why people listen to individuals and media that affirm their viewpoints. And it's also why it's so hard to refrain from jumping in to refute speakers with whom you disagree before hearing them out, much less keep from nonverbally communicating your resistance by folding your arms, sighing, or rolling your eyes. We almost can't help ourselves because when our deeply held beliefs or positions are challenged, if there's even a whiff that we might be wrong, it feels like an existential threat.

Neuroscientists at the Brain and Creativity Institute at the University of Southern California in Los Angeles recruited subjects with staunch political positions and, using an fMRI scanner, looked at their brain activity when their beliefs were challenged. Parts of their brains lit up as if they were being chased by a bear. And when we are in this fight, flight, or freeze mode, it's incredibly hard to listen. ("So tell me, Mr. Bear, why are you chasing me?")

Student protestors in recent years have said listening to opposing views and opinions made them feel "unsafe." According to a nationwide survey of college and university students conducted by the Brookings Institution, more than half, 51 percent, thought it was "acceptable" to shout down a speaker with whom they disagreed and almost a fifth, 19 percent, supported using violence to prevent a speaker from delivering an address.

Politicians likewise refuse to consider their opponents' proposals, calling their ideas "dangerous." It's inconceivable today for political adversaries to be cordial, like the Democratic Speaker of the House Tip O'Neill and Republican president Ronald Reagan, who often had drinks together at the White House. After a particularly partisan fight, O'Neill told Reagan, "Old buddy, that's politics—after six o'clock, we can be friends." That willingness to engage, let down their guards, and listen is why historians say the two were able to compromise and pass landmark Social Security reform legislation.

Senator John McCain of Arizona served during the Reagan years and embraced the spirit of bipartisanship throughout his career. Before he died of brain cancer in 2018, he exhorted his colleagues to return to "regular order" under which legislation is drafted by committees with members from both parties. He called upon his congressional colleagues to listen to those across the aisle rather than drafting one-party legislation that was dead on arrival, often never even offered up for a vote. "We might not like the compromises regular order requires, but we can and must live with them if we are to find real and lasting solutions," McCain wrote in an editorial that appeared in *The Washington Post*. "All of us in Congress have the duty, in this sharply polarized atmosphere, to defend the necessity of compromise before the American public."

McCain would likely have been disappointed if he knew how his colleagues subsequently behaved during the infamous "talking stick" incident. During the first of two government shutdowns in 2018, Maine senator Susan Collins presented a colorful, beaded talking stick to colleagues assembled in her office for bipartisan budget negotiations, hoping to inject some civility into the proceedings. Talking sticks are an indigenous tribal tradition in North America and Africa. Only the holder of the stick can speak while everyone else listens. But in Collins's office, it wasn't long before one senator had hurled the stick at another senator, chipping a glass elephant on her shelf.

Of course, no one has to wait their turn or listen to views that make them uncomfortable on social media. It's democratic in that everyone can air an unmediated and unedited opinion. But it's undemocratic in that people selectively listen to only those who make them feel secure in their positions, which breeds insular thinking and so-called alternative facts. President Donald Trump famously said, "My primary consultant is myself." A prolific tweeter, Trump represents a transformation in the body politic: people on the right and the left can create their own realities online and drive their own unchallenged narratives—maligning, blocking, or deleting content and commentary they don't like.

The result is we are no longer drawing on common sources of information. Anyone and any bot can instantaneously blast out opinions and critiques. These posts, often only as nuanced as what can be crammed into a 140-character tweet (with exclamation points!), are then retweeted or "liked" without consideration of source, motivation, or accuracy. The discourse is harsher—flying between disembodied Twitter handles and Facebook feeds—than it would be if people were face-to-face. The result is increasingly uncivil and extreme political and cultural debates that breed distrust, vitriol, and fear.

Which brings us back to feeling like you're being chased by a bear. The Pew Research Center found that large shares of the population now feel not only frustrated with and angry at members of the opposing political party but also afraid of them. A majority of Democrats, 55 percent, said they are fearful of the GOP, while 49 percent of Republicans are scared of the Democratic Party. In interviews with one thousand people about political dialogue, longtime political researcher Frank Luntz found that nearly a third said they had stopped talking to a friend or a family member because of disagreements over politics since the 2016 election.

The National Institute for Civil Discourse* at the University of Arizona–Tucson has seen a surge in requests since 2016 to intervene in situations where political rancor is turning family members, church congregants, and coworkers against one another. Essential Partners, a similar organization in Cambridge, Massachusetts, has also reported a sharp increase in calls to help organize respectful dialogues between people riven by their opposing political views.

Carolyn Lukensmeyer, executive director of the National Institute of Civil Discourse, told me her organization's work previously had been limited mostly to working with state legislators who had become hopelessly partisan and deadlocked. "But now the big shift we're seeing is hyperpartisanship in

---

* National Institute of Civil Discourse was founded in 2011 after the shooting of former Arizona congresswoman Gabrielle Giffords.

everyday situations—at work, at home, at school, at church—where people vilify and demonize each other," she said. "The level of antipathy and shutting each other out is extreme and corrosive."

Toning down the inner alarm, or the "No, *you're* stupid!" impulse that leads to ideological entrenchment is possible, as Gillien Todd tells her students, when you remind yourself to take a calm, open, and curious stance rather than an angry, aggravated, or alarmed stance. It's far more useful to listen to find out how other people arrived at their conclusions and what you can learn from them—whether it changes or shores up your own thinking. At the moment you feel you are going to react with hostility toward those who disagree with you, take a breath and ask them a question, not to expose flawed logic but to truly expand your understanding of where they are coming from.

The truth is, we only become secure in our convictions by allowing them to be challenged. Confident people don't get riled by opinions different from their own, nor do they spew bile online by way of refutation. Secure people don't decide others are irredeemably stupid or malicious without knowing who they are as individuals. People are so much more than their labels and political positions. And effective opposition only comes from having a complete understanding of another person's point of view and how they came to develop it. How did they land where they landed? And how did you land where you landed? Listening is the only way to have an informed response. Moreover, listening begets listening.

Someone who has been listened to is far more likely to listen to you.

————

Disagreements and sharp differences of opinion are inevitable in life whether they are over political ideology, ethical issues, business dealings, or personal matters. When engaged in any kind of dispute, the father of listening studies, Ralph Nichols, advised listening for evidence that you might be wrong rather than listening to poke holes in the other person's argument, much less plugging your ears or cutting someone out of your life entirely. It requires a certain generosity of spirit, but if you remain open to the possibility that you might be wrong, or at least not entirely right, you'll get far more out of the conversation.

This approach is backed up by science. Engaging higher-order thinking is what tamps down activity in your amygdala, one of two almond-shaped structures in the primitive part of the brain that primes us to react (racing pulse, tense muscles, and dilated pupils) when we perceive a threat. The amygdala is what makes you instinctively jump when you see a snake or reflexively duck out of the way if someone hurls something at you. But it's also what propels people into a blind rage when someone cuts them off in traffic or makes someone tweet a bit of vitriol so out of proportion, it defies reason.

Research shows there is an inverse relationship between amygdala activity and activity in areas of the brain involved in careful listening. If one of these brain regions is hot, the other is not. Amygdala activation clouds judgment, rendering us unthinking and irrational. When trial lawyers put clients through grueling mock cross-examinations, they are essentially training their clients' amygdalae to tone it down, so during the actual trial they won't get provoked into giving flustered or antagonistic answers that would harm their cases.

Interestingly, people with an overactive amygdala are more apt to suffer from anxiety and depression, according to the research of Ahmad Hariri, professor of psychology and neuroscience at Duke University. His lab studies the amygdala and how individuals may vary in the degree to which their amygdalae get goosed during times of stress. For example, children who have so-called helicopter parents tend to have overactive amygdalae when faced with adversity. They have an exaggerated sense of threat likely because Mom and Dad have always run interference for them. Also notable is the discovery that people with autism have an excess of neurons in their amygdalae during childhood—making them overreactive—and then too few neurons when they are adults—often making them underreactive, or flat, in affect.

Hariri told me that in the not-too-distant past, our amygdalae helped us fight or flee from existential threats like lions, tigers, and bears; but today, our biggest worries tend to be social rejection, isolation, and ostracism. "Our ascendancy to the apex of the animal kingdom has to do with our sociability, our ability to learn from each other and help one another, but, at the same time, it makes us more vulnerable to slights and insults," he said. "Other people now represent the biggest threat to our well-being, and that manifests in these social-related anxieties."

This explains why people can get in vein-popping, eyes-bulging shouting matches when they disagree, rather than listening to each other. In the moment, the primitive brain interprets a difference of opinion as being abandoned by the tribe, alone and unprotected, so outrage and fear take over. It's why political differences can ruin family dinners and friends can get in fistfights over something as insignificant as which is a better sci-fi franchise, Star Wars or Star Trek (this really happened in Oklahoma City, leading to an arrest for assault and battery). But listening is actually what keeps us safe and successful as a species, if we can overcome our amygdala-activated defensiveness.

According to Carl Rogers, the psychologist who coined the term *active listening,* listening to opposing viewpoints is the only way to grow as an individual: "While I still hate to re-adjust my thinking, still hate to give up old ways of perceiving and conceptualizing, yet at some deeper level I have, to a considerable degree, come to realize that these painful reorganizations are what is known as learning."

Not that it's easy to listen and to consider different opinions. Not for politicians who are often elected by promising to remain steadfast in their views. Not for people in the media whose audiences want affirmation of their beliefs. And not for the rest of us, as people increasingly limit their social circles to those who agree with their political leanings and ideologies.

In today's world, to associate with someone who holds opposing views is seen as an almost traitorous act. A landscape designer who leans left politically told me she would never speak to a childhood friend again after she saw on Facebook that he had attended a Trump rally. "He can't take that back," she said. "There is no explanation he can give me that would make that okay." Likewise, a corporate pilot told me he will not fly with copilots who are supporters of Far Left politicians like Bernie Sanders or Alexandria Ocasio-Cortez. "Shows they have poor judgment and lack basic analytical skills," he said.

The English romantic poet John Keats wrote to his brothers in 1817 that to be a person of achievement, one must have "negative capability," which he described as "capable of being in uncertainties, mysteries, doubts, without any irritable reaching after fact and reason." Good listeners have negative capability. They are able to cope with contradictory ideas and gray areas. Good listeners know there is usually more to the story than first appears and are not so eager for tidy reasoning and immediate answers, which is perhaps the opposite to being narrow-minded. Negative capability is also at the root of creativity because it leads to new ways of thinking about things.

In the psychological literature, negative capability is known as *cognitive complexity,* which research shows is positively related to self-compassion and negatively related to dogmatism. Because they are able to listen without anxiety and are open to hearing all sides, people who are more cognitively complex are better able to store, retrieve, organize, and generate information, which gives them greater facility for making associations and coming up with new ideas. It also enables them to make better judgments and sounder decisions.

Apple cofounder Steve Jobs famously hired people who

weren't afraid to push back on his ideas as hard as he pushed, often brutishly, on theirs. There was even an award given out every year by Apple employees to whomever did the best job standing up to him. Jobs knew about it and loved it. It's as if he was looking for people who would force him to listen when his nature was to run roughshod over them. In one instance, an employee reportedly argued with Jobs but eventually backed down, exhausted by the fight but still convinced Jobs's logic was flawed. When it turned out the employee was right, Jobs berated him. "It was your job to convince me I was wrong," Jobs said. "And you failed!"

By contrast, Apple's former chief design officer, Jony Ive, who oversaw the development of Apple's most important products, including the iMac, iPhone, iPod, and iPad, has said a manager's most important role is to "give the quiet ones a voice." While Jobs and Ive had different approaches to—and perhaps different tolerances and aptitudes for—listening, they both seemed to understand its importance. Listening is the engine of ingenuity. It's difficult to understand desires and detect problems, much less develop elegant solutions, without listening.

To listen does not mean, or even imply, that you agree with someone. It simply means you accept the legitimacy of the other person's point of view and that you might have something to learn from it. It also means that you embrace the possibility that there might be multiple truths and understanding them all might lead to a larger truth. Good listeners know understanding is not binary. It's not that you have it or you don't. Your understanding can always be improved.

8

Focusing on What's Important

Listening in the Age of Big Data

At a yucca- and cactus-landscaped resort atop a rust-colored butte in Tempe, Arizona, the annual conference of the Qualitative Research Consultants Association, or QRCA, was a cacophony of networking. For a gathering of professional listeners, it was surprisingly loud and frenetic. Attendees darted between events in the conference center's warren of Native American–themed meeting rooms, leaving zigzag scuff trails in the nap of the wall-to-wall carpeting. According to the conference brochure in my swag bag, we were there to "focus on mastering the art and science of uncovering, and sharing, insights." And there would be sunrise yoga and an ice-cream sundae bar in the afternoon.

Qualitative research consultants are who businesses, government agencies, and political candidates hire to listen for them. When they want to know what people think about their products, platforms, logos, or ad campaigns, they call a "qual." The gold standard for conducting qualitative research has for decades been to conduct a series of focus groups, but at the QRCA conference, it was clear the trend now is toward quicker and cheaper approaches that depend more on technology than inviting people to sit around a table and share their views.

The conference's exhibition hall was packed with vendors selling products that promised to reveal people's opinions, motivations, beliefs, and desires without having to listen to them. One booth had a Google Glass–type of biometric device that tracked physical signs of arousal like pupil dilation, body temperature, blood pressure, and heart rate. There was also a computer program where users could drag and drop images to express how they felt about a product or service. Kitten, good. Snake, bad.

In one of the conference's breakout sessions, a millennial with a nose ring gave a presentation on how to use apps like Tinder, Snapchat, and Couchsurfing for qualitative research. She coached us on how to use social media to reel in subjects to answer questions about, say, feminine hygiene products or frozen dinners. As part of her PowerPoint presentation, she showed us her own Tinder profile. As is typical on Tinder, her profile picture was an enhanced version of reality. And she was astride a motorcycle. A woman in the audience wearing half glasses and sensible shoes asked how likely it was that anyone would swipe right if the profile picture was of an older person like her. A voice behind me muttered that there are plenty of "horned toads" on Tinder who will swipe right on anything.

At that moment, I imagined Robert Merton, the father of

focus groups, turning over in his grave. Merton, a sociologist at Columbia University, was hired by the United States Office of War Information in the 1940s to research propaganda, specifically to find out what anti-Nazi messaging would be most effective on the American people. His approach was the so-called focused interview, where he convened a small group and asked particular, probing questions and noted the responses. It proved spectacularly more effective than the previous approach, which was to bring in much larger groups of people and let them push green (like) or red (don't like) buttons in response to more general questions.

For example, while it was thought that portraying the Nazis as bloodthirsty savages would make people want to go to war, the opposite was true. People pushed the red button. Through focused interviews, Merton was able to find out it was because people worried our boys would be slaughtered by the Nazi heathens. What he found would really rally the public was messaging that emphasized America's values such as honor, democracy, and rationality.

It wasn't long before corporate America and advertisers got wind of Merton's magic.* One of the earliest examples of how focus groups shaped a product is Betty Crocker cake mixes, which originally contained powdered egg. All you had to do was add water. But the mixes weren't catching on with American housewives. A focus group in the 1950s found out why— the women said they felt guilty because the mixes were too easy.

---

* Fun fact: Merton was a magician before he became a university professor.

So, General Mills, which owned the Betty Crocker brand, reformulated its mixes, leaving out eggs to give homemakers more of a role in the baking process. Having to crack some eggs as well as add water made it feel like more of an honest effort. It didn't hurt that the fresh eggs made the cake fluffier, but still, it took listening to consumers in a focus group to bring about the change.

In no time, focus groups came to determine the look, shape, and content of many of the products on store shelves. They still have an enormous influence on product development, how services are delivered, and what television shows and movies we get to watch. Political candidates use focus groups to decide what issues to champion and how to part their hair.

Today, though, decisions are increasingly made based on big data. The trend has been away from qualitative research methodologies like focus groups and toward more quantitative approaches, such as online analytics, social media monitoring, and telecom tracking. This is in part because of the explosion of available online and consumer data from both public and private sources. But it's also because focus groups are expensive, typically costing $5,000–$9,000 per group. Moreover, it's getting harder to recruit so-called virgin focus group participants. Focus groups have become so ubiquitous that there are individuals who have made a side hustle out of giving their opinions, getting paid $50–$100 for two hours of opining (plus free granola bars and peanut M&Ms).

A screening process is supposed to prevent anyone from serving on more than one focus group within a six-month period. But people lie. "If they ask you something off-the-wall, like 'Have you purchased a treadmill in the past year?,' say yes; they wouldn't ask if that weren't [*sic*] the answer they wanted," wrote one veteran focus group participant in an online how-to. His record was four focus groups in one week.

And yet, flawed as focus groups are, marketing and advertising executives told me listening, even to a "focus groupie," can often be more illuminating than a spreadsheet of numbers. Ironically, even technology companies that sell data hold focus groups to find out how to better serve their customers. As one marketing executive at a financial services firm in Boston put it, "The great advantage of focus groups is you get to listen to actual responses instead of seeing a checked box or unexplained click on a link."

I sat through several focus groups, and it was fascinating how quickly the participants forgot they were being observed from behind a two-way mirror. They checked their teeth, fixed their hair, and made pouty faces at their reflections, never mind that I and at least a half dozen advertising and marketing people were watching and, admittedly, trying not to laugh.

More important, the participants were as unselfconscious when they discussed topics ranging from public utilities to underarm antiperspirants. Despite my strong suspicion that some of the participants were old hands at the process (like the guy who asked a woman to get out of his usual seat), I never left a focus group without feeling I had learned something relevant to selling the product or service in question.

But how much I learned was entirely dependent on the

moderator. Some of the moderators I watched were breathtakingly bad listeners—interrupting, sometimes mocking, asking leading questions, or no questions when participants gave clear indications they had more to say. I imagine these were the kinds of moderators who led the focus groups before the rollouts of such product flops as New Coke, Cheetos lip balm, and Harley-Davidson perfume. Other moderators, though, were virtuosic in their ability to listen and elicit information. They were the ones who coaxed the timid out of their shells and bridled the blowhards so the anecdotes and insights flowed.

Which brings me to Naomi. To the rest of the world, she's Naomi Henderson. But in the qualitative research community, she has first-name status like Beyoncé, Rihanna, Cher, and Madonna. As she moved through the QRCA conference in Arizona, people would stop mid-sentence and elbow one another. "It's Naomi," they'd whisper out of the corners of their mouths. Attendees crowded around asking her to sign dog-eared copies of her self-published book, *Secrets of a Master Moderator.*

At seventy-six, Naomi has been moderating focus groups for nearly fifty years and, worldwide, is still possibly the most sought-after moderator, either to lead focus groups or train others to be moderators. People in the qualitative research field tell you they attended Naomi's RIVA Training Institute in Rockville, Maryland, with an air of superiority similar to how someone else might tell you they attended Harvard or Yale.

Tall and striking-looking with dyed auburn hair and amber eyes, Naomi moderated the focus groups that determined the looks of the modernized Aunt Jemima and the American Express centurion. Her questioning led to the Kentucky Fried Chicken slogan "We Do Chicken Right!" and informed Bill Clinton's operatives that voters were put off when he played up his Southern accent when he first ran for president.

"Here Clinton was a Rhodes Scholar, attended an Ivy League school, and he was the governor of Arkansas, and the focus groups wanted to know what part of that made him want to pretend to sound like a country guy who chews straw and drinks beer and drives a pickup truck," Naomi told me in her velvety, deep voice. "The people in the groups said, 'We don't need someone we can relate to, we'd rather have someone we can look up to.'"

Spend time with Naomi and you notice how easily she connects with people. Whether talking to a high-profile client or a checker at Trader Joe's, she has an uncanny ability to shift her frame of reference to see things as they would. It's a skill born of moderating six thousand focus groups, including ones comprised of prostitutes, men who have had reverse vasectomies, housewives who obsessively clean their homes, women who have had two stillborn children, tax cheats, and guys who drive monster trucks. In all, she's professionally listened to more than fifty thousand people.

One of her greatest talents is asking questions that don't rob people of their stories. For example, when moderating a focus group for a grocery store chain that wanted to find out what motivates people to shop late at night, she didn't ask participants what would seem like the most obvious questions:

"Do you shop late at night because you didn't get around to it during the day?" "Is it because stores are less crowded at night?" "Do you like to shop late because that's when stores re-stock their shelves?" All are logical reasons to shop at night and likely would have gotten affirmative responses had she asked.

Nor did Naomi simply ask why they shopped late at night because, she told me, "Why?" tends to make people defensive—like they have to justify themselves. Instead, Naomi turned her question into an invitation: "Tell me about the last time you went to the store after 11:00 p.m." A quiet, unassuming woman who had said little up to that point raised her hand. "I had just smoked a joint and was looking for a ménage à trois—me, Ben, and Jerry," she said. Insights like that are why people hire Naomi.

Born a mixed-race child in Louisiana in the 1940s, her fa-ther was Joseph Henry Hairston, the first African American helicopter pilot in the United States Army. Because of his military service, Naomi attended fourteen different elemen-tary schools before she was ten. And after that, she was one of seven black children who integrated her Washington, D.C., middle school in the 1950s. "I feel my childhood trained me for my career," Naomi said. "I had to learn to easily establish rapport with people." Being the new kid and, later, the kid who was the object of protests, she said, taught her how to "listen and size people up pretty quick."

Naomi told me this while we were seated at the dining room table in her colonial-style home in Rockville. It was rain-ing outside, and the water I tracked in was quickly dispatched with a Swiffer, another product Naomi's moderating skills helped shape. Swiffers are a popular line of cleaning products based on the "razor-and-blades" model where customers buy the long mop-like handle and then have to keep buying the disposable cleaning cloths that go on them. "I didn't create Swiffers, but I was there at the birthing," said Naomi.

Swiffers sprang in part from a focus group of so-called super cleaners, women for whom a clean house was not only "next to Godliness" but also a measure of being a good wife and mother. As Naomi encouraged these women to talk about their lives and cleaning rituals, one participant mentioned she felt guilty when she used paper towels instead of cloth rags that she could wash and reuse. Guilty? Naomi wanted to know more about that. The woman explained that to make herself feel less wasteful, she saved "lightly used" paper towels—the ones she used to dry her hands, pat down lettuce, or wipe up water splashed on the counter—and at the end of the day, she threw the damp towels on the floor and used her foot to mop up any accumulated grime. The other women in the focus group chimed in that they did the same thing. "And that led to a paper towel on a stick," Naomi said, aka the Swiffer.

Naomi's mantra is: "What matters in life cannot be counted." She has nothing against quantitative methods, which she's used many times for clients, usually in the form of surveys. But those experiences taught her that it takes "a whole lot of listening" and not just tallying numbers to understand people's quirky feelings, habits, and motivations. A survey or poll couldn't have predicted that homemakers' skating around on damp paper towels to assuage their guilt would give rise to a half-billion-dollar brand sold in fifteen countries. "If you poll enough people, then you can tell a story; it's not the truth, it's just a story," Naomi said. The power of qualitative research— the power of listening—is that it explains the numbers and possibly reveals how the numbers come up short. Combining quantitative and qualitative approaches may not get you the whole truth, Naomi said, but you will get a "truer truth."

That's also the view of Matthew Salganik, a professor of sociology at Princeton University, who is affiliated with several of Princeton's interdisciplinary research centers, including the Center for Information Technology Policy and the Center for Statistics and Machine Learning. He wrote about the limitations of big data in his book, *Bit by Bit: Social Research in the Digital Age.* He explained to me that, broadly speaking, the difficulty with looking for answers in data sets is you become like a drunk looking for his keys under a lamppost. Ask the drunk why he's looking for his keys under the lamppost, and the drunk says, "Because that's where the light is." Data sets shed light only on what's in the data set.

This means that algorithms, which are derived from data sets, are similarly limited. Go back and look at Charles Darwin's wide-ranging reading list and you can imagine that had he made buying decisions based on Amazon's algorithmic recommendations, we might not have *On the Origin of Species.* In addition to many books pertaining to zoology and titles like

Thomas Malthus's *Population* and Adam Smith's *The Theory of Moral Sentiments,* Darwin also read French studies on the influence of prostitution on morals and public hygiene, Daniel Defoe's *Robinson Crusoe,* Shakespeare's works, and novels by Jane Austen. He was following the threads of his own idiosyncratic and unpredictable interests, which fed his creativity and informed his scientific output. Darwin was human, and humans will surprise you. Our ways of thinking and the paths we take in life are hard to fathom, much less forecast using a reductive formula.

It's a sobering lesson for companies that rely on so-called social media listening tools. These are algorithms that monitor and analyze data from sites like Twitter, Instagram, and Facebook to gauge customers' inclinations and attitudes. Salganik told me using social media data to learn about human behavior is like learning about human behavior by watching people in a casino. They are both highly engineered environments that tell you something about human behavior, but it's not typical human behavior.

Listening is the opposite of algorithmic approaches. "Algorithms aspire to make guesses that will be as accurate as possible," Salganik said. "They don't aspire to understand." Moreover, he said, many quantitative analysts don't even want to know what the data is. All they want is a spreadsheet of numbers with data populating, say, the first 100 columns, so they can come up with a formula for what goes in column 101. It's irrelevant to them what or who the data represents or the real-life problems the data might help solve. Based on his experience, Salganik said, that kind of blind approach generally doesn't work out very well: "I think the more you understand about what you're doing, the better the statistical model you will build, and if you actually really, deeply understand the people represented by the data, it will probably work even better." In other words, even in the era of abundant data, we need to listen to get to understanding.

For Naomi, the hardest thing about listening is resisting the urge to insert her point of view instead of just taking in what people have to say. That's an advantage of purely quantitative approaches—when you know nothing but the numbers, your ego and beliefs are less likely to influence the results. But when you're face-to-face with someone, this can happen directly by straight-up voicing your opinion, or indirectly by asking questions in a leading way. Or you can telegraph your bias nonverbally with an encouraging nod or disapproving sigh. "It's hard to hold it inside," said Naomi. "But when you get good at it, you can pull back the curtain to people's lives and see what's in there; and my goodness, I've learned things about our world that I would never have learned in another job."

Naomi has what I have come to recognize as the listener's demeanor. By that, I mean she's exceptionally calm and has an expression that transmits interest and acceptance. Her eyes don't dart, her fingers don't fidget, and her body seems always relaxed and open. I spent several hours interviewing her and observing her interactions with others, and not once did I see her cross her legs or arms. When she was with someone, she never gave the slightest indication she was on a schedule or there was somewhere else she'd rather be. My most vivid image of Naomi is her sitting with her elbows bent in front of her on the table, cheeks resting in her hands, eyes wide, listening like a rapt teenager. "The real secret to listening I've learned is that it's not about me," Naomi said at one point. "I'm holding my cup out in front of me. I want them to fill my cup and not pour anything in their cup."

In a position now to pick and choose, Naomi has given up political work to focus exclusively on clients who sell consumer products. "The political arena even for market research can get a little smarmy," she said. "They are listening for something, not to people." She also travels widely to train employees at Fortune 500 companies how to moderate their own focus groups. Holding focus groups in-house rather than hiring qualitative research consultants is becoming more common and not something Naomi necessarily endorses because it creates all kinds of biases. "You tend to not listen very well when it's your boss's idea you're asking people about," she said. "You ask questions in a way, and hear answers in a way, and write your reports in a way that will make your boss happy."

Information is only as useful as how it's collected and interpreted. Algorithms are only as good as the scope and reliability of the data sets to which they are applied. So, too, the findings of a qualitative researcher are only as good as that individual's neutrality, perceptiveness, and skill at eliciting anecdote and emotion—in other words, how well the qualitative researcher listens. At best, a quant can give you broad brushstrokes while a good qual can provide finer detail. Both approaches are valid and when used in concert can be extremely revealing. But when it comes to human interactions and divining individuals' unique motivations, proclivities, and potentials, listening is, so far, the best and most accurate tool.

9

Improvisational Listening

A Funny Thing Happened on the Way to Work

Back in 2012, Google commissioned a study to find out what made a great team. Most of Google's projects are carried out by teams, and the company wanted to understand why some groups got along and got things done while others developed animosities and petty resentments that led to infighting, backbiting, and passive-aggressive dysfunction. What was the special alchemy of personalities, process, and protocol that made people work well together?

A task force (code-named Project Aristotle) comprised of statisticians, organizational psychologists, sociologists, and engineers examined 180 of Google's employee teams. They scrutinized team members' personality traits, backgrounds, hobbies, and daily habits and found no predictive patterns of a group's success or failure. How teams were structured, how they measured their progress, and how often they met were also all over the map.

After three years of collecting data, the researchers finally reached some conclusions about what made for cohesive and effective teams. What they found was that the most productive teams were the ones where members spoke in roughly the same proportion, known as "equality in distribution of conversational turn-taking." The best teams also had higher "average social sensitivity," which means they were good at intuiting one another's feelings based on things like tone of voice, facial expressions, and other nonverbal cues.

In other words, Google found out that successful teams listened to one another. Members took turns, heard one another out, and paid attention to nonverbal cues to pick up on unspoken thoughts and feelings. This led to responses that were more considerate and on point. It also created an atmosphere of so-called psychological safety, where people were more likely to share information and ideas without fear of being talked over or dismissed.

While this was a revelation at Google, our friend Ralph Nichols, the father of listening research, said the very same thing in the 1950s. The only difference is that back then, Nichols said listening would make you better at your job. In today's economy, listening likely *is* your job. Nearly all job growth since 1980 has been in occupations with higher levels of social interaction, whereas positions that require predominantly analytical and mathematical reasoning—that can be turned into an algorithm—have been disappearing.

Few products or services today are made or carried out end-to-end by one person. Google is not an exception. Most businesses rely on teams of employees to get things done. A study published in *Harvard Business Review* found that during the last two decades, "the time spent by managers and employees in collaborative activities has ballooned by 50 percent or more." At many companies, employees can spend as much as 80 percent of their day communicating with others.

But recognizing the importance of listening and getting employees to actually do it are two very different things. Some employers have added sections on "active listening" to their employee handbooks, but, as mentioned earlier, the concept tends to be vaguely or inaccurately defined. Employers also sometimes bring in career coaches and business psychologists to help employees listen better. But employees tend to resist and resent any suggestion that they might have "issues." Which brings us to one of the more interesting and effective methods for improving employees' listening skills: improvisational comedy. Many large companies, including Google, Cisco, American Express, Ford, Procter & Gamble, Deloitte, and DuPont, have given it a try.

To find out more, I went to Second City, the improvisational comedy mecca in Chicago where Tina Fey, Stephen Colbert, Steve Carell, Amy Poehler, and so many other famous comedians and comedy writers got their starts. There, I met artistic director Matt Hovde, who, in addition to directing comedy shows at Second City, also oversees the improv training program. He was gripping a coffee and looking a bit weary, having spent the previous week auditioning 350 people for just six cast openings. He pinched the bridge of his nose when he told me a lot of would-be comedians aren't as funny as they think they are.

But Hovde rallied when we started talking about listening. It's a skill he considers essential to his art. "Improv actors don't know what's going to happen next in a scene," he said. "We train ourselves to be very sensitive to what's happening onstage; to listen to what our scene partners are saying and what they mean, because if we miss those details, scenes will make less sense and will seem less magical or funny to an audience."

In a typical beginner improv class, Hovde told me people miss their scene partners' cues again and again because they formed incorrect assumptions about where the scene was going, talked over their partners, rushed their partners, or were intent on getting in the last word. "In many art forms, there is the perception that the artist must be selfish or self-centered, but in improvisation, it works the opposite way," Hovde said. "We focus a lot in improv on taking care of and making our scene partners look good, and listening is a fundamental skill in being able to do that."

When teaching a class, Hovde holds out his arm and asks students, "If a story someone is telling you starts at the shoulder and ends at the fingertips, where do we stop listening?" They generally agree that they stop listening at the elbow and start thinking of what they want to say. To stop them from doing that, Hovde has them play a game of group storytelling. He gives them a title, and when he points at someone, it is that person's turn to be the narrator of the story, making it up as they go along. Hovde can switch narrators at any time, even when someone is mid-sentence. The following person has to have been listening carefully to pick up the thread. Not surprisingly, there are a lot of deer-in-the-headlights looks when people get tapped.

"It's really hard for people to do it successfully because they want to control where the story is going and they are already filling in the blanks about what the story should be about," Hovde told me. "At first, people tend to freeze up a little bit because they have to rewind their brain and surrender what they wanted to happen and submit to where the last person left off. They have to give over control and really be in the moment."

To understand what he was talking about, he recommended I take, and not just observe, a class. And so I did, along with a dozen others, many of whom said they were there for "professional development"—that is, their employer had told them they needed to work on being a team player. Our instructor was Stephanie Anderson, a veteran improv performer who managed to be quick-witted without being cutting or unkind, putting the class at ease even as she asked us to do things outside our comfort zones.

Like Hovde, Anderson had us do the group storytelling exercise. But in our class, the problem was more often people grabbing for attention than losing the thread of the narrative. Some of my classmates said things that were so silly, absurd, or out of nowhere that the next person had a really hard time coming up with something logical to follow. They went for a cheap, quick laugh at the expense of a bigger, funnier payoff later, built on each person's contribution. It was like that train-wreck moment during a work meeting or dinner party when someone says something so weirdly out of context or inept that it makes everyone else laugh uncomfortably and shift in their seats.

Two other listening-intensive exercises Anderson had us do were speaking with one voice and mirroring. In the former, you pair up with another person and try to talk as if you are one being. Seated in chairs facing each other, one person starts speaking, and you try to say everything your partner says as simultaneously as possible. And then you switch. Mirroring is similar, only you must match each other's facial expressions and body movements. Maintaining eye contact during these exercises is crucial because only by using your eyes can you signal that you're handing off the leader role. The intent, of course, is to get people to focus on each other; to listen so carefully that they sync up mentally and physically. Maintaining focus is as important for the leader as the follower because the leader has to be sensitive to avoid doing or saying something that makes the other person uncomfortable.

But again, our class had its attention grabbers. During the mirroring exercise, for example, I watched as one woman—let's call her Ms. Yoga Pose—took her foot in the palm of her hand and slowly raised it over her head. Her less flexible partner grimaced and struggled as he tried to match her movements. All the while, Ms. Yoga Pose smiled brightly and insistently motioned with her head for him to continue to lift his foot despite his clear agony.

"Listening is a long learning curve," Anderson told me after class. She said it's one of the toughest parts of teaching improv and a frequent topic of discussion in staff meetings as she and other instructors brainstorm ways to make people more attentive and aware of their impact on others. "I like to think of improv as medicine," Anderson said. "Instead of thinking, 'This person is a jerk and out for themselves,' I think, 'Oh, man, this person is really struggling to be seen.'" In her experience, it all boils down to insecurity. "Their concern is they are not enough," she said. "So they will use whatever tactics they think will work for them." The most common tactics are showing off, withdrawing into a corner, or sometimes even getting hostile when others don't think they are funny— "What's wrong with you? Don't you get it?"

Anderson has particular insight because she used to work as an aide on a teen psychiatric unit. She first took improv classes as a de-stressor but soon realized that part of what was making her job stressful was she was more reactive than active in her listening. "At work, it was like I was this boulder on some shore and stormy water was crashing down on me," she said. "I didn't see trouble before it started because I wasn't present. I was always thinking about the next thing."

With improv training, she said, she became more aware of and sensitive to signs of an impending outburst or aggression so she could intervene before a patient acted out or before a fellow staff member got too overwhelmed. "It's an amazing thing to realize that you get to set the tone within your space," Anderson said. "People don't realize the power they have when they learn to listen."

She was promoted to be the ward's education coordinator and began teaching improv to combined classes of patients and staff members, which transformed the climate on the unit. "It humanized an authoritative nurse who was mostly known for yelling at everybody because the kids would see that he was also afraid to be in the moment and think on his feet," Anderson said. "I think it helped patients talk about their feelings in group therapy because everyone had already taken a low-level risk of listening and responding to each other during the improv exercises." Interestingly, another mental health worker, the famous psychoanalyst Carl Jung, early in his career, did a kind of therapeutic improv with patients who wouldn't speak. He mirrored their gestures and movements until they felt "heard" by him and started to talk.

Now at Second City, Anderson teaches classes to professionals hoping to improve their performance at work as well as classes for those with social anxiety or Asperger's syndrome. She has also been recruited to teach improv to students at the University of Chicago Booth School of Business, the University of Illinois at Chicago College of Business, and at Northwestern University Feinberg School of Medicine.

No matter who is in the class (including a journalist doing research for a book), her approach is fundamentally the same: getting people to listen to one another and have meaningful exchanges. Anderson is not far off when she describes improv as medicinal or therapeutic. Week by week, in doing the exercises, people start to realize the behaviors that keep them from connecting with people. Remember Ms. Yoga Pose? At the conclusion of the class, during which she tried to turn her partner into a human pretzel, she said, "I'm beginning to think my need to show what I can do is keeping me from finding out what other people can do and what we can do together."

To be successful at improvisational comedy and also the improvisation that is your real life, listening is critical. Controlling the narrative and grabbing for attention make for one-sided conversations and kill collaboration. Rather than advancing your agenda, it really just holds you back. The joy and benefit of human interactions come from a reciprocal focusing on one another's words and actions, and being ready and willing to respond and expand on every contribution. The result is mutual understanding and even appreciation. As fun as it is to watch talented improv performers effortlessly riff off each other, it's even more satisfying to be in a good conversation where you are both listening and helping to develop each other's thoughts.

Moreover, listening is essential to being funny. A vast body of evidence indicates humor is an asset in forming and maintaining relationships both professionally and personally. In work environments, successful attempts at humor lead to perceptions of competence and confidence. In romantic relationships, successful humor is a gauge of intimacy and security. But the operative word here is *successful*. Unsuccessful humor has the opposite effect. Taking an improv class taught me that people don't so much have a fixed sense of humor as a variable ability to sense humor, depending on how well they listen. Whether telling jokes in front of a crowd at a comedy club or just trying to inject a little levity into a normal conversation, you won't be funny unless you accurately read your audience.

The cartoon and humor editor for *Esquire* and former *New Yorker* cartoon editor, Bob Mankoff, told me, "Dating is a ritual of getting to know another person well enough to laugh." To have an inside joke, to be able to make someone smile even when that person is mad at you, to have license to let down your guard and be silly, requires the investment of listening. "You have to listen to them long enough to be able to repeat back something they said and put a funny twist on it and also to know what the lines are that you'd better not cross," said Mankoff, who has a background in experimental psychology and has taught humor theory at Fordham University and Swarthmore College.

Making a joke also involves being vulnerable. You're putting yourself out there, hoping your humor will be appreciated. You are more likely to take that risk if the other person has proven an attentive and responsive listener and vice versa. Indeed, shared humor is a primary indicator of feelings of connectedness. People who fear intimacy tend to use divisive, put-down, or mean humor, which discourages listening by making people defensive.

If you think of the people in your life who can make you burst out laughing, it's usually your closest confidants. That's because you feel free enough to let loose with them but also because the things that are the funniest to us are often the most personal. There are likely inside jokes and familiar gags you have with your romantic partner or best friend that are side-splittingly funny to the two of you but leave others scratching their heads. And when you try to explain it, they are still baffled because they haven't been listening in on the long-running conversation that has defined your relationship. They don't have the same deep, mutual understanding. When people say, "I guess you had to be there," it's true. Funny is a by-product of honesty, intimacy, and familiarity.

Shared humor is a form of connectedness born out of listening. It's a collaborative dynamic that involves the exploration and elaboration of ideas and feelings. The same improvisational interplay is required for any cooperative endeavor, which is why listening is so crucial in the modern workplace. Those who preempt, dominate, or otherwise curb the conversation are unlikely to succeed in their careers, much less have fulfilling personal relationships. Intimacy, innovative thinking, teamwork, and humor all come to those who free themselves from the need to control the narrative and have the patience and confidence to follow the story wherever it leads.

10

Conversational Sensitivity

What Terry Gross, LBJ, and Con Men Have in Common

In a near-dark recording studio at WHYY in Philadelphia, Terry Gross, host of the popular National Public Radio program *Fresh Air,* was interviewing a film director who was sitting in another studio on the West Coast. Lights blinked, needles jumped, and bars rose and fell in the control room as Gross, all but invisible behind an enormous microphone, talked to the director about a wide range of subjects, including his artistic process, his personal insecurities, an unsettling childhood experience, and the fact that horses will go up, but not down, stairs.

As the interview progressed, two of the show's producers, Lauren Krenzel and Heidi Saman, clicked away on their laptops, keeping track of what the director was saying and noting the times during the interview when he was saying it. He talked for about an hour and fifteen minutes. It was Krenzel and Saman's job, along with executive producer Danny Miller, to decide how to edit what he said down to the forty-five minutes that would eventually be broadcast.

Why put three people on a job any one of them could do on their own? Because they didn't all hear the same interview. Katherine Hampsten, associate professor of communication studies at St. Mary's University in San Antonio, Texas, has a good analogy for what happens when we listen. She says it's like a game of catch with a lump of clay. Each person catches it and molds it with their perceptions before tossing it back. Things like education, race, gender, age, relationship with the other person, frame of mind, connotations of words, and distractions all influence how the clay is shaped. Add more people to the game of catch and the complexity and range of meanings increases.

There are eight people on *Fresh Air*'s production staff, many of whom came to their jobs without much, and sometimes without any, radio experience. Miller told me the key qualification he looks for when hiring producers is "good ears," meaning a superior ability to listen and detect what's really going on in conversations. Miller calls it having *command of conversations*. Psychologists call it *conversational sensitivity*.

People who have conversational sensitivity not only pay attention to spoken words, they also have a knack for picking up hidden meanings and nuances in tone. They are good at recognizing power differentials and are quick to distinguish affectation from genuine affection. They remember more of what people say and tend to enjoy, or at least be interested in, the conversation. Conversational sensitivity is also thought to be a precursor to empathy, which requires you to summon emotions felt and learned in previous interactions and apply them to subsequent situations.

Not surprisingly, conversational sensitivity is related to cognitive complexity, which, as discussed earlier, means you are open to a range of experiences and can cope with contradictory views. You can't be good at detecting intricate cues in conversation if you haven't listened to a lot of people. It is said that intuition, often called the sixth sense, is nothing more than recognition. The more people you listen to, the more aspects of humanity you will recognize, and the better your gut instinct will be. It's a practiced skill that depends on exposure to a wide range of opinions, attitudes, beliefs, and emotions. *Fresh Air* producers and associate producers fit this profile, coming from many different backgrounds, including a former waitress, film director, and folklorist.

"When we meet to discuss the edit, we are making sure we are all on the same page about what the conversation was about," said Miller. "There's lots of comparing notes. We're different ages and come from different places in life. We want to have different perspectives coming to it." He described the process as "a combination of interpretation of what was said and how you felt about it." He added diplomatically, "We have pretty active discussions about how to cut the interview."

After the conclusion of Gross's interview with the film director, producers Krenzel and Saman emerged from the darkened studio into the bright sunshine pouring through the floor-to-ceiling windows that front WHYY's offices. They settled at a table to discuss their impressions. Krenzel, who is in her sixties and originally from Philadelphia, has had a long career in audio. Before *Fresh Air,* she produced audiobooks, broadcasts of professional sporting events, and several radio shows for WNYC in New York. Saman is in her thirties and a first-generation Egyptian American who grew up in Los Angeles. Her background is in filmmaking, and she continues to write and direct films. The two of them went through the interview line by line. "We could take that out . . . Let's definitely keep that . . . Could that quote be shorter? . . . He said that twice . . . We'll pick that part up later . . . Maybe that's not as interesting . . . I thought that part was cool . . . That part surprised me . . . Is that important?"

They were taking the conversation and distilling it to its most essential, checking in with each other to make sure they didn't cut something that, while perhaps not interesting to them, might be interesting to someone else. "We are looking for what represents the interview best and what represents the person interviewed best," Krenzel told me. "We obviously want it to make sense in terms of a narrative arc, but we also want to get people hooked into the emotion of it, so we might have to shape it or shorten it to fit in all the really great moments."

Miller, a dervish of energy, walked up and made a few laps around the table where Krenzel and Saman were seated, providing input, quoting parts of the interview he liked from memory. His recall and sensitivity to conversational nuance reflect forty years working on the daily show. He started as an intern at WHYY in his twenties. I could almost see the three of them tossing Hampsten's lump of clay around the table. "Really? . . . I didn't get that . . . Oh yes . . . Wow, no . . . What did you think about that? . . . I get what you're saying."

While they may not agree on everything they want in the final cut of an interview, there's generally unanimity when it comes to including parts that reveal the emotional depth of the person. This is in line with research that indicates conversational sensitivity is most aroused when personal stuff is discussed. Other things that make us alert in conversation are more variable, depending on the situation and our individual quirks, such as whether we happen to be in a good mood, can relate to what is being said, or find the subject matter surprising. Personal stuff, though, always perks up our ears.

The worst interviews, according to Krenzel, are those where people "don't want to open up or reveal anything about their lives." They just drum the beats their publicist has given them, she said, "and it all feels so disconnected and it's just dry as dust because there's no emotional resonance." Lack of emotional resonance, of course, is what makes normal conversations dull and boring. You have probably had exchanges with people who sound as if they are speaking from a script— delivering well-worn lines rather than sharing spontaneous thoughts and feelings unique to a back-and-forth with you. If you overheard them talking to someone else, you'd likely hear the same stories told the same way about their jobs, kids, dietary habits, medical issues, and so on.

More than 6 million people tune in to *Fresh Air* each week because Gross has a knack for getting guests to go off script. Listening to her do interviews pre-edit, you notice how she subtly nudges guests off their tired talking points. "That's when the tape can get really interesting for us," Saman told me. "Terry is trying to find the zone where they are comfortable. You can really hear it with the rhythm of their talking once she gets them in that place; sometimes it's personal, or early work, anything that engages them. She's trying to get them out of their head." A good listener has the ability to elicit more than superficial or anxious chatter so people reveal more of who they really are.

Working to Gross's advantage is the preparation she and her producers put into every show. Guests know by Gross's questions that she has done her homework and is knowledgeable and keenly interested in their work. When people feel known and appreciated, they are more willing to share. Gross also assures them before the interview starts that they are free to stop her at any time if she ventures into an area that feels uncomfortable. So right there, she's established that she cares about their feelings. These are things anyone who wants to be a better listener can emulate. Demonstrate interest either by learning about people beforehand or being inquisitive in the moment. Try to find what excites them. It doesn't matter if it's their bottle cap collection; if they are passionate about it, it will be interesting. And also respect boundaries by backing off if you suspect you've stumbled into a touchy area. Gently change the subject and be gracious in not knowing. Intimacy can't be forced.

By the time a *Fresh Air* episode is finally aired, all three producers might listen to an interview three to four times. With each rewind and replay, they pick up not just subtleties in expression and meaning but also telling inhalations, pauses, and perhaps barely audible fidgeting in the background. Sitting with Saman while she deftly polishes an interview using a digital sound-editing program, you get down to the granular of conversations. When is an *um* or *uh* significant? Is that breath right there important? Why did he keep repeating that word? It makes you aware of how much information can be hidden in a single sentence. You also realize why it's so much easier to listen to an edited interview than an ordinary, everyday conversation. Real conversations are not as clear or as clean. They are murkier and messier, and they meander.

———

Conversations in English, in particular, can get messy because of the complexity and expansiveness of the language. Linguists and lexicographers estimate that English has about a million words and is expanding all the time. The literary critic Cyril Connolly wrote that the English language is like a broad river "being polluted by a string of refuse-barges tipping out their muck." But the writer Walt Whitman more charitably described English as "the accretion and growth of every dialect, race, and range of time, and is both the free and compacted composition of all." Either way, English is one of the easiest languages to misunderstand even if you're a native speaker.

Just within the borders of the continental United States, there are dozens of regional dialects that offer all kinds of opportunities for confusion. For example, west of the Ohio River, *caramel* begins shedding syllables. And how you say *pecan* pretty much depends on your time zone—from PEE-can to pa-CON to PICK-on. In some parts of the South, you'll hear *waste* something instead of *spill* something. And a *traffic circle* is just that in the mid-Atlantic states but becomes a *rotary* in the Northeast and a *roundabout* in the West. On the way to Grandma's house, drive slow around the rotary, or you'll waste the CAR-mel pa-CON pie all over the seat of the car.

Personal interpretation also messes us up. Like when someone says, "I'd like to get to bed at a decent hour." You could be thinking a decent hour is 10:00 p.m. when the other person has 2:00 a.m. in mind. The meaning of *hard labor, good sex, not far,* and *spicy food* all depends on who's saying it. And, of course, euphemisms like *monthly visitor, passed away, bigboned,* and *between opportunities* abound, as people are always coming up with alternative and sometimes cryptic ways of saying what they don't want to come out and say. Virginia Woolf said, "Words are full of echoes, of memories, of associations. They have been out and about, on people's lips, in their houses, in the streets, in the fields, for so many centuries."

Things get even more complicated when you try to communicate with someone who grew up speaking a different language from yours. Then you get into linguistic relativity, also known as the Sapir-Whorf hypothesis, which holds that a person's native language influences how they see or experience the world. A clever study by South African and British researchers demonstrated linguistic relativity quite elegantly. They had Swedish and Spanish speakers estimate the amount of time that elapsed while watching two animations: one of a line increasing in length and another of a container filling from the bottom. Because Swedish speakers describe time using distance terms like *long* or *short* and Spanish speakers use volume-related terms like *big* or *small,* the Swedish speakers tended to think the line that grew longer took longer, when it actually took less time, while the Spanish speakers thought that the fuller vessel took longer to fill when, in fact, it didn't.

But what most gets in the way of understanding is your emotions and personal sensitivities. Given that you interpret things according to your background and psychology—and you can't convene a team of producers to collaboratively dissect conversations like they do on *Fresh Air*—knowing yourself and your vulnerabilities is an important aspect of being a good listener.

Say someone tells you that your outlook is "original." If you are the type who often feels somewhat out of step, then you might take *original* to mean *oddball* when the person might have meant you were refreshingly unique. Knowing you have that tender point can help you to think more broadly about what the person meant and to engage further to find out for sure. It's sort of like repositioning a rearview or side mirror on your car to help minimize blind spots.

Research indicates that people who have a higher degree of self-awareness, and a related concept known as *self-monitoring,* are better listeners in part because they know the sorts of things that lead them to jump to the wrong conclusions and thus are less likely to do so. Cultivating self-awareness is a matter of paying attention to your emotions while in conversation and recognizing when your fears and sensitivities—or perhaps your desires and dreams—hijack your ability to listen well. A spouse or close friend may have insight into what shuts you down or sets you off, or you may prefer a good psychotherapist. While it can be difficult to do this kind of self-assessment, the reward is a greater capacity to understand and connect with other people. You can only be as intimate with another person as you are with yourself.

Psychoanalysts have to go through their own analyses so their personal issues don't get in the way of understanding the problems and feelings of those who seek their help. In his 1948 book, *Listening with the Third Ear,* Theodor Reik, an Austrian psychoanalyst who was one of Freud's first students, wrote that to listen well is to note the feelings that bubble up from one's own unconscious: "To observe and to record in memory thousands of little signs and to remain aware of their delicate effects." For him, awareness of one's reflexive reactions and intuitions is like having a third ear with which to listen.

Similarly, CIA recruits are subjected to an intense screening process, including psychological tests to weed out those who are not self-aware enough to tame their weaknesses in tense situations. During our conversation at the Four Seasons in Washington, D.C., former CIA agent Barry McManus told me, "If you don't know your own stuff, you can't do the job. We all have weaknesses, flaws, and vulnerabilities. I have them. You have them. But in this game, I've got to get to yours before you get to mine."

Which brings us to the listener's power to manipulate. In describing telephone recordings that revealed how Lyndon Johnson worked his influence in the Senate, his biographer Robert Caro said, "People think Johnson talks all the time. If you listen to these tapes, he often doesn't talk at all for the first few minutes. You hear him, all he has is this sound—'Mmmm-hmmm. Mmmm-hmmm.' And you get the feeling, and then you see what's coming, he's listening for what the guy really wants, what he's really afraid of."

In much the same way, con artists, hustlers, and scammers also tend to be superb listeners. They pick up on subtle nonverbal cues and the deeper meanings in offhand comments to find out exactly what you most fear or desire. And with that understanding, they know exactly how to play you. But it must be said that lying is often a cooperative act. There's the liar and the person who hears what they want to hear. People say, "Oh, I'd never fall for that," not realizing how seriously their listening is impaired when they so want to believe somebody loves them or will make them rich or will cure what ails them.

The infamous con artist Mel Weinberg* had a wily under-standing of the cooperative dynamic between liar and listener. It's why the FBI drafted him in the late 1970s to help ensnare a U.S. senator and six U.S. congressmen in the Abscam sting. "When a guy is in a jam and lookin' for money, it's my philos-ophy to give hope," he told *The New York Times Magazine* in 1982. "If you say you can't do nothin', you're killin' his hope. Everybody has to have hope. That's why most people don't turn us in to the cops. They keep hopin' we're for real."

It's not that con artists are somehow inherently more skilled listeners and diviners of human frailty than their victims. The difference is that cons are more practiced and more motivated listeners, because they know it pays. Several studies have shown that people who are well motivated tend to be more accurate in their perceptions. Victims of cons are less motivated listeners because the fiction the con is feeding them at that moment in their lives is so appealing.

So you could say, good listeners are better at both deceiving and detecting deceit. If you think back to the times in your life when you were fooled, if you're honest, there were likely things you missed or chose to miss. The too-urgent tone. The facts that didn't quite add up. The hostility or exasperation in the person's voice when you asked questions. The facial expression that didn't quite match what the person was saying. The slight

---

* Weinberg was inspiration for Christian Bale's character in the film *American Hustle*.

discomfort in the pit of your stomach that you couldn't quite put your finger on.

We often miss lies, as well as truths, because when someone says something that doesn't make sense, most of the time, we don't stop the conversation and say, "Wait. Back up. I don't understand." In unedited versions of *Fresh Air* interviews, you frequently hear Terry Gross stopping her guests to get them to explain what they meant. But in everyday conversations, people more often shrug and move on because it doesn't seem worth the trouble or they think they can guess what the other person meant. People are also reluctant to ask for clarification lest they appear dense. How many times has someone laughed at something you said that wasn't intended as a joke? And how many times have you nodded when you had no idea what someone was talking about? Probably more times than you can count. "For whatever reason, often we are hesitant to stop and ask when we're not sure what someone meant," said communication researcher Graham Bodie at the University of Mississippi.

In addition to his academic work, Bodie also does corporate consulting, particularly training salespeople to become more effective listeners. He said one of the major things he warns against is glossing over points in conversations that don't make sense because it's a leading cause of costly mistakes. "You've got to assume everything is relevant. If something doesn't quite make sense to you, you need to pay attention," he said. "Most of the time when it happens, we keep going even though we think there's something weird here. But you should stop and clarify. Say something like 'When you said *X,* I was confused.'"

We hear about disasters resulting from the failure to clear up confusion all the time: the *Challenger* explosion, the collapse of Lehman Brothers, and medical errors that cause around 250,000 deaths in the U.S. each year. But what about all the micro-miscommunications that fill our days? While the repercussions may not be as catastrophic, they are nonetheless consequential. For all the times we have that moment of "Oooh! *Now* I get it," there are many more misunderstandings we fail to catch. We are oblivious to all the hurt feelings, missed opportunities, and botched jobs. All because we couldn't be bothered to make sure we understood.

Misunderstandings, like differences of opinion, are valuable reminders that others are not like us, or even remotely like us. Because we only really know ourselves, it's a natural tendency to have a solipsistic view of the world. We incorrectly assume other people's logic and motivations resemble our own. But, of course, they have different backstories and baggage.

Intellectually, we know this, but nonetheless it's always a rude awakening when someone thinks or behaves in ways that are beyond our expectations or imaginations. Misunderstandings, then, can be seen as an opportunity. They are an inspiration, or perhaps an aggravation, to listen more closely and inquire more deeply. In the words of Miles Davis, "If you understood everything I said, you'd be me."

11

Listening to Yourself

The Voluble Inner Voice

I have a good friend who, like a lot of accomplished people, is really hard on herself. She's enormously successful, attractive, warm, and witty, but when things go wrong in her life, her default is to self-loathe. All of a sudden, she's an idiot, a complete failure, and can't do anything right. When she gets on these self-critical jags, I tell her to stop listening to Spanky. *Spanky* is code for her mean inner voice—the one that pipes up during times of stress, mercilessly chastising her and making her feel small.

We all have voices in our heads. In fact, we talk to ourselves constantly about things mundane and potentially profound. We have moral arguments and absurdist debates. We assign blame and make rationalizations. We analyze past events and rehearse future ones. The voices in our heads can be encouraging or defeating, caring or criticizing, complimentary or demeaning. Psychologist Charles Fernyhough at Durham University in the UK knows this better than most. He studies inner dialogue.

His interest sprang from his doctoral thesis, which looked at how children talk out loud to themselves to work through problems and regulate their emotions. We continue talking to ourselves when we grow up, we just learn to do it in our heads—though it still occasionally slips out of our mouths. Who hasn't found themselves wondering aloud where they put their keys or audibly cursing at something they heard on the news? "I have a constant inner dialogue that spills out into external speech," Fernyhough told me. His wife has gotten used to it, but he gets funny looks when it happens on the bus. "Inner speech and talking to yourself is something we all do," he said. "It's a give-and-take. We are talking and listening inside our heads."

Indeed, we engage the same parts of our brains when we talk to ourselves as we do when we talk to another person. These are the brain regions involved with so-called theory of mind, or social cognition, which allow us to empathize and read other people's intentions, desires, and emotions.

In his book *The Voices Within,* Fernyhough writes that many great philosophers and social theorists, including William James, Charles Sanders Peirce, and George Herbert Mead, believed the self generates conversations with itself by taking the perspective of another. An example is an athlete who might internalize the voice of a coach. Or you might have a back-and-forth with yourself that resembles exchanges you've had with your mother, boss, spouse, sibling, friend, or maybe a therapist.

Listening to others, then, determines the tone and quality of our inner dialogues. Our previous interactions teach us how to question, answer, and comment so we can do the same with ourselves when we need to solve problems, manage ethical dilemmas, and think creatively. *This will work. Oh no, this way is better . . . I'm going to ask for a raise. But they only hired you two months ago . . . I want some ice cream. It'll spoil your dinner . . . I'm really attracted to her. Move on, man, she's married.*

This kind of private or inner speech is associated with higher performance on cognitive tasks by children as well as adults. The research suggests that the more people you listen to in the course of your life, the more sides to an issue you can argue in your head and the more solutions you can imagine. Inner dialogue fosters and supports cognitive complexity, that valuable ability to tolerate a range of views, make associations, and come up with new ideas.

More sophisticated private speech has been found to be associated with having more involved parents and higher socioeconomic status. Private speech development is hindered in children who have grown up in circumstances where their listening opportunities were limited. For example, children brought up in low-income Appalachian families, a culture where children can be isolated and treated as better "seen and not heard," show delays in private speech, as do children from low-income urban families with a history of neglect.

This is significant because how you talk to yourself affects how you hear other people. For example, someone who has a critical inner voice will hear someone else's words very differently than someone whose inner voice tends to blame others. *It's all your fault* versus *It's all their fault.* In other words, our inner dialogue influences and distorts what other people say and thus how we behave in relationships.

Remember psychologist and attachment expert Miriam Steele from chapter 2? Her research, building on the work of other attachment experts dating back to the 1950s, indicates that the voices that get replayed in one's head echo those heard in childhood. When early attachments are secure—if you had parents or caregivers who listened and attended to your wants and needs—then you develop an inner voice that is, as Steele put it, "friendlier."

We all have guilt and wrestle with ourselves, Steele told me, but an inner voice that says, *Are you sure you want to do that? Why don't you put yourself in their shoes?* and *Yeah, that was hurtful, but maybe they didn't intend to hurt you,* is a very different voice from the one that says, *They are all out to get me* and *I'm no good.* The latter voice is the one that makes you react in ways that are not to your benefit.

People's inner voices have tremendous influence in part because they're actually perceived as louder. Researchers in the United States and China found that subjects who were asked to imagine repeating the syllable *da* rated external sounds as softer. Their internal voices dampened, or drowned out, what they heard. Moreover, their brains showed less auditory activation when the external sounds were played. If this is the effect of saying a single syllable to yourself, imagine what happens when a full-on dialogue is going on inside your head. *He seems standoffish. Did I offend him? Maybe he's just having a bad day. No, I think he's mad at me.*

Some theorists argue that reading is a form of inner speech. Research indicates that we sound out words in our heads as we read. If a word takes you longer to say, it will take you longer to read. Another study showed that when subjects heard recordings of two people, one who spoke rapidly and another who spoke very slowly, and then were asked to read excerpts of works supposedly written by the slow or fast talker, the subjects read at a pace consistent with the speech rate of whoever they thought the writer was.

Many readers who come to love a particular writer report that they hear that author's unique voice, or the voice they imagine the writer has. They also might hear the distinct voices of the writer's characters. Indeed, studies have found that the voice-sensitive areas of the auditory cortex are activated more when reading direct versus indirect speech—that is, your brain reacts as if it's hearing an actual person speak when you read: "He said, 'I'm in love with her,'" but not so much if you read: "He said he was in love with her."

Fernyhough and colleagues teamed up with *The Guardian* newspaper to survey 1,566 readers, and 89 percent said they heard the voices of characters in books, often vividly. Fifty-six percent of respondents said some characters' voices stayed with them even when they weren't reading, influencing the tone and content of their inner speech. Of course, many fiction writers say their characters talk to them and determine the course of their novels. When asked about his daily writing routine, Ray Bradbury responded that his morning ritual was to lie in bed and listen to the voices in his head. "I call it my morning theater," he said. "My characters talk to one another, and when it reaches a certain pitch of excitement, I jump out of bed and run and trap them before they are gone."

The tenor of our inner voices comes not only from listening to the actual people in our lives but is also likely influenced by the voices we regularly hear in the media. The tone and dialectical style of, say, Sean Hannity, Oprah Winfrey, or Judge Judy might begin to reverberate in your head, depending on how avid a follower you are. Who does your inner voice remind you of? What does it tell you? Does your inner voice sound different in different situations? Is it friendly? Is it critical? These are all important things to ask yourself because your inner voice influences how you ponder things, interpret situations, make moral judgments, and solve problems. This, in turn, influences how you are in the world; whether you see the best or worst in people and whether you see the best or worst in yourself.

The trouble is, really tuning in to one's self is something people go to great lengths to avoid. This was borne out in eleven experiments involving more than seven hundred people conducted by psychologists at the University of Virginia. The majority of subjects did not enjoy spending just six to fifteen minutes in a room by themselves with nothing to do but think. In one experiment, 64 percent of men and 15 percent of women began self-administering shocks rather than be alone with their thoughts.

This suggests a lot of people have inner voices that sound like my friend's tormenter, Spanky. Even if your inner voice is friendlier, the dialogues you have with yourself often have to do with what's weighing on you—things like relationship problems, professional disappointments, health concerns, and the like. Human beings are by nature problem solvers, so in quiet moments, this is where our minds go. Our fixation on what needs to be fixed is why some people can't abide downtime and always have to have something to do so they won't think about what's wrong. However, trying to suppress your inner voice only gives it more power. It gets louder and more insistent, which makes some people get even busier and overscheduled to drown it out. It never works, though. Your inner voice is always there and, if it can't get your attention during the day, it will roust you at 4:00 a.m. *Hello! Remember me?*

Cognitive behavioral therapy is all about learning how to talk to yourself differently. An unhelpful inner voice that sounds like a belittling parent or negative friend is replaced by a voice that sounds more like your therapist, suggesting kinder or more open ways of thinking, which in turn has proven effective at fostering a greater sense of well-being. Listening to a wide variety of people, too, is helpful. Many voices bring many perspectives. Questioning people and considering their responses is how you get better at doing the same when you have dialogues with yourself. As difficult as a problem may be, having a dialogue with yourself is ultimately the only way to solve it, or at least come to terms with it.

When the great physicist and Nobel Prize winner Richard Feynman was examined for his fitness to serve in the military during WWII, a psychiatrist asked him, "Do you talk to yourself?" As Feynman told his biographer, "I didn't tell him something which I can tell you, which is I find myself sometimes talking to myself in quite an elaborate fashion: 'The integral will be larger than this sum of the terms, so that would make the pressure higher, you see?' 'No, you're crazy.' 'No, I'm not! No, I'm not!' I say. I argue with myself. I have two voices that work back and forth."

Feynman said the conversations he had with his father, wife, friends, and colleagues all influenced and found echoes in his inner dialogues. In his book of essays, *The Pleasure of Finding Things Out,* Feynman wrote, "By trying to put the points of view that we have in our head together and comparing one to the other, we make some progress in understanding and in appreciating where we are and what we are."

12

Supporting, Not Shifting, the Conversation

In the memoirs of American socialite Jennie Jerome, otherwise known as Lady Randolph Churchill, Winston Churchill's mother, she described dining separately with archrival British politicians Benjamin Disraeli and William Gladstone: "When I left the dining room after sitting next to Gladstone, I thought he was the cleverest man in England. But when I sat next to Disraeli, I left feeling that I was the cleverest woman."

No surprise she preferred Disraeli's company. The two-time Tory prime minister was a brilliant orator but also a keen listener, solicitous and adept at steering conversations toward whomever he was with. It also made him a favorite of Queen Victoria's, whose undisguised preference for Disraeli over Gladstone during elections some said verged on unconstitutional. But it wasn't just aristocracy and royalty to whom Disraeli paid scrupulous attention. *The Times* of London famously wrote he was able to see a conservative voter in the working-man as a sculptor discerns "the angel in the marble."

Disraeli was master of what sociologist Charles Derber at Boston College calls the *support response*. Since the 1970s, Derber has been interested in how people behave and compete for attention in social settings. By recording and transcribing more than a hundred informal dinner conversations, he identified two kinds of responses. More common was the *shift response*, which directs attention away from the speaker and toward the respondent. Less common, and Disraeli's forte, was the *support response*, which encourages elaboration from the speaker to help the respondent gain greater understanding. Here are some hypothetical examples:

John: My dog got out last week, and it took three days to find him.

Mary: Our dog is always digging under the fence, so we can't let him out unless he's on a leash. (shift response)

John: My dog got out last week, and it took three days to find him.

Mary: Oh no. Where did you finally find him? (support response)

Sue: I watched this really good documentary about turtles last night.

Bob: I'm not big on documentaries. I'm more of an action-film kind of guy. (shift response)

Sue: I watched this really good documentary about turtles last night.

Bob: Turtles? How did you happen to see that? Are you into turtles? (support response)

Good listeners are all about the support response, which is critical to providing the kind of acknowledgment and evaluative feedback discussed in chapter 5 as well as avoiding the types of misunderstandings identified in chapter 10. According to Derber, shift responses are symptomatic of *conversational narcissism,* which quashes any chance of connection. Shift responses are usually self-referential statements while support responses are more often other-directed questions. But they have to be truly curious questions meant to elicit more information and not subtly impose your own opinion—open-ended questions like "What was your reaction?" not "Didn't that piss you off?" The goal is to understand the speaker's point of view, not to sway it.

Fill-in-the-blank questions are useful in this respect. "You and Roger got in a fight because . . . ?" That way, it's like you're handing off a baton, allowing the speaker to go in whatever direction the person wants. Try to avoid asking about incidental details that knock people off their train of thought and feeling state: "Were you and Roger arguing at the coffee shop on

Fifty-fifth Street or Sixty-seventh Street?" Where they were, what time, what they ordered—none of it matters as much as what happened and how it felt.

Because people like to appear knowledgeable, they like to ask questions that suggest they already know the answer. Or they frame questions in ways that prompt the answers they want. Good questions don't begin with: "Don't you think . . . ?" "Isn't it true . . . ?" "Wouldn't you agree . . . ?" And good questions definitely don't end with "right?" These are actually camouflaged shift responses and will likely lead others to give incomplete or less-than-honest answers that fit the questioner's opinions and expectations.

Also deadly are long questions that contain a lot of qualifying or self-promoting information: "I have a background in landscape architecture and am an admirer of Frederick Law Olmsted, who designed Central Park and is an underrecognized genius in my opinion, and I travel extensively and I'm struck by the enduring vibrancy and popularity of the great parks like New York's Central Park and St. James's Park in London and the Bois de Boulogne in Paris, so I'm wondering if you agree that we need to have more grand ambitions when we think about green spaces?" This was an actual question someone stood up and asked at a sustainable development forum. Don't be that person.

Beware, too, of questions that contain hidden assumptions. Another noted sociologist, Howard Becker, reprimanded me once for asking him just such a question. We were sitting in his sunny study overlooking San Francisco's famously steep and switchbacked Lombard Street when I asked him, "What made you decide to become a sociologist?" Becker's face contorted as if he'd just smelled something dreadful. "You're assuming it was a decision," he said. "Better to ask, 'How did it happen that you became a sociologist?'"

Becker, who spent much of his long career at Northwestern University, is known for embedding himself for months, if not years, within various subcultures and then writing about them like an insider. His subjects have included jazz musicians, pot smokers, artists, actors, and medical students, among others. "I'm not sure I'm a better listener than anyone else, but if I hear something I don't understand, I ask about it," he told me. For him, the worst questions are the ones that are never asked.

Ninety-one and feisty, Becker doesn't understand why people are so reluctant to ask questions. Having traveled widely and lived in four countries as a lecturer and researcher, Becker said reticence seems to be a global, and globally unproductive, tendency. He now divides his time between homes in San Francisco and Paris,* and he said the shuffle between cultures and languages keeps him from getting complacent about what he knows. "So much is taken for granted in ordinary discourse, particularly if it's in your native language," he said. "Things go by you and you don't know exactly what was meant, but you let it go because you think it's not important, don't need to know it, or feel embarrassed."

Or people are anxious about the answer. Asking open-ended

---

* Becker's work and research methods, or "Beckerisme," is required reading at many French universities.

questions means the conversation can go anywhere, particularly into emotional territory. To listen openly takes a certain amount of adventurousness and even some courage because you don't know where you may end up. "A lot of people aren't comfortable with it," Becker said. "Quite a few men are not very good at it. That's why instead of doing fieldwork, [male sociologists] tend to get into demography, the statistical study of populations, so they don't have to develop intimate knowledge of people."

This is not just Becker's opinion. Research indicates both women and men view women as more open and empathetic listeners. Some evidence suggests women focus more on relational and personal information whereas men are more attentive to fact-based information. As a result, women are more likely to gain people's trust and be privy to more self-disclosure, which makes their conversations more interesting and, thus, reinforces their willingness to listen.

But there's considerable disagreement over whether this is nature or nurture. Some blame cultural influences that teach boys to man up and not be interested in or affected by the emotions of others, while others argue that the greater social sensitivity of women, even infant girls, cannot be entirely attributed to societal or parental influence. Some have even argued that autism, characterized by difficulty picking up emotional cues in verbal and nonverbal communication, is a severe form of the male brain.

In all the interviews I did for this book, the idea that women were better listeners than men was a recurring theme. A real estate investor in Houston told me, "I don't interview tenants. I send one of my female employees because they are much better at reading people than I am. I don't listen the way they do." Like-wise, a venture capitalist in San Francisco said that when sizing up founders of start-ups, he always defers to a female partner at his firm. "She is off-the-charts unbelievable at being able to read people. Founders barely start speaking and she understands their motivations and whether they are good or bad. It's incredible. I've asked her to explain it to me, and she can't really. She's like my mom. She just knows. Maybe it's a female thing."

But to say all women are better listeners than men is like saying all men are taller than women. I've interviewed and known personally many women who were horrible listeners and many men who were exceptional listeners. It has much more to do with background, life experience, and even the sit-uation. Some people might be great listeners but only when listening to certain people or in certain circumstances.

Everyone, though, to a greater or lesser extent, has some anxiety about, or some discomfort with, the strong feelings that can tumble out of people when they find a willing listener. Humans beings, as much as we try to contain it or pretend otherwise, are brimming with emotion. It can sometimes feel like too much to take on someone else's inner chaos when we can barely cope with our own.

According to researchers at Université de Lausanne in Switzerland, sounds that convey negative emotions are per-ceived as significantly louder than those that are more neutral or positive in tone, even when they have the same amplitude. Similarly, researchers at the University of Minnesota and Uni-versity of Illinois at Urbana–Champaign found that employees were five times more upset by negative interactions at work as they were made happy by positive interactions. This dovetails with the findings of marriage and family researcher John Gottman at the University of Washington in Seattle whose decades of observational studies indicate good interactions must outnumber negative ones by at least five to one for a relationship to succeed. It explains the instinct to shut out others rather than risk the disproportionate intensity of feeling hurt.

In the book *There Is No Good Card for This: What To Do and Say When Life Is Scary, Awful, and Unfair to People You Love,* authors Kelsey Crowe and Emily McDowell indirectly identified another kind of shift response that arises from just this kind of avoidant behavior. Derber characterized the shift response as a narcissistic attempt to redirect the conversation back to one's self. But the shift response Crowe and McDowell described occurs when people, uncomfortable with others' emotions, respond by trying to solve or explain away problems rather than listening and letting the upset or aggrieved feel what they feel and, through dialogue, find their own solutions. The authors advise squelching the impulses to:

- suggest you know how someone feels
- identify the cause of the problem
- tell someone what to do about the problem
- minimize their concerns
- bring perspective to a situation with forced positivity and platitudes
- admire the person's strength

Being aware of someone's troubles does not mean you need to fix them. People usually aren't looking for solutions from you anyway; they just want a sounding board. Moreover, you shut people down when you start telling them what they should do or how they should feel. No matter how good your intentions or how sage you think your advice, people reflexively resist and resent directives, even if gently delivered. You may be able to help someone fix a leaky faucet, edit a résumé, or find a good accountant, but you can't help someone salvage a ruined career, repair a broken marriage, or emerge from the depths of despair. Your answer to someone else's deepest difficulties merely reflects what you would do if you were that person, which you are not.

The best you can do is listen. Try to understand what the person is facing and appreciate how it feels. This in itself can lead to solutions. The listening approach to problem solving underlies the Quaker practice of forming "clearness committees." It started in the 1900s as a way for church elders to determine the compatibility of couples who wished to marry. But over the years, clearness committees have expanded their mandate to consider whatever concerns a member of their community might have—whether it's about a relationship, career, or matters of faith.

Upon receiving a request, a clearness committee of about a half dozen members convenes to listen to the so-called focus person lay out the problem. Then the committee members ask what they call "faithful" questions. It's essentially a full-court support response. There is no wise counsel or sharing of similar personal experiences, nor is the questioning meant to guide or influence the person's thinking. Rather, the clearness committee's questioning is intended to help the focus person go deeper so an answer might emerge; so clearness can arise from within.

Quaker educator and author Parker Palmer told me about his experience with a clearness committee in the 1970s when he was trying to decide whether to accept an offer to become president of a large educational institution. At first, the questions were about the position and what he hoped to accomplish. Then someone asked what seemed like a simple question: "Parker, what would you like about being president?" He listed the things he wouldn't like—the politics, raising money, not being able to teach. When asked again, "But what would you like?" he again talked about aspects he wouldn't like. "Well, I wouldn't like to give up my summer vacations." The committee members persisted, "But, Parker, what would you like about it?"

Finally, appalled by what he realized was the truth, he said, "I guess what I'd really like most is getting my picture in the paper with the word *president* under it." There was an uncomfortable quiet. Finally, another questioner broke the silence. "Parker, can you think of an easier way to get your picture in the paper?" Palmer laughed recalling it. "I knew right then that taking the job would be a totally bogus career move," he said. So he went home, talked it over with his wife, and called the institution and withdrew his name. "I look back with enormous gratitude for an experience of being deeply listened to, but more than that, having this rare opportunity to listen to myself," he said. "It saved me from making an enormous mistake."

Had someone on the committee said to him, "You know, Parker, I don't think you're really interested in that job," the outcome likely would have been different. "When people tell you how you feel or what you should do, I think most of us know that it makes us defensive," Palmer told me. "We start defending the indefensible. 'That's arrogant. You don't know me. Of course I'm interested. This is a great opportunity.' We start to talk ourselves into something. It totally changes the dynamic."

His experience being the focus of a clearness committee and serving as a questioner on dozens of other clearness committees moved Palmer to develop a curriculum to teach the process to people outside the Quaker community. It is now taught at retreats sponsored by the Center for Courage & Renewal, a Seattle-based nonprofit Palmer founded twenty-five years ago to support people in the helping professions, such as doctors, teachers, and social workers. The idea is not so much to teach people how to hold formal clearness committees but rather to teach them the listening techniques involved so they are more effective in their jobs and more attuned to people in their personal lives.

More than two hundred thousand people have attended the retreats, and it turns out the most difficult part of the curriculum is learning how to ask "faithful" questions, which, in keeping with the secular nature of the retreats, are referred to as "open and honest" questions. A neurosurgeon from Seattle who participated in one of the retreats told me, "You don't realize how the questions you ask can reduce your interactions to sterile transactions. In your professional and also your personal life, everything gets so binary—this or that—so you don't hear people's stories and you lose sight of what's important."

It's hard to ask open and honest questions because most people ask questions that are really recommendations or judgments in disguise. For example, "Have you thought of seeing a therapist?" and "Why don't you divorce him?" are not open and honest questions. Open and honest questions don't have a hidden agenda of fixing, saving, advising, or correcting. "It deprives us of all the things we love to do," Palmer said. But open and honest questioning is essential for basic understanding. It allows people to tell their stories, express their realities, and find the resources within themselves to figure out how they feel about a problem and decide on next steps.

―――――

Say your son or daughter jumps into the car after soccer practice and says, "I hate it. I'm never going back. I quit." This always strikes a nerve with parents who are likely to respond with: "You can't quit. Where's your team spirit?" or "Oh my God, what happened? I'm going to call the coach!" or "Are you hungry? Let's go eat. You'll feel better." None of that is listening. Grilling them about what happened is interrogating. Telling them they shouldn't feel how they feel is minimizing. And changing the subject is just maddening. Kids, like all of us, just want to be heard. Try instead, "Have you always felt this way?" or "What would quitting mean?" Look at it as an invitation to have a conversation, not as something to be fixed or get upset about.

Again, the solutions to problems are often already within people, and just by listening, you help them access how best to handle things, now and also in the future. Researchers at Vanderbilt University discovered that when mothers just listened, providing no assistance or critique, while their children explained the solutions to pattern recognition problems, it markedly improved the children's later problem-solving ability—more so than if the children had explained the solution to themselves or repeated the solution over and over in their heads. Previous research has shown that adults provided with an attentive listener gave more detailed solutions with more alternative ideas and better justifications than solutions generated in isolation.

Whether it's your child, romantic partner, friend, colleague, or employee who comes to you with a personal problem, if you ask open and honest questions and listen attentively to the answers, it communicates, "I'm interested in hearing more from you," and "Your feelings are valid." If you jump in to fix, advise, correct, or distract, you are communicating that the other person doesn't have the ability to handle the situation: "You're not going to get this without me." And you're also telling them, "There's no room for honest emotion in our relationship." By questioning and listening carefully to the answers, the other person might in return begin to ask you questions so they can benefit from your experience. And that's okay, too. In this way, you have earned the right to reflect on your own approaches to problems and offer counsel or consolation. And it also ensures the stories and sentiments you share are truly relevant and helpful.

Julie Metzger, an infectiously enthusiastic registered nurse in Seattle, specializes in encouraging parents and adolescents to listen to one another. For nearly thirty years, her nonprofit, Great Conversations, has offered classes and presentations in the Pacific Northwest to help teens, preteens, and their parents talk about sex and "other growing-up stuff." Despite the often blush-worthy subject matter, her classes are packed. It's partly due to Metzger's sense of humor (she's been known to give talks with sanitary pads comically stuck to her sweater) but also her ability to nail family dynamics, particularly the tendency to ask questions that are based more on logistics than on trying to connect with one another.

Think of when your child comes home from school—you might ask a string of rapid-fire questions: "How was school?" "Have you eaten?" "Do you have homework?" "What did you get on your French test?" "Did you bring home your lunchbox?" Similarly, when greeting your spouse, you might ask, "How was work?" "Did you finish your proposal?" "Do you want to have the Murrays over for dinner on Friday?" "Do you have dry cleaning?" It sounds super friendly, caring, and curious, but Metzger said, "It is actually you running down a checklist to determine where things stand and what needs to happen next. It's not a real conversation, and it's not listening."

Not that practical questions shouldn't be asked. Of course they should. It's just when those are the only kinds of questions you ask, the relationship suffers. Open, honest, and exploratory questioning and the genuine curiosity and careful listening it presupposes can not only bring about greater clarity of what's on someone's mind but is also the very basis of intimacy. The question can be as simple as: "What did you learn today?" Another good one is: "What was the best part and what was the worst part of your day?"

The more you know about and understand where someone is coming from, the closer you feel to them whether they are loved ones or strangers. Arthur Aron, a professor of psychology at the State University of New York at Stony Brook, conducted an experiment in which he paired students, who didn't know each other, and had them ask each other thirty-six expansive questions like:

- Before making a telephone call, do you ever rehearse what you are going to say? Why?
- What would constitute a "perfect" day for you?
- When did you last sing to yourself? To someone else?
- If you were able to live to the age of ninety and retain either the mind or body of a thirty-year-old for the last sixty years of your life, which would you want?

After this reciprocal listening exercise, the paired strangers reported intense feelings of closeness, much more so than subjects paired for the same amount of time to solve a problem or accomplish a task. Indeed, two of the participants in the experiment later got married. The research received little notice when it was published more than twenty years ago, but it got an enormous amount of attention when it resurfaced in a 2015 essay in *The New York Times* headlined TO FALL IN LOVE WITH ANYONE, DO THIS. Aron's questions, subsequently renamed, "The 36 Questions That Lead to Love," have become an internet meme, as people continue to use them to spark new romantic relationships and reignite existing ones.

Good listeners are good questioners. Inquiry reinforces listening and vice versa because you have to listen to ask an appropriate and relevant question, and then, as a consequence of posing the question, you are invested in listening to the answer. Moreover, asking genuinely curious and openhearted questions makes for more meaningful and revelatory conversations—not to mention prevents misunderstandings. This, in turn, makes narratives more interesting, engaging, and even sympathetic, which is the basis for forming sincere and secure relationships.

You can't have meaningful exchanges with people, much less establish relationships, if you aren't willing to listen to people's stories, whether it's where they come from, what their dreams are, what led them to do the work they do, or how they came to fear polka dots. What is love but listening to and wanting to be a part of another person's evolving story? It's true of all relationships—romantic and platonic. And listening to a stranger is possibly one of the kindest, most generous things you can do.

People who make an effort to listen—and respond in ways that support rather than shift the conversation—end up collecting stories the way other people might collect stamps, shells, or coins. The result is they tend to have something interesting to contribute to almost any discussion. The best raconteurs and most interesting conversationalists I have ever met are the most agile questioners and attentive listeners. The exceptional listeners highlighted in this book, named and unnamed, kept me enthralled with their stories. It's in part because they've collected so much material but also, they seemed to have consciously or subconsciously learned the tones, inflections, cadences, pauses, and turns of phrase that rivet your attention.

Many celebrated writers, including Tom Wolfe, John McPhee, and Richard Price, have said that listening is the generative soul of their work. Pulitzer Prize–winning author Elizabeth Strout told an interviewer, "I have listened all my life. I just listen and listen and listen." One of her characters, Jim Burgess, in her novel *The Burgess Boys,* says, "People are always telling you who they are." Strout said she loved giving him that line because people really do tell you who they are, often in spite of themselves. "If you listen carefully, you can really get an awful lot of information about other people," she said. "I think most people just aren't listening that much."

The stories we collect in life define us and are the scaffolding of our realities. Families, friends, and coworkers have stories that bind them together. Rivals and enemies have narratives that keep them apart. All around us are people's legends and anecdotes, myths and stark realities, deprecations and aggrandizements. Listening helps us sort fact from fiction and deepens our understanding of the complex situations and personalities we encounter in life. It's how we gain entrée, gather intelligence, and make connections, regardless of the social circles in which we find ourselves.

13

Hammers, Anvils, and Stirrups

Turning Sound Waves into Brain Waves

The passenger pickup zone at Houston's George Bush Intercontinental Airport was pandemonium. Cops bellowed and blew whistles, diverting traffic around construction. Workers in hard hats and orange vests jackhammered concrete. A belching backhoe sent heaps of ashy rubble crashing into the bed of a rumbling dump truck. Shuttle buses idled and hissed. Cars honked. Drivers rolled down their windows and yelled expletives.

I saw my father exit the terminal about one hundred yards from where I was stuck in a line of cars. He was dragging a roller bag that roused a flock of pigeons pecking on the pavement. I stood on the running board of my car and called out, "Dad!" My voice was lost in the surrounding din. And yet, my father snapped his head in my direction. He waved and strode determinedly to the car. "You can always hear your puppies," he said.

Certainly, there are animals that have better hearing than humans. A dog, for example, could hear its puppy yelp from a much greater distance than my dad could hear me, his grown daughter. Elephants' hearing is so sensitive they can hear approaching clouds. But humans are particularly adept at discriminating between and categorizing sounds, and—perhaps most important—we imbue what we hear with meaning.

When my dad exited the airport, he plunged into a roiling sea of sound waves, undulating at various frequencies and amplitudes. But it was the unique sonic properties of my voice that got his attention. My voice triggered a cascade of physical, emotional, and cognitive reactions that made him take notice and respond. It's easy to take for granted our ability to perceive and process auditory information in this way. We do it all day, every day. Nevertheless, it's a feat that's astounding in its specificity and complexity.

There's been extensive research over the years on where in the brain we make sense of auditory information. The processes that underlie the recognition and interpretation of sound have been studied in a variety of species (monkeys, mice, rabbits, harpy eagles, sea lions, dogs, etc.), and you can read hundreds of papers about everything from the neural pathways auditory signals take to how your genes respond depending on the input. And yet, there's still little understanding of just how we listen and connect with one another during a conversation. Processing what someone says, it turns out, is one of the most intricate and involved things we ask our brains to do.

What we do know is that each side of your brain has an

auditory cortex, conveniently located near your ears. If it is injured or removed, you will have no awareness of sound, although you might have some reflexive reaction to it. You'll flinch at a clap of thunder, but you won't know why. Critical to the comprehension of speech is Wernicke's area, located in the brain's left hemisphere. It's named for the German neurologist Carl Wernicke, who, in 1874, published his discovery that stroke patients with lesions in that area could still hear and speak but were unable to comprehend what was said to them. It's unknown exactly how many other areas of the brain are recruited in speech comprehension or how much variability there is between humans, though it's reasonable to suspect a fantastic listener who is picking up every nuance in a conversation is firing off more neurons in more parts of the brain than a bad listener.

But it's not only words our brains are processing when we listen to people. It's also pitch, loudness, and tone as well as the flow of tone, called *prosody*. In fact, human beings can reliably interpret the emotional aspect of a message even when the words are completely obscured. Think of the various ways a person can say, "Sure." There's the peppy, higher-pitched "Sure!" said when someone is eager to help with a request. There's the tentative and lower-pitched "Suuuure" that stretches out for a couple of beats when someone is somewhat ambivalent or reluctant to help with the request. And then there's the clipped, level-pitched "Sure" that precedes a "but" when someone is probably going to argue about how to help with the request, or is not going to help at all.

Researchers are just now discovering that specialized clusters of neurons in the brain are responsible for detecting those slight changes in pitch and tone. The more practiced a listener you are, the better these neurons get at perceiving the kinds of sonic variations that carry the emotional content, and much of the meaning, of what people say. For example, musicians, whose art depends on detecting differences in pitch and tone, more readily pick up on vocal expressions of emotion than nonmusicians, lending some truth to the notion that musicians tend to be more sensitive souls. Perhaps not surprisingly, musicians unfamiliar with Mandarin Chinese also tend to be better than nonmusicians at discerning the language's subtle tonal differences, which can change the entire meaning of a word in addition to signaling emotion.

There's also evidence that you use different parts of your brain depending on how you interpret what you hear. Uri Hasson, the neuroscientist who showed us how listeners' and speakers' brain waves sync when there is understanding, conducted another intriguing fMRI experiment in his Princeton lab that showed the mind-altering effects of prejudicial information. He and his colleagues had subjects listen to an adapted version of the J. D. Salinger short story "Pretty Mouth and Green My Eyes," which describes a telephone conversation between Arthur and Lee. Arthur tells Lee he suspects his wife is having an affair while an unidentified woman lies in bed next to Lee. Before hearing the story, half the subjects were told the woman in bed with Lee is Arthur's wife. The other cohort was told Arthur is paranoid and the woman is Lee's girlfriend.

That one differing detail was enough to significantly change the subjects' brain patterns while listening to the story so that Hasson could easily tell who thought the wife was a two-timer and who thought she was faithful. If that was all it took to separate people into neurally distinct groups, just think what's happening in the brains of people habitually listening to, say, Fox News versus CNN. If you tell both factions the exact same thing, their brains will measurably hear it differently, as the signals are routed through distinct pathways depending on what they had previously heard. "It will reshape your mind," Hasson told me. "It will affect the way you listen." It's an argument for listening to as many sources as possible to keep your brain as agile as possible. Otherwise, your brain becomes like a car that's not firing on all cylinders or a computer circuit board where electrical impulses run through a limited number of channels, wasting its full capacity.

Another interesting aspect of how we process auditory information is the right-ear advantage. Our language comprehension is generally better and faster when heard in the right ear versus the left. It has to do with the lateralization of the brain so that what one hears in the right ear is routed first to the left side of the brain, where Wernicke's area is located. There's a left-ear advantage when it comes to the recognition of emotional aspects of speech as well as the perception and appreciation of music and sounds in nature. The opposite may be true for left-handed people whose brain wiring may be reversed.

So, you may be better at picking up on the meaning of speech versus the emotional feelings that underlie speech depending on which ear you use. This finding comes from studies of subjects listening to voices piped into either the left or right side of headphones as well as studies of patients who have had brain damage in the right or left side of the brain. Those with right-side injuries, for example, had the most trouble picking up on emotions.

There was also an ingenious study by Italian researchers that showed, in noisy nightclubs, people more often offered their right ear when someone walked up and tried to talk to them and were also more likely to give someone a cigarette when the request was made in the right ear versus the left ear. It was a clever way of demonstrating the right-ear advantage in a natural setting, since there are not many environments where it's possible to make a request into only one ear and have it not seem totally weird.

This may have implications for which ear you want to incline toward a speaker or which ear you use to talk on the phone. For talking to your boss, tilt your head to the left so your right ear is up. If you're having trouble figuring out whether your romantic partner is upset, switch your phone to the left ear. Do the reverse if you are left-handed. But you probably subconsciously choose the most advantageous ear already. For example, a left-handed female executive who works in the male-dominated, take-no-prisoners oil industry in Houston told me she always holds the phone to her left ear—which, for lefties like her, is the more logical, less emotional ear. "When I put a phone to my right ear, it seems like I can't hear," she said. "That's not true, of course, but it feels that way."

Naomi Henderson, the focus group moderator, told me she's noticed that when people tilt their heads to the right so their left ear is up, it usually signals that they are tapping into more emotional parts of themselves, which is the kind of information that is most valuable to her clients. So when she sees someone cock their head right, lifting that left ear, it prompts her to zero in and inquire what memories or images the product or issue they were discussing brought to mind. She discovered this through experience rather than a scientific experiment, but it makes sense given the left ear is usually the more emotional ear.

Which ear do you use to talk on the phone? Which ear do you put forward when you're straining to hear something? Do you use a different ear in different circumstances or with different people? It's an interesting experiment and might indicate how you are processing information, or rather, what aspects of the information are taking precedence at that moment. Equally fascinating is to notice which ear others incline toward you and how that may change depending on the topic of the conversation.

We should probably back up at this point to talk about the actual mechanics of hearing, which is the necessary precursor to listening. We've talked about how auditory information is processed once inside the brain, but it's worth taking a moment to appreciate how it gets in there. Let's pause to consider the miracles that are our ears, the openings on either side of our heads that help us not only hear but also maintain our physical balance. You could say our ears help us get our bearings both physically and emotionally.

The earliest vertebrates had inner ears, which were the beginnings of the vestibular—or balance—system. People who have had vertigo know all too well the importance of a functioning vestibular system. It senses the body's acceleration and orientation in space and sends signals to the musculoskeletal system to keep us upright. Our slithering forebears' primitive vestibular systems not only sensed which way was up but could also vibrate in response to pressure, first underwater and then in the open air. This was the beginning of hearing because what are sound waves but compressions of air? A Bach sonata, a garbage truck backing up, a mosquito's whine—they're all just air particles being scrunched together at regular intervals, kind of like an invisible inchworm moving up-down, up-down through space.

When sound waves reach our ears, the air compressions are funneled down the stiff, fleshy outside part of the ear known as the *pinna,* increasing the relative acoustic pressure by up to twenty decibels by the time it reaches our ear canal. The nerve endings in there are incredibly dense. David Haynes, a professor of otolaryngology, neurosurgery, and hearing and speech sciences at Vanderbilt University in Nashville, Tennessee, told me that there are more nerve tendrils reaching into the ear per square centimeter than just about anywhere else in the body. "It developed that way over time to make us more protective because our ears are super important real estate," he said. And those sensory nerves can refer sensations throughout the body, including to internal organs and erogenous zones, which is why people persist in sticking Q-tips in their ears despite dire warnings from doctors like Haynes that it can be harmful. It just feels so darn good to root around in there. They don't call it "eargasm" for nothing.

At the other end of the ear canal, about an inch inside your head, the sound waves strike the *tympanic membrane*—your beautiful, pearlescent little eardrum—which vibrates neighboring bones with wonderfully descriptive names like the *hammer,* the *anvil,* and the *stirrup.* From there, the waves spiral around the fluid-filled *cochlea,* which looks like a snail shell (*cochlea* is Greek for *snail*). The cochlea is lined with tiny hair cells, each tuned to a different frequency. Given how important communication and cooperation have been to our species' survival, it should come as no surprise that the hair cells tuned to the frequencies of human sounds are the most sensitive.

Protruding from each hair cell is a bundle of bristles, called *stereocilia,* with each strand only as wide as the smallest wavelength of visible light. When sound waves nudge these filaments back and forth, it tickles nerve endings to set all sorts of cognitive and emotional processes in motion. So in the midst of all that ruckus at the airport, tiny hair cells tens of microns long registering infinitesimally small changes were how my dad recognized and responded to my voice.

Most hearing loss comes from damage to those hair cells caused by loud noises. Viewed through an electron microscope, healthy stereocilia look like soldiers, standing at attention in precise formation. But when exposed to sounds as loud as an ambulance siren, they look like they've suffered an enemy attack, bent and flopped over.

Your hair cells might recover if the noise wasn't too loud and didn't last too long. A typical conversation occurs at sixty decibels and doesn't cause damage, but listen to music through earbuds at high volume, which is around one hundred decibels, and you'll have permanent damage after just fifteen minutes. Lower the volume to a more moderate eighty-eight decibels and you'll have damage in four hours. A jackhammer or jet engine can cause damage in less than thirty seconds.

A distressing number of everyday activities can damage your precious stereocilia, including drying your hair, using a blender, going to a rock concert, vacuuming, watching a movie in a movie theater, eating at a noisy restaurant, riding a motorcycle, and operating a power tool. Over time, the noisy insults can add up to significant hearing loss. This, of course, inhibits your ability to listen and disconnects you from the world. But audiologists say inserting a cheap pair of foam earplugs into your ears in noisy situations can go a long way toward preserving your hearing.

You can also have earplugs custom made to fit your ears' unique pinnae for $40–$200. The higher-priced versions have noise-filtering systems built in, which allow you to hear clearly but at reduced volume. These kinds of plugs are often used by people who have noisy professions, such as musicians, pilots, dentists, factory workers, and computer technicians. But noise-filtering plugs are not a bad investment for anyone who wants to go to a movie or music concert without damaging their ears. If you download a noise meter app onto your phone, you'll find that the sound level during many movies far exceeds the upper limit recommended by the Centers for Disease Control and Prevention's National Institute for Occupational Safety and Health.

Experts have begun referring to teenagers today as "Generation Deaf" because near chronic earbud or headphone use is ruining their hearing. The World Health Organization has warned that 1.1 billion young people are at risk of hearing loss because of earbud abuse. A good way to tell if kids are damaging their hearing is if you can hear any noise emanating from the earbuds or headphones they are wearing. The volume is at a safe level if you can't hear anything. But of course, it's not just young people. Adults, too, routinely crank up the volume on their phones to drown out ambient noise, or because the connection is bad.

Fifteen percent of Americans, around 48 million people, have hearing loss. Sixty-five percent of them are under age sixty-five. As a result, hearing loss is viewed as a major public health issue, ranking as the third most common chronic physical condition after high blood pressure and arthritis.

Many people aren't aware that they are losing their hearing

until it's severe. This is because when you have light to moderate hearing loss, your brain takes up the slack by filling in the words you don't hear in conversations. The problem is that your brain is not always accurate. In fact, it often isn't. Your brain goes with what it expects to hear rather than what is actually said or sometimes hears things when nothing is said at all. As far back as the 1890s, researchers have demonstrated humans' susceptibility to auditory hallucinations by pairing a tone with some sort of stimulus, such as a pulse of light. Before long, subjects start to "hear" the tone when only the light flashes. You've probably experienced a similar phenomenon when you hear your cell phone ring, ping, or burble when it hasn't.

Before he died, the neurologist Oliver Sacks kept a notebook of his "mishearings" when his own hearing was failing. He wrote what he misheard in red, what was really said in green, and in purple, he recorded the resulting misunderstandings, some worthy of a sitcom episode. They included him hearing "choir practice" instead of "chiropractor" and "cuttlefish" instead of "publicist." My personal favorite example of a mishearing was when I told a friend I was growing baby seedless watermelons in my garden and he said, "Baby Jesus watermelons? Do you have to grow them in a manger?"

A common form of mishearing happens when we're unable to make out the lyrics of songs and our brains substitute something that makes some sort of sense. A classic example is hearing "'Scuse me while I kiss this guy," in Jimi Hendrix's "Purple Haze" instead of "'Scuse me while I kiss the sky." The phenomenon even has a name: *mondegreen*. American writer

Sylvia Wright coined the term in 1954, describing how as a girl she misheard the lyric "—and laid him on the green" in a Scottish ballad as "—and Lady Mondegreen."

Mishearings are also sometimes due to the McGurk effect, which occurs when people get conflicting visual and auditory stimuli. For example, if the syllables *ba-ba* are spoken over the lip movements of *ga-ga,* our perception is *da-da.*

The lesson in all this is that many people may be poor listeners because they truly can't hear well and their brains are working in strange ways to make up for it. While some mishearings can be humorous, hearing loss, in the long run, leads to a litany of poor emotional and social outcomes, including, but not limited to:

- irritability, negativism, anger, fatigue, tension, stress, and depression
- avoidance or withdrawal from social situations
- social rejection and loneliness
- reduced job performance and earning power
- diminished psychological and overall health

These symptoms are not so much the result of hearing loss per se but the resulting inability to connect with people. So it's enormously important to protect your hearing by keeping volume on sound systems in a safe range (no more than 60 percent of maximum volume) and wearing earplugs when in noisy environments. It's also a good idea to get your ears checked if you suspect your listening problems have a physiological component.

Earwax buildup all by itself can cause hearing loss. You'd be surprised how a good ear cleaning once or twice a year by an otolaryngologist can improve your hearing.

―――――――

While our ears are obviously essential to hearing, it's worth noting that listening is as much a visual as aural enterprise. It's probably not by accident that Wernicke's area, where speech is processed in the brain, is located at the juncture of the visual and auditory cortices. During perfectly audible conversations, lipreading is responsible for as much as 20 percent of your comprehension. Moreover, it's widely thought that at least 55 percent of the emotional content of a spoken message is, in fact, transmitted nonverbally. So, even if you've had your ears checked and your hearing is perfect, if you are looking at your phone or out the window while someone is talking to you, you're not getting the whole story.

As much as we like to think we can control how much we reveal, our facial expressions, respiration, perspiration, gestures, posture, and numerous other types of body language usually give us away. As Sigmund Freud said, "No mortal can keep a secret. If his lips are silent, he chatters with his fingertips; betrayal oozes out of him at every pore." Good listeners pick up on the subtle signals others miss.

There are universal facial expressions people make when feeling authentic emotion. Among the most obvious are the furrowed brow, pursed lips, and raised chin of wounded pride and the soft wrinkling around the eyes and open, upturned mouth of genuine delight. We share many spontaneous facial expressions (smiling, grimacing, raising your eyebrows in surprise) with primates, which suggests our facial expressions are an involuntary pre-language.

Charles Darwin believed that the ability to communicate, "Danger!" or "Don't mess with me!" or "Let's mate!" was key to human survival long before we developed the ability to talk. Researchers have measured the rate at which people's facial muscles contract to form expressions and found that they occur in conjunction with, and at the same frequency as, spoken or signed words in a sentence. It's called the *grammaticalization* of facial expressions.

Expressions of authentic emotion are discernibly different from those people "put on." They are a special combination of minute muscle contractions, particularly around the eyes and mouth, over which you have no control. You can fake a smile, put on a brave face, and feign surprise, but it's not going to look the same as it would if you actually felt the emotions.

People tend to be pretty good at telling when someone is putting on a fake face as well as reading people's real emotions, provided they have experience. People who were raised by, say, emotionally flat parents or parents who were depressed or angry all the time tend to have trouble reading the full range of facial expressions. Studies have shown this is also true for people who spend too much time looking at screens.

But the effects are reversible if one seizes opportunities to listen and engage with a wide variety of people. For example, in one study of children at a device-free outdoor camp, researchers found that after just five days without phones or tablets and interacting with their peers, the kids were able to accurately read facial expressions and identify the emotions of people in photographs and videotaped scenes significantly better than controls who had not attended the camp and continued using their devices.

The face not only changes its expression in response to emotion, it also changes color. Not just beet red with embarrassment and ghostly white from shock but more subtle shades corresponding to a range of emotions. The changes occur due to slight shifts in blood flow around the nose, eyebrows, cheeks, and chin. Moreover, the color patterns, or color ratios, indicating different emotions are the same regardless of gender, ethnicity, or overall skin tone. Attentive listeners perceive those shifts, usually subconsciously.

Researchers at Ohio State University superimposed the color signatures of various emotions on neutral faces and subjects were able to accurately tell what the person was feeling up to 74 percent of the time. Our faces have more blood vessels close to the surface of the skin than just about anywhere else in the body. That, along with the fact that we have less facial hair than apes, suggests there is an evolutionary advantage to showing our true colors. But you won't perceive it if you aren't listening using all your senses.

You get a flood of signals when you listen to someone, many outside of your conscious awareness, but nevertheless, informing your impression of the person and interpretation of the message. Sometimes, though, all that incoming information can get overwhelming, particularly when the subject of the conversation is intense. It's why people sometimes, without realizing it, attempt to dial it back by, for example, bringing up emotional topics while driving, cooking, or doing some other task where they won't have to look at the other person straight on. Likewise, romantic partners might have serious talks while they are lying side by side in a darkened bedroom. The lessening or softening of visual cues keeps them from going into sensory overload.

Many journalists, including *Fresh Air*'s Terry Gross, prefer telephone to in-person interviews so they don't get biased or distracted by the other person's appearance or nonverbal tics. They may also not want to inadvertently influence the other person with their own body language or unsettle them by taking notes or consulting notes they'd taken in preparation for the interview. It's the same idea behind the confessional booth in the Roman Catholic Church, where a screen divides priest and penitent so there's nothing but the words passing between them. It can make people less self-conscious and encourage a more open and honest exchange.

It's a balance, though, between what you lose and what you gain by listening blind. Because nonverbal signals typically carry more than half, or 55 percent, of the emotional content of a message, if you take them out of the equation, you're missing out on a lot of information. But on occasions when nonverbal indicators would get in the way of the articulation of the message or affect how accurately the message is interpreted, you need to take that into account.

If you have to listen to someone remotely, phone is better than text or email because as much as 38 percent of someone's feelings and attitudes are conveyed by tone of voice. This means that during many conversations, you get just 7 percent of the meaning from the actual words, which could be typed. Recall that the way someone says *sure* can indicate whether that person is eager, ambivalent, or resistant to help with a request. Font styles notwithstanding, the word *sure* always looks the same on a screen.

Of course, picking up on intonations during a phone call depends on a decent connection, which is getting harder to come by. Terry Gross has the advantage of talking to people on an integrated services digital network, or ISDN, line which gives her exceptionally high-quality audio. But for those placing calls on mobile phones, the distortions, delays, and breaks make it harder to pick up on the nuances in tone that enhance understanding.

Jerry Gibson, an electrical engineer and distinguished professor at the University of California–Santa Barbara, told me one of the reasons why it's so hard to have a decent cell phone conversation is because voice calls are a low priority for service providers. There is higher demand for video and data, he said, so wireless providers have gotten stingy on the bandwidth, or bit rates, they allot for voice calls. The result is poor sound quality but fewer interruptions in service.

"Their calculation is you will be less frustrated by a bad connection than a dropped connection," said Gibson, who is an expert in mobile communication technology and author of several books on the subject with titles like *Information Theory and Rate Distortion Theory for Communications and Compression*. In other words, there are technological reasons contributing to your disinclination to talk on the phone. "You get low enough bandwidth and the call is tinny, breaks in and out, and doesn't sound very good," Gibson said. "It's no wonder people would rather text."

While the technology used to digitally transmit the human voice between mobile phones is complicated, it's nothing compared to the complexity of how human beings perceive speech, process it, and ultimately derive meaning. Science still hasn't figured it all out. But what is known is listening is intricate and multisensory. We also know the mechanics of listening—the structures within our ears—are fragile and should be protected. And finally, and most reassuringly, we know that our listening ability, measured by the accuracy of our understanding, is improvable with motivation and practice.

14

Addicted to Distraction

There was a time when, during idle or anxious moments, people reached for a cigarette. They lit up while fretting over a problem, drinking a cup of coffee, waiting on a friend, driving a car, mingling at a party, and unwinding after sex. Now, in those same situations, people just as reflexively reach for their phones. Like smokers nervously patting their pockets for cigarettes, people get jittery without their phones. Indeed, mental health experts say device dependency has many of the same behavioral, psychological, and neurobiological components as substance abuse.

While our smartphones may not allow us to have a decent conversation ("Can you hear me now? How about now?"), they seem to offer us just about everything else—social media, games, news, maps, recipes, videos, music, movies, podcasts, shopping, and pornography, if you're so inclined. In the end, none of it is as emotionally satisfying or as essential to our well-being as connecting with a live human being. And yet, like any addict, we keep tapping, scrolling, and swiping as if pulling a lever on a slot machine, hoping to eventually hit the jackpot.

This compulsion, driven by a fear of missing out, prevents sustained attention, making listening—or any task requiring thought—difficult. It's hard to concentrate on what's happening in the real world when you're preoccupied with what could be happening in the virtual one. Experts have raised concerns that we are even losing our ability to daydream, as fantasizing, too, requires some level of attention. Many of the greatest advances in science and arts and letters have come by way of daydreaming. Albert Einstein, Alexander Graham Bell, Charles Darwin, Friedrich Nietzsche, T. S. Eliot, and Lewis Carroll all attributed their genius to long periods of uninterrupted musing. Could you put away your phone for an hour? A half hour? Five minutes?

Research conducted by Microsoft found that since the year 2000, the average attention span dropped from twelve to eight seconds. For context, a goldfish has an attention span of nine seconds, according to the report. While journalists, psychologists, and neuroscientists have since quibbled with how one measures attention (of a human or a goldfish) and whether it's really a declining ability or simply more divided, advertisers and media companies are living with the reality that it's harder than ever to capture people's attention.

It's why *The New York Times* online now has daily briefings of a couple of sentences accompanied by lively visuals, video, and animated graphics, replacing the previous paragraph-long teasers of top stories that were standard a decade ago. Experts in web analytics say the majority of internet users give articles online about fifteen seconds before deciding to stay or go, and if a website takes more than three seconds to load, people get utterly exasperated and move on. A study by a British advertising buyer found that, on average, when people are at home, they switch between devices (phone, tablet, or laptop) twenty-one times per hour, all while the television is on in the background. So if you're still reading this book so many pages in, I'm ecstatic.

Comedy skits performed onstage at Second City in Chicago have gone from fifteen minutes to five minutes. Acutely aware of their audiences' diminished attention spans, directors told me they have to keep the action moving at a rapid clip as well as provide more active (moving, flashing, rotating) lighting. There is no thought of letting a joke slowly build to a big payoff. Directors and performers said people would be checking their phones before actors could arrive at the punch line.

Websites, mobile apps, video games, and social media platforms are designed to grab and keep your attention. Companies like Facebook, Google, and Epic Games (the creator of the popular third-person-shooter video game Fortnite) comingle computer science, neuroscience, and psychology to develop strategies to hook you, often by playing on your social anxieties, vanity, and greed. They do it because your taps, swipes, scrolls, and clicks are how they make money. Like it or not, we are participating in an attention economy, where advertisers pay billions to media companies to steal us away from whatever else we might want to focus on. Attention has become a commodity, bought and sold on sophisticated electronic exchanges where bidding occurs in real time based on data provided by your cell phone or web browser. The quality of your attention doesn't matter. Indeed, the more divided your attention, the more persuadable you are. The more likely you are to click *Buy Now*.

Our human brains are not equipped to manage the onslaught. A stay-at-home mom in Boise, Idaho, told me, "It used to be you just knew the narratives of the people in your immediate world, but now it's the universe, with updates every minute. Things are pushed on us. There are constant, urgent interruptions. What did President Trump do now? A typhoon in Asia killed how many people? I feel like I'm always being buffeted about. You feel busier trying to keep up, but it just keeps you from getting anything done."

As machines have increasingly competed for our attention over the past century, the average amount of time people have devoted to listening to one another during their waking hours has gone down almost by half, from 42 percent to 24 percent. And now even the time spent listening to recorded speech is going down, as speed-listening has become the new speed-reading. People listen to audiobooks at twice the original speed, often while doing something else like exercising or driving. Apps like Overcast allow people to listen to podcasts in double or triple time; a practice called *podfasting*. And the audiobook retailer and producer Audible has a "Take Me to the Good Parts," feature that lets listeners jump to the steamy sections of romance titles in the company's collection.

Though live and in-person stories can be infinitely more

interesting, they take a degree of patience that can be hard for people accustomed to speeding up or sexing up audio content on their smartphones. Research suggests that after people listen regularly to faster-paced speech, they have great difficulty maintaining their attention when addressed by someone who is talking normally—sort of like the feeling you get when you come off an expressway and have to go through a school zone. Moreover, you lose your ability to perceive and appreciate nuance in conversation because things like tonal shifts, subtle sighs, foreign accents, and even voices made raspy by whiskey and cigarettes all but disappear when heard in double time.

Conversational partners become just another device to toggle between. People periodically check their phones rather than fully attending to whoever is talking, which only makes it more likely they'll have slow and soul-sucking conversations. A study by psychologists at the University of Essex found that the mere presence of a phone on the table—even if it's silent—makes those sitting around the table feel more disconnected and disinclined to talk about anything important or meaningful, knowing if they do, they will probably be interrupted. It's a weird loop of the phone creating a circumstance where people will talk about things that aren't worth listening to, which in turn makes you more likely to stop listening and look at your phone.

Several studies of caregiver-child interactions in public spaces like playgrounds and fast-food restaurants found that the vast majority of caregivers ignored their children in favor of their phones. Pediatric experts say such behavior impairs children's development, which depends on being attended to by their parents. As mentioned earlier, we tend to listen as we were listened to as children, which suggests the so-called screen generation now coming of age may have greater difficulty connecting with others.

———

But it's not just mobile devices and the associated online distraction that are getting in the way of listening. It's also the modern aural environments we have created for ourselves. Workplaces today, for example, from the smallest start-ups to the largest corporations, are typically "open office" designs, with few walls or enclosures, so every telephone call, keyboard click, and after-lunch belch contributes to a constant daily racket. It's hard to hear yourself think, much less pay full attention to someone who might want to tell you something important.

Having a quiet conversation at a restaurant is even less likely. According to food industry research and investigative reporting by several news outlets, sound levels average 80 decibels at restaurants in the United States (recall that the typical conversation averages about 60 decibels). The most popular, trendy restaurants have sound levels that exceed 90 decibels, which can cause hearing loss before dessert is served. Indeed, the most recent Zagat Dining Trends Survey found that noise in restaurants was ranked as diners' top complaint. There is also evidence that the clamor makes diners overeat and make less healthy food choices.

Stores like Abercrombie & Fitch, H&M, and Zara can have

noise levels in the high 80 to low 90 decibels. Similarly, you can't go to a coffee shop, grocery store, or even a car dealership without piped-in background music, which even at low levels divides attention and makes full comprehension of conversations difficult. The distraction makes customers more vulnerable to the hard sell and more prone to impulse buy. I can tell you from experience that you are at a disadvantage negotiating the price of car while Survivor's "Eye of the Tiger" blares in the dealer's showroom.

People haven't made their homes refuges of quiet either. Televisions are almost always on with the drone of cable news, reruns, looping weather reports, or cooking shows. Most people now also have some form of sound system, even if it's just a small, portable speaker plugged into an iPhone. Streaming services like Apple Music, Pandora, and Spotify have allowed even those without large music collections to have constant ambient music—excellent for setting a mood but a distraction if you want to listen closely to a family member or friend.

While you may think you can tune out these kinds of things, research consistently shows that you cannot. The ability to multitask is a delusion. Each input degrades your attention. Psychologist Daniel Kahneman memorably wrote, "The often used phrase 'pay attention' is apt: you dispose of a limited budget of attention that you can allocate to activities, and if you try to go beyond your budget, you will fail."

All this is to say that you must cultivate the right environment if you want to truly listen, which is as much about a receptive physical space as a receptive state of mind. You need quiet and freedom from interruption. There shouldn't be background noise, much less the intruding *ping* of a mobile device. It seems obvious, but how often do we actually do it?

It's not that you can only effectively and meaningfully interact with people in secluded or soundproof spaces. That's impossible. But you can wave someone into your office and put your computer to sleep. You can choose quiet restaurants and silence your phone and keep it out of sight. You can find a park bench, take a walk on a quiet street, or just duck into a doorway away from the stream of pedestrian traffic to have a word. All are ways of signaling your receptiveness; your willingness to listen to what someone has to say. Whether the conversation is long or short, about business or more personal, contentious or sedate, in offering a quiet moment, or a quieter moment in the surrounding chaos, you create a better opportunity to connect with that person and understand where they are coming from.

A group of Harvard researchers in 2010 collaborated on a pilot program they called the Family Dinner Project, formed to encourage device-free and listening-focused family meals. The impetus was a number of studies over the past fifteen years that showed families eating together and sharing stories led to lower rates of substance abuse, teen pregnancy, and depression while improving kids' vocabularies, grade point averages, resilience, and self-esteem.

The project has since evolved from the original fifteen families in and around Cambridge, Massachusetts, to a nationwide initiative that provides resources, workshops, and tips on how to get families to share meals and have uninterrupted conversations. "I know you're thinking, 'Oh my gosh, have we gotten to the point where we need a workshop for that?'" said John Sarrouf, who was a director of the Family Dinner Project during its early years. "Yes, we have gotten to that point."*

Among the conversation starters recommended by the Family Dinner Project are questions like "What is the best gift you ever received?" and "If you went back in time one hundred or two hundred years and could only bring three things with you, what would you bring?" Similar to the "The 36 Questions That Lead to Love" mentioned earlier, the conversation starters are curious rather than appraising, seeking to find out not what someone has achieved but who the person really is. So, it's not just eating together that is beneficial. Anyone who's suffered through a tense family meal knows that's not the case. The potential to improve relationships and health outcomes results from using the meal as an opportunity to ask questions and truly listen to one another in a curious and openhearted way.

At a family dinner or any gathering, the gift of your full attention is a form of hospitality, according to literary scholar Ronald Sharp, who, with Eudora Welty, coedited *The Norton Book of Friendship,* an anthology of works on the importance and meaning of friendship in which listening figures prominently. "You're

---

* Sarrouf is now co-executive director at Essential Partners, one of the groups mentioned in chapter 7 that helps individuals in communities and organizations listen better to get beyond the "us versus them" mentality.

welcoming another person's words and feelings into your consciousness," he told me. "You are allowing that person to cross over the threshold and take up residence in your world."

Welty was legendary for extending that kind of hospitality. Sharp said she was one of the most attentive listeners he has ever known, which was not only the basis of her intelligence and humor, so evident in her writing, but also her capacity for friendship. "So many people thought she was the most amazing friend they ever had," he said. Sharp echoed others who were close to her, recalling how she always made time for him and expressed genuine interest in what he had to say. "She never rushed you or tried to finish your thoughts," Sharp said. "She invited you to tell your story, and, more importantly, she actually let you tell your story."

An invitation like that can have a lasting influence. An example is former Dallas police chief David Brown, who gained national attention following the 2016 fatal shootings of five local police officers during a protest against racially motivated police violence. Brown, who is African American, was widely praised at the time for encouraging people to sit down and listen to one another rather than protest in the streets and online. He famously invited protesters to join the police force to bring about meaningful change. Following his nationally televised press conference, applications to the Dallas Police Department soared.

Brown later told an interviewer that what he was asking people to do was no different from what a white classmate did when he invited Brown home for dinner when they were eleven years old. Approaching his friend's house, Brown said he felt like Sidney Poitier in the movie *Guess Who's Coming to Dinner,* worried he might get uninvited when his friend's parents found out he was black. But they welcomed him, served him a potpie, and were interested in what he had to say. "Why aren't we smarter than sixth graders? Why can't we figure this out?" Brown said. "It takes not a big group, not yelling and screaming, but 'Let's sit down and listen to each other and invite someone home for dinner.'"

Back when Chief Brown had dinner with his childhood friend, there weren't cell phones on the table. No one was checking newsfeeds between bites or taking pictures of the potpies to post on Instagram. When Ronald Sharp visited Eudora Welty, she didn't have cable news on in the background or have a MacBook open on her lap. In both instances, there were no distractions. The focus was on, and the abiding interest was in, the guest. That simple courtesy made a lasting impression on the two men. They remembered the people who listened to them decades later with affection and gratitude.

15

What Words Conceal and Silences Reveal

It was the holiday shopping season, and I was seated at a highly polished cherrywood dining table at Gallery Furniture in Houston, Texas. Also seated at the table was Greg Hopf, Gallery Furniture's top salesman, which is saying something in a megastore that does more than $200 million annually in sales. With us were Mrs. Horton, seventy-six, perched tentatively on the edge of her chair, and Mr. Horton, eighty-three, standing behind her and rocking heel to toe, heel to toe in his Roper work boots. They were considering buying the table for their breakfast nook. They were also thinking about a bureau for their guest bedroom that Hopf had shown them earlier.

Apparently gripped by indecision, the couple hadn't said anything for maybe five to ten minutes. The quiet was getting oppressive, and I was getting fidgety. I was only there as an observer, but it was taking everything I had not to make a gentle comment or suggestion that might get them to make up their minds already. Hopf works on commissions that escalate with the number of sales he makes during the day. I knew he was missing out on other potential customers who, this being the holidays, were coming through the front door in droves.

But Hopf's expression was as placid as a lake on a windless day. He looked at the couple with earnest concern; his liquid eyes seemed even more sympathetic magnified behind his large glasses. It was the same expression he'd had while Mrs. Horton told us how her leg still troubled her some six years after breaking it. And also while Mr. Horton described being on foot patrols during his military service in Korea. "Mud was up to here," he said, indicating his mid-thigh. "And then'd rain, and then'd freeze."

Just when I thought I was going to lose my mind in the awkward silence, certain these two weren't going to buy anything, Mrs. Horton piped up. She'd take the table and also the matching chairs and oh, the bureau, too, and, what the heck, an entertainment console, just, well, because. I was stunned. Hopf, who has been selling furniture for thirty years, was not. "I've learned to be quiet," he told me after we delivered the couple to the cashier. "I guarantee you if I'd said something while we were sitting there, they would have just bought the bureau or nothing at all."

Hopf doesn't quite fit with Gallery Furniture's somewhat carnival atmosphere—there are caged parrots and monkeys, free cake and candy, and what looks like an acre of mattresses pushed together for kids to jump on. Gallery Furniture's owner, Jim McIngvale, known locally as Mattress Mack, jumps up and down on mattresses in TV ads clutching fistfuls of cash while shouting, "Gallery Furniture saves you money!"

Hopf is more sedate, purposely shepherding customers to relatively quiet corners of the store and just letting them talk—or not talk—on occasions when they are mulling or just plain muddled. He doesn't interrupt, wheedle, cajole, correct, or interject. When customers go off on tangents, he just listens, gathering intelligence. An older guy said he didn't own a computer because computers were ruining the world, so Hopf knew it was pointless to show him a complicated HD television. A harried young mother complained about getting stuck in traffic while taking her four preschool-age kids to their grandmother's house, and Hopf steered her toward sofas that are covered in durable materials that resist dirt and Popsicle stains.

"It may seem like it would take longer to let people go on, but it's actually quicker and easier, and you make fewer mistakes," Hopf said. I noticed, too, that his willingness to hear customers' stories made them less guarded and more trusting toward him. It's not a bad bet because, as Hopf told me, "when you hear people's stories, you tend to want to do right by them."

What's most striking about Hopf is his unusually high tolerance for silence, remaining totally unperturbed when customers like the Hortons go mum. It's a rare quality, particularly in Western cultures, where people get extremely uncomfortable when there are gaps in conversation. We call it *dead air*. A hesitation or pause is seen as unbearably awkward and something to actively avoid. People are poised to jump in at the slightest indication that a speaker might be trailing off, even if the person hasn't quite completed a thought.

When researchers graphed around fifty thousand pauses or transitions that occurred during English language conversations, they got a dramatic bell curve between -1 and +1 seconds (negative numbers indicating the times people began talking before the other person stopped talking). The highest peak was around 0–200 milliseconds, which means there was no pause at all between speakers or there was a pause that lasted less than the blink of an eye. Studies of Dutch and German speakers yielded similar results.

People in Japan, by contrast, allow longer gaps in conversation. Studies have shown that Japanese businesspeople tolerate silences that last nearly twice as long as those Americans can withstand, 8.2 seconds versus 4.6 seconds. Doctor-patient interactions in Japan contain more silences than in America, 30 percent versus 8 percent. In America, we say, "The squeaky wheel gets the grease," while in Japan, "The silent man is the best to listen to."

There's a similar comfort with silence in Nordic countries, most notably Finland. Like the Japanese, Finns place greater value on listening, modesty, and privacy than Americans and many Western Europeans. There's some truth in the joke about two Finnish men on their way to work and one says, "It is here that I lost my knife," and on the way home that evening, the other man says, "Your knife, did you say?" It's considered impolite and overbearing in Finland to be too quick to jump in when someone finishes a thought, much less to interrupt.

Silences are not only okay there, they are basic decorum. But researchers have also suggested that people in quieter cultures may have greater fear of losing face or being humiliated, which makes them more reluctant to speak.

Regardless, when we talk about culturally determined tolerances for silence, the differences are usually only on the order of seconds, if not fractions of seconds. People universally don't like so-called loss of conversational flow. If the silence goes on too long, longer than what the norm is in that culture, it makes people uneasy, particularly if they are talking to someone who is not a close friend. Intimacy and trust with a conversational partner make it less likely you will feel the need to rev up the chitchat when the conversation slows. Research shows that being able to comfortably sit in silence is actually a sign of a secure relationship. Higher-status people also aren't as likely to get agitated by gaps in conversation, presumably because they are more secure in their position.

In Western cultures, people tend to interpret silences longer than about half a second as disapproval, sanction, or ostracism, so they rush to say something to try to raise their standing. A silence of just four seconds is enough for people to change or nuance their expressed opinion, taking the quiet to mean their views are out of line. Former tech executive turned author and career coach Kim Scott has written about Apple CEO Tim Cook's propensity for silence: "A friend warned me that Tim tended to allow long silences and that I shouldn't let it unnerve me or feel the need to fill them. Despite this warning, in our first interview I reacted to a long period of silence by anxiously talking nonstop, and in the process inadvertently told him far more about a mistake I'd made than I had intended."

A Dutch study showed people's feelings of belonging and well-being diminished during video chat sessions with gaps or delays between responses. This occurred even when the subjects were told the conversational flow disruptions might be due to technical difficulties. The lead researcher, social psychologist Namkje Koudenburg, told me people might feel similarly unsettled and insecure, albeit subconsciously, when talking to someone on a cell connection that has a delay or even when someone doesn't respond right away to a text.

Certainly there are times when silences mean disapproval— think of the cricket silence after someone tells an inappropriate or off-color joke. But there's a big difference between being "silent with" and being "silent to," just like there's a big difference between "laughing with" and "laughing at." It's more often the case in normal conversation that gaps are because the other person is just thinking or taking a breath before continuing. People pause while figuring out what, or how much, to tell you, or perhaps they need a moment to manage their emotions. Composer Gustav Mahler said, "What's best in music is not to be found in the notes." It's often in the spaces between the notes; when the strands of sound attenuate and disappear. So, too, in conversation, it's important to pay attention to what words conceal and silences reveal.

To be a good listener is to accept pauses and silences because filling them too soon, much less preemptively, prevents the speaker from communicating what they are perhaps struggling to say. It quashes elaboration and prevents real issues from coming to the surface. Just wait. Give the other person a chance to pick up where they left off. As a journalist, it took me too long to realize that I didn't have to say anything to keep the conversation going. Some of the most interesting and valuable bits of information have come not from my questioning but from keeping my mouth shut. You get so much more out of interactions when you allow people the time and space to gather their thoughts.

Christianity, Judaism, Islam, and, in fact, most of the world's religions from Bahá'í to Zen Buddhism incorporate some form of meditative or contemplative silence where the faithful try to listen to some higher order or, at least, to their best selves. Trappist monks believe silence opens the mind to the inspirations of the Holy Spirit. There is a teaching in the Talmud that says, "A word is worth one coin, silence is worth two."

The Quakers have something called *waiting worship* where congregants assemble and sit in silence so they are open and available to divine insight. But even Quakers can be uncomfortable with silence. A member of a Quaker congregation in Richmond, Indiana, told me that there's no problem finding a seat on the one Sunday a month devoted to waiting worship because "a lot of people don't go because they find the quiet too challenging."

This discomfort with silence has been known to trip up Western businesspeople when they try to negotiate deals with their less loquacious Asian counterparts. Charles Freeman, the U.S. Chamber of Commerce's senior vice president for Asia, said Westerners—particularly Americans—can't tolerate silence while Asians tend to embrace it. He said time and again he's watched as Americans gab their way into bad bargaining positions during foreign trade negotiations.

"Americans generally speak to fill up silence as if silences are bad things, but Asians are very different," Freeman told me. "In a negotiating context, Asians actually get a lot of stuff done by just sitting there, being deferential and taking everything in. It's a genuine advantage." By remaining silent, he added, you can learn a lot about the other side's mood and willingness to compromise as well as what will make them walk away, just by how they frame the issue. "If you are not listening in a negotiation context, you're kind of screwed," he said.

For Canadian composer and music educator R. Murray Schafer, silence is a "pocket of possibility," and to make the point, he sometimes required his students to remain silent for one day. His students at first didn't like it because their thoughts were more audible and intrusive. Some said they felt hollow listening to themselves. But at the end of twenty-four hours, many students reported a greater awareness and appreciation of not only environmental sounds like the hiss of a lawn sprinkler or murmur of simmering soup but also subtleties in conversation that they would have missed had they been able to talk.

An aspiring singer and songwriter in Los Angeles told me she had a similar experience when she had to go without speaking for six weeks after surgery on her vocal cords. She carried around a whiteboard that said, "Hi. I'm on vocal rest."

Forced silence, she said, made her realize that she wasn't a very good listener. "As opposed to really listening, you tend to be always sharpening your knife, thinking how to prove your point; why you're right," she said. "I started understanding people better because I didn't have the option to tell them my opinion, and it also made me more accepting of others because I was able to listen." Like Schafer, she encourages taking a day to dive into the "pocket of possibility" that is silence. "If you can bear to do it for just twenty-four hours, you will learn to be a better listener," she said. "You will learn the unimportance of your words and the importance of other people's words."

If a full day seems daunting, try staying silent during a single conversation. Don't say anything unless asked a question. See what happens. Take it from bartenders—the other person probably won't notice. On slow nights, bartenders can listen to a customer go on for hours without having to utter a word. "You could say it's because beer loosens the tongue," said a longtime bar owner in New Orleans. "But I think it's more that people aren't used to being listened to, so they end up telling you stuff they don't even tell their parents or significant others."

Bartenders I interviewed also said that on busy nights, patrons don't so much talk *to* one another as talk *at* one another, neither having much idea what the other is saying or what they, themselves, are saying. "People frequently talk to take up the empty space between them and a stranger," said a bookbinder turned bartender in Asheville, North Carolina. "They are trying to fill the void of a relationship that has not started yet—or isn't very deep—with noise." She added, "It's the people who are comfortable in their own skins that are okay with quiet."

Somehow lost in our self-promoting culture is the fact that you can't talk your way into a relationship. Garrulousness fills the silence but erects a kind of word wall that separates you from others. Silence is what allows people in. There's a generosity in silence but also a definite advantage. People who are comfortable with silence elicit more information and don't say too much out of discomfort. Resisting the urge to jump in makes it more likely you will leave conversations with additional insight and greater understanding. And if you're Gallery Furniture's Greg Hopf, you'll outsell everyone else on the floor.

16

The Morality of Listening

Why Gossip Is Good for You

Good gossip smells like bourbon to me. Both were served, straight up, during cocktail hour at my great-great-aunt's house in Galveston, Texas. People angled for invitations, as much for the banter as the booze. Until her death at age ninety-seven, my great-great-aunt and I spent many uninterrupted hours together—deep-sea fishing in the Gulf of Mexico, cutting sweet peas in her garden, cruising with the top down in her vintage, electric-blue Oldsmobile convertible. Although she'd certainly bristle at being called a gossip, all we talked about was what we loved and what we loathed about other people.

While gossip often has a negative connotation, it actually has a positive social function. There's a reason why as much as two-thirds of adult conversation is gossip, defined as at least two people talking about someone who is absent. Men gossip as much as women, and children are adept gossipers by age five. We all do it (although not with as much flair as my great-great-aunt) because gossip allows us to judge who is trustworthy, who we want to emulate, how much we can get away with, and who are likely allies or adversaries. In this way, listening to gossip contributes to our development as ethical, moral members of society.

We are socialized by the gossip we hear from our families, friends, colleagues, teachers, and religious leaders. What are the Jesus parables and Buddha stories but recorded gossip? Dutch researchers found that listening to positive gossip made people try to behave in a similar way, and negative gossip made people feel better about themselves. Another study showed that the more shocked or upset you are by gossip, the more likely it is that you'll learn a lesson from it.

Of course, you are also likely to reform if you are the subject of gossip. Researchers at Stanford University and the University of California–Berkeley found that subjects, when given the opportunity, readily gossiped about others who were untrustworthy in a financial game, which in turn led the cheaters to play nice to get back into everyone's good graces. The conclusion was that organizations that allow their members to gossip will be more cooperative and deter selfishness better than those that don't.

This is the case even when the gossip is not always entirely true. Social psychology and economics researchers in Australia and the UK collaborated on a study that showed any kind of gossip, accurate or not so accurate, creates a demand for "reputability." They had subjects play a trust-based game involving the distribution of rewards, and when people could freely impugn or praise the integrity of fellow players, even if falsely, they behaved better and operated more efficiently compared to those who were not allowed to gossip. The researchers observed that inaccuracies were most often motivated by a desire to more severely punish bad actors (people sometimes made cheaters sound worse than they were). There's also the thought that listening to how people talk about others, true or untrue, may say as much, or more, about them than the people they are talking about.

No wonder gossip makes people reflexively lean in and lower their voices to a conspiratorial whisper. It's valuable. My great-great-aunt and I would almost touch foreheads when discussing something particularly sensitive, even when no one else was around. Rather than being trivial, superficial, or simpleminded, a surprisingly large body of evidence indicates listening to gossip is an intelligent activity and essential to adaptation. Gossip scholars (there are more than you would think) say talking about people is an extension of observational learning, allowing you to learn from the triumphs and tribulations of those you know and even those you don't know.

British anthropologist and evolutionary psychologist Robin Dunbar, who you met in chapter 4, has studied gossip in conjunction with his work on friendship, and he told me that despite the widely held view that gossip is mostly malicious, only 3–4 percent of it is truly mean-spirited. "Gossip is hanging over the yard fence, sitting on the stoop, rocking in the rocking chair," he said. "Most of it is discussing some difficulty going on between you and another person, but it's also about what's going on in the community and the status of people in the network—who's fallen out with whom."

Social dynamics change rapidly and are incredibly complicated. Every interpersonal decision and behavior is the result of myriad factors coming together at a particular moment between particular people. Depending on a number of variables, the same interaction can be insignificant or spin wildly out of control. Trying to understand this complexity is extremely challenging, Dunbar said, and that's why "we're so interested in listening to and examining lots and lots of examples to try to understand how the game is played so we can handle it better." Indeed, people came to my great-great-aunt's cocktail parties to gather just such intelligence. Galveston may be a sleepy coastal town, but it was, and still is, hard to keep up with all the antics and intrigues.

According to Dunbar, to understand the origins of gossip, we need look no further than the grooming behavior of apes. It's thought early humans—like apes—bonded socially by grooming one another. Mutual stroking and nitpicking fostered goodwill so that later on, the two might share bananas or come to each other's defense. But as humans grew more intelligent and the complexity of our activities and the size of our communities grew, language—and, more specifically, gossip—replaced grooming as a way to establish and maintain alliances, although we still pet and stroke those closest to us.

The advantage of gossip over grooming, Dunbar said, is that it is a more "efficient mechanism for our social bonding and social learning." Grooming is very much a one-on-one activity that can take quite some time (depending on how tangled or louse-infested your partner is), whereas face-to-face conversations are quicker and can accommodate up to four individuals (one speaker and three listeners). Any larger and people tend to break off into smaller groups. You've probably seen this in action at large parties where guests naturally form various conversational pods of two to four people.

This perhaps explains why social media is so seductive. The speed with which gossip can be accessed online, and the sheer quantity, is more than you could ever muster or manage in face-to-face interactions. It creates this imperative to keep checking to make sure you are still in the loop. But, of course, you can never keep up with it all, and with so many narratives and interpretations, the quality and value of the information plummets.

———

The social science literature often talks about gossip in economic terms, subject to the law of supply and demand. So, for example, the things that my great-great-aunt told me one-on-one and in strictest confidence were more valuable to me than what she tossed off at a cocktail party where everyone there was essentially free to tell anyone they wanted. You can probably guess how comparatively little economists would say gossip is worth on the internet. The value of information is inversely related to its availability and its triviality.

University of Chicago sociologist Peter Michael Blau originated social exchange theory in the 1960s, which applied economics to social interactions, including the information we disclose to one another. Blau was a student of Robert Merton, the father of focus groups, and he maintained that listening to people's stories was essentially a privilege that had to be earned. People start with minor transactions where the information isn't so sensitive; therefore, it wouldn't be a big deal if word got out. But as both partners prove their trustworthiness by their attentiveness, sensitivity, and discretion, their relationship deepens, which leads them to engage in more significant transactions (i.e., disclosing more tightly held information).

Listening, then, is not only how we learn to be virtuous members of society, it is in itself a virtue that makes us worthy of the most valuable information. The French philosopher Emmanuel Levinas believed human interactions are the foundation of personal ethics and that listening, and the understanding and empathy it engenders, gives our lives meaning and direction. Levinas, who was Jewish and was a prisoner of war during WWII, stressed the importance of experiencing the "other." By this, he meant engaging with other people face-to-face and learning how all our stories are different and yet the same in terms of underlying emotions. Listening to the "other" is what reminds us of our common human vulnerability and fragility, and it imposes the ethical imperative, or duty, to do no harm.

Integrity and character are not things you are born with; they develop day by day through the choices you make, and that very much includes to whom and how well you choose to listen. Ethical behavior requires that you take into account how your words and actions affect others, and you can't get a

sense of that without listening. In a purely practical and evolutionary context, we survived as a species by cooperating as we
foraged for food and hunted big game. Early humans had to
listen and collaborate or die. Norms of behavior and rules of
civility emerged from those early joint activities, which later
informed our ideas of morality.

The contemporary French intellectual Pascal Bruckner
argues in *The Temptation of Innocence* that modern individ-
ualism may be taking us backward. He observes that when
one's duty is foremost to one's self, there is no sense of social
obligation and "guided only by the lantern of his own understanding, the individual loses all assurance of a place, an order,
a definition. He may have gained freedom, but he has lost security." In our self-reliant society, we believe we are responsible for our own happiness and prosperity. "Everyone must sell
himself as a person, in order to be accepted," Bruckner writes.
But this constant self-promotion and image cultivation comes
at a cost. We lose touch with others and ultimately our sense
of belonging and connection, which was all we really wanted
in the first place.

Our modern selves talk more and listen less despite the fact
that understanding and responsiveness to one another's stories,
ideas, and concerns have defined all our achievements from
hunting woolly mammoths to putting a man on the moon. Not
listening to one another diminishes what we can achieve and in
that way, too, can be seen as a moral failing. We not only fail
one another as individuals, we also fail to thrive as a society.

Moreover, when people feel the urgency to always sell

themselves, they tend to exaggerate, which lowers the level of discourse and fosters cynicism. When asked his IQ score, the physicist and cosmologist Stephen Hawking said, "I have no idea. People who boast about their IQ are losers." This is from a man whom many considered the smartest person in the world. My great-great-aunt also observed that those who bragged the most were usually the least accomplished. Something to keep in mind when you're tempted to promote yourself instead of finding out what's great about whomever is in front of you.

People tend to regret not listening more than listening and tend to regret things they said more than things they didn't say. It seems giving people a piece of your mind isn't all it's cracked up to be. While you may feel a sense of urgency to tell people how you feel, it's not always helpful. You are putting your ego ahead of the other person's vulnerability. This doesn't mean you have to be dishonest or self-effacing, but you do need to listen enough to know when the other person is ready to hear what you have to say. Not everything needs to be said as you are feeling it. In fact, sometimes it's better to wait until you aren't feeling it quite so strongly.

Regret came up repeatedly when I interviewed people for this book. So many of them expressed profound regret that they didn't listen at a critical point in their lives. They were too distracted or maybe they had to "speak their truth" and neglected to take into account the potential impact. They reflected on a person who died, a relationship that ended, a job they lost, or a fight they had and wished they could go back and ask more questions and listen more carefully to the answers.

According to psychologist Amy Summerville, director of the Regret Lab at Miami University in Oxford, Ohio, social regrets, which have to do with relationships, tend to be more intense than nonsocial regrets, such as where you went to school or an investment you made. Moreover, research shows that you regret most the things you could have done differently but can't go back and do over. Not listening is ripe for regret because once you let the opportunity slip away, you can never re-create the moment and often don't realize what you missed until it's too late.

"Not listening is in that sweet spot of things that can really stir up regret over time," Summerville told me. "It's essential to relationships, and we can readily recognize it's something fully under our control." Regret is the second-most common emotional state, after love, she said, and the two feelings are intertwined since the most intense regret comes from neglecting those we love. Relationships most often fail due to neglect, and one of the principle kinds of neglect is not being attentive. Whether viewed as an evolutionary survival tactic, basic moral virtue, or what we owe the ones we love, listening is what unifies us as human beings.

Which brings me to a final note on my great-great-aunt. We were having breakfast, just the two of us, huddled at one end of the mahogany expanse that was her dining room table. It was springtime, and the smell of wisteria wafted through the open windows. We had been talking about someone who had lived to sorely regret some things he had done. I asked my great-great-aunt, then in her nineties, if she had any regrets. "What good would that do?" she said.

17

When to Stop Listening

A few years ago, I was working on a story for *The Times* about fake laughter. Curious why we so often laugh when nothing is funny, I called a psychologist and university professor who studies laughter. He began by telling a few jokes. Perhaps not surprising coming from a guy who studies laughter for a living, but they were not funny jokes. They were lame jokes. I did that forced *ah-ha-ha* you do to be polite. In other words, a fake laugh.

The professor then launched into a lengthy lecture on how human laughter evolved from apes panting. "I think that answers your question," he said finally. "Well . . . not exactly," I said, and I tried again to tell him that my story was about fake laughter, particularly why people laugh when they are uncomfortable. He corrected me. You can't fake laughter. "You've laughed during this conversation, real laughter, and that's a positive thing. Okay?" he said, not doubting the sincerity of my earlier *ah-ha-ha*. He went on, "Men are the most effective laugh getters. It's not a matter of sexism in the entertainment industry; it's just harder for women to get laughs than men. Around the world, class clowns are males. Males are the best laugh getters, whether as comedians or at the next cocktail party. Okay?"

On a deadline and my question still unanswered, I thanked him very much for his time. Not that the call wasn't useful. He spectacularly proved my thesis about fake laughter. But it was time to stop listening to him. Four psychologists, three neuroscientists, and one humor expert later, I had new insight into why we laugh for real and for show, and how to tell the difference (hint: fake laughter has speech sounds in it like *ah-ha-ha* or *eh-heh-heh* or *tee-hee-hee*). I also learned there is likely no gender monopoly on humor, but women are more likely to fake laughter, as I had so ably demonstrated.

But the larger point here is sometimes you need to make the call to stop listening. While you can learn something from everyone, that doesn't mean you have to listen to everyone until they run out of breath. Obviously, you can't. As George Eliot wrote in *Middlemarch:* "If we had a keen vision and feeling of all ordinary human life, it would be like hearing the grass grow and the squirrel's heart beat, and we should die of that roar which lies on the other side of silence." Moreover, there are only so many hours in a day. So we make choices, consciously and unconsciously, about who gets our time and attention.

According to the British language philosopher and theorist Paul Grice, human beings, without realizing it, have certain expectations in conversation that, when violated (as happened with the unfunny laughter expert), make us less inclined to listen. It stems from the fact that communication is fundamentally a cooperative endeavor, so if we perceive our partners aren't keeping up their ends of the bargain, we are going to feel cheated and want out of the deal. Grice summarized our conversational expectations in four maxims:

1. Maxim of Quality—we expect the truth.
2. Maxim of Quantity—we expect to get information we don't already know and not so much that we feel overwhelmed.
3. Maxim of Relation—we expect relevance and logical flow.
4. Maxim of Manner—we expect the speaker to be reasonably brief, orderly, and unambiguous.

Some scholars have argued for the inclusion of politeness and fairness in turn taking, but Grice's four maxims are widely recognized as what most people expect in civilized society, even if they aren't aware of it. It explains why it's so difficult to talk to people suffering from dementia or psychosis. No longer tethered to reality and social norms, they may spout fantastic, disorderly, ambiguous, vague, and/or disconnected ideas. It's also why calling tech support is so incredibly aggravating. The scripted responses often have no logical link to what you said, provide too little or too much information and are often untrue—"It's your equipment, not ours."

The social contract implied by Grice's maxims applies

across cultures, whether the exchange is friendly or antagonistic. People can be really angry with one another but still
follow the rules to have a productive argument. While Grice's
maxims are pretty universal, they are also universally flouted,
to a greater or lesser extent, perhaps because people can have
very different ideas about what is truthful, relevant, logical,
brief, orderly, or unambiguous. But still, in our own minds,
this is what we expect. And when we detect total bullshit in a
conversation or someone throws out a non sequitur or drones
on in mind-numbing detail about something we don't care
about—we tend to get annoyed, and we check out.

Strange as it may sound, most people who violate Grice's
maxims are not so much bad speakers as bad listeners. The
best communicators, whether addressing a crowd or a single
individual, are people who have listened, and listened well, in
the past and continue to listen in the moment. They are able
to engage, entertain, and inspire because they first try to get
a sense of their audience and then choose their material and
style of delivery accordingly.

And they also remain attuned to their audience while they
are speaking, paying attention to verbal and nonverbal cues as
well as the energy in the room to assess whether people are following them and care about the subject. It's sort of like when
you adopt a different narrative approach when talking to, say,
your grandmother versus your girlfriend, a coworker versus a
customer, or your liberal friend versus your conservative friend.

The stories you tell and the way you tell them depend on
your read of your audience—or at least they should. You can

have strong values and convictions, but you can't make yourself compelling, clear, or convincing if you don't take into account who is in front of you. Not everybody has the same interests, sensibilities, or level of understanding, and to not try to discern and respect those differences is the surest way to bore or aggravate people or otherwise make them shut down.

Listening is not just something you should do when someone else is talking; it's also what you should do *while* you are talking. Is the other person indicating any real interest in hearing more about your kid's oboe recital? Did the other person wince when you started talking about politics? Was that a sigh of relief you heard when you said, "To make a long story short . . ."? If you're not good at reading other people's reactions as you speak, then just ask them. Check in. "Have I lost you?" "Did I overstep?" "What do you think?" "Are you still with me?" "Had enough?" "Am I boring you?" "Make sense?" "Too much?"

Conversation, at its best, is a continual listening feedback loop that shapes what people say and how they say it. Ralph Waldo Emerson wrote, "'Tis the good reader that makes the good book." Likewise, 'tis the good listener who makes the good conversation. When both parties in a conversation are focused and engaged, it's like a fantastic dance where the two of you are listening intently to each other regardless of who is speaking. Not only are your brain waves in sync—as Uri Hasson and his colleagues discovered—but research shows you also start to physically and tonally align. You mirror each other's speaking style, body posture, gazes, and gestures.

Conversing with someone who doesn't listen well—who

doesn't follow what you are saying or take into account how you feel about what you are hearing—is like dancing with someone who is keeping to a different rhythm or has no rhythm. It's awkward. And watch out for your toes. The person may have valuable things to say, but it takes much more energy and self-discipline to listen and find out what it is.

Or the person could just be a jerk. People rarely are, though. Their self-centered conversational style more often speaks to deep insecurities, anxieties, or blind spots. Sometimes just by listening, they begin to listen, too—not only to you but also to themselves. And when they do, the conversation becomes more coherent, relevant, and responsive. The power of the listener is that you get to decide how much effort you want to put in and when you've had enough.

Anyone who has suffered through a bad date knows how much work it is to be with someone when you are hopelessly out of sync. If you've forgotten, tune in to a few episodes of *Second Date Update*. For the uninitiated, it airs during morning drive time on pop and country music radio stations in larger markets like Houston, Seattle, Chicago, and Boston. What happens is a man or woman calls in after having a great time on a date and can't understand why the other person isn't responding to texts or calls for a second date. The morning radio hosts then call the guy or gal in question to ask what went wrong. This, while the person hoping for a second date and countless commuters eavesdrop on the conversation. It's by turns fascinating and appalling, comic and tragic, as people, so hoping for connection, so utterly fail to listen to the objects of their desire.

Take Jonas, who didn't pick up on Mary's discomfort during their first date when he introduced her to his "little bandits," which is what he called the wild raccoons that he hand-fed and liked to watch frolic in the raccoon playland he'd constructed in his yard. And then there was Hannah, who failed to register Nate's disapproval when she started networking—handing out business cards and working the room—at a children's charity event he had invited her to. One could argue whether consorting with animals known to carry rabies and tireless self-promotion are problematic in relationships, but the inability to attend to your date's words and reactions surely is.

It's what makes *Second Date Update* so cringeworthy. The callers didn't listen to their dates when they were with them, all but guaranteeing no second date. Undeterred, they ask radio hosts to listen for them and then, when they overhear their dates explaining their feelings, they still don't listen, usually breaking in on the call to insist that the other person has got it all wrong. "We can readily accept the fact that we can be wrong," the Polish-born social psychologist Robert Zajonc wrote, "but we are never wrong about what we like or dislike." Better to listen to how people feel than try to convince them to feel differently. You can't argue your way into affection, but truly listening is the surest way to form a bond.

———

As great as it is to find someone, a romantic partner or just a good friend, who is easy to talk to and gets you just as you get them, don't expect that the two of you will be able to sustain that degree of connection all the time. Careful listening is draining, regardless of your personality, aptitude, or motivation. You can't do it continuously. Indeed, air traffic controllers are limited to one-and-a-half-hour to two-hour shifts before they must take a break. Newer controllers can manage even less time because they haven't built up enough stamina. Controllers not only have to listen for information like pilots' requests and read backs of instructions, they also have to listen for any trace of unease or confusion in pilots' voices to assess when things could be getting dicey in the cockpit.

"You get mentally exhausted and mushy listening too long," an air traffic controller in the Dallas–Fort Worth area told me. "You have to be careful because it happens to some people sooner than others." He said he often feels like he has used up his capacity to listen once his shift is over. "There are days when I come home and the last thing I want is to engage with my family," he said. "It makes everyone walk on eggshells around Dad, but I just can't listen to anyone else."

Naomi Henderson, the focus group moderator, told me a downside of being a good listener is people are always calling her with their problems. She has been known to carry her phone to the front door and ring the bell so she can say, "Uh-oh. There's someone at the door. I have to go." Otherwise, she said, "You're like a bowl of chocolate mousse and everybody's got a spoon." When someone listens to you, it can feel so much like love, some people may not know the difference. Part of being a good listener is knowing your limits and setting boundaries.

Not listening because you don't agree with someone, you are self-absorbed, or you think you already know what someone will say makes you a bad listener. But not listening because you don't have the intellectual or emotional energy to listen at that moment makes you human. At that point, it's probably best to exit the conversation and circle back later. If you half listen to someone or listen as if you are skimming through a book, the other person will pick up on it. Even small children know when you're not listening. Take, for example, my friends' toddler who has repeatedly thrown his parents' cell phones in the toilet—no other objects, just the cell phones. He knows precisely what keeps Mom and Dad from listening to him.

There are also times when you have to admit that, try as you might, you can't get on someone's wavelength. It could be that something inside you is preventing you from listening, or it could be that the other person doesn't want to be heard and is being withholding. Or it could be the person is just toxic. These are people who, whenever you listen to them, you feel depressed, diminished, or distressed. You can't listen someone out of being abusive or cruel. Kathryn Zerbe, professor of psychiatry at Oregon Health & Science University in Portland, echoed several psychotherapists I interviewed when she said, "In our business, there are some patients you can't treat. But also in life, there are some stories you just can't hear. Every person has to know that. That's the limit of human experience, and that's okay."

The problem is that we tend to give up too soon. Few people, if any, are effortlessly eloquent and often need time to build up enough trust in you, and maybe also in themselves, to talk freely. Whether you are listening to your boss, colleagues, friends, loved ones, or strangers, it takes a while for people to get it out. They may beat around the bush or hide behind humor. They may say too much or too little. And they can even say things they don't mean. A good listener takes the time and makes the effort to help people find their voice, and in so doing, intimacy and understanding are earned. Listeners, through the gift or by dint of sustained attention, receive in return other people's confidences. And besides, wouldn't you want people to hang in there with you while you figured out or worked up to what you wanted or needed to say?

Sometimes it takes more than one conversation to hear someone. I have left interviews feeling like I understood everything and then, after thinking about it awhile, gone back to ask additional questions or even asked the same questions again, perhaps in a different way, hoping for more clarity. Listening can continue even when you are no longer in the presence of the speaker as you reflect on what the person said and gain added insight. This is not to recommend obsessive rumination or picking apart conversations, which psychiatrist Zerbe said usually has more to do with insecurity than honest reflection. You know you're doing this when you are spinning your wheels going over and over how you feel about something someone said instead of considering the feelings that drove the other person to say it.

Journaling is a form of reflective listening for Anthony Doerr, author of the Pulitzer Prize–winning book *All the Light We Cannot See.* Now forty-seven, he has kept a diary since he was sixteen. "It's really a way to train yourself to look and listen," he told me. "You slow down and translate a big confusing world, almost like a prayer." Good journalism has the same quality. Profiles in *The New Yorker,* for example, are the writer's reflections on conversations with the subject, laying out not only what the person said but also noting what the person did not say, as well as mannerisms and demeanor. Perhaps not surprisingly, Gillien Todd tells students in her negotiation class at Harvard Law School to listen to the opposing side as if they were going to have to write a newspaper or magazine article about them.

I, myself, am an inveterate quote collector—I jot down any interesting, funny, or thought-provoking thing I hear, or overhear, during the course of the day. I have several notebooks as well as files on my computer filled with pithy and profound quotes from friends, family, colleagues, strangers, and, of course, people I have interviewed. When you start paying attention, you'd be surprised how many things you will find worth recording. And reading back over your quote collection, you start to pick up interesting themes that are as revealing about yourself as the people you are quoting.

When you reflect on what someone said, the person's thoughts and feelings take up residence in you. It's an extension of the idea of listening as a form of hospitality. You are inviting someone into your consciousness. And the conversations you care about are the ones you carry with you in memory. Alexander Nehamas, a professor of philosophy at Princeton University and author of the treatise *On Friendship,* once told me, "The best friendships are those where you are able to immediately pick up the conversation where you left off because the person's words have remained with you." Indeed, one of the most gratifying things you can say to another person is: "I've been thinking about what you said." Likewise, friends are people who can connect what you are saying in the moment to things you've said in the past to help you work through problems or clarify your thinking or, in some cases, just make you laugh at the association.

But in an age when listening is seen as a burden, people often feel ashamed, embarrassed, or guilty when someone listens to them, much less reflects on what they said. They might empty their souls into the digital black hole that is the internet, but revealing themselves to someone in the same room, who is giving them full attention, is another thing entirely. "It may really be too hard and too late, not even desirable, after such long, familiar cold, to be known, and heard, and seen," wrote Amy Bloom in *Love Invents Us.*

Jerry Jacobs, a hairstylist in New York City, told me many of his clients apologize for unloading during their appointments. "It seems like they think they are doing something wrong," he said. "I tell them not to worry about it. It helps to talk. I don't run away from other people's trouble." Visit his salon and you can easily see how people might end up releasing pent-up thoughts and emotions. First, there is a perceived intimacy when someone stands so close to you and touches your head. And Jacobs asks very personal questions: "How do you feel about how you look?" and "How do you want to look?"

Facing a mirror, his clients seem to respond by talking to themselves as much as to him. "I get the sense, for a lot of them, they don't have other people who listen to them, or maybe don't listen very well," Jacobs said. Whether the person in the chair is a young woman who wants to experiment with turquoise streaks or a middle-aged man wanting to camouflage his bald spot, details about their failing relationships, issues with their kids, health concerns, social anxieties, or money problems accumulate like piles of hair on the floor.

When you don't interrupt or talk over people, you don't keep them from finishing their sentences and thoughts. They sometimes say things that they didn't expect and maybe didn't even know themselves. It can be disconcerting, and they may not appreciate it. I have interviewed people who later became embarrassed by what they said or, worse, insisted they never said what they said, even when I had them on tape and knowingly on the record. Similarly, in social situations, people may apologize for saying too much or might later act distant or coolly toward you, resentful that you know what you know. Psychotherapists told me that when patients divulge particularly sensitive information during a session, it's not unusual for them to cancel their next few appointments or maybe not come back at all. "They feel exposed, so you may not hear from them for ages," said Zerbe.

This vulnerability brings up the importance of keeping people's confidences. There's a world of difference between gossip (talking about other people's observed behavior to try to understand it) and betraying someone's trust by divulging what the person told you in private. According to communication privacy management theory, private information is kind of like money. If you are indiscreet with other people's private information, it's like you are spending their money without their consent. You can give up as much information as you want about yourself, just as you are free to spend your own money any way you like. But when you start drawing from other people's accounts, they are going to get upset. This is true even if you believed the information was already widely known or thought that it was not embarrassing or sensitive information. The information is still not yours to give away unless given explicit permission. Better to be a reliable confidant. Otherwise, people will think twice about telling you anything of significance, or they may cease communicating with you altogether.

With all its potential perils and pitfalls, listening may seem like too much to ask. And sometimes, with some people, it is. But more often, listening is a rewarding endeavor. Hearing how other people deal with struggles helps you figure out how to deal with your own problems, either by adopting their coping strategies or doing the opposite when you observe it's not working out for them. Listening helps you see we are all dealing with similar issues—wanting to be loved, looking for purpose, and fearing the end. You learn you are not alone. By listening, you acknowledge and embrace the world that is going on outside your head, which helps you sort out what's going on inside your head. And unlike most things in your life, listening is fully under your control. You get to decide who deserves your attention. Listening is your gift to bestow. No one can make you listen.

But just as you should be mindful and intentional when you grant the gift of your attention, you should try to be as mindful and intentional when you withhold it. While not listening is justified and a matter of practicality in some circumstances, there's no getting around the fact that it's a form of rejection. Consciously or unconsciously, you are choosing to attend to something else, which implies that person is not as interesting, as important, or as worthwhile, at least not at that moment.

Not listening to someone can be hurtful even when you don't mean to be, and it can be cruel if used as a weapon. It's why ghosting, where someone cuts off all communication with another person without warning or explanation, is so incredibly painful. A study published in *Journal of Research in Personality* found that compared to other breakup strategies, ghosting (technically, the *avoidance/withdrawal strategy*) was the most wounding and provoked the most anger and resentment from those on the receiving end. Those who were given the benefit of an explanation and the opportunity to have their say were less angry and aggrieved.

One of the most common reasons people withdraw is in response to criticism. But it's important to remember sometimes the things we least want to hear can be the most beneficial.

A rebuke can sting, but if we really listen without letting our egos get in the way and reflect on what was said, even if indelicately, we might realize how we are coming up short. Or if we feel the criticism is unfair, it gives us the opportunity to acknowledge how we came across and explain our true intent. Also, good listeners, because they expose themselves to a range of thoughts and opinions, are more resilient when they are criticized. They know one person's words are not necessarily definitive or entirely accurate.

A good exercise is to think about the people in your life who you have a hard time listening to and ask yourself why that is. Are they judging? Do they tell the same stories over and over? Do they exaggerate? Give too much detail? Do they only talk about how great they are? Do they get their facts wrong? Are they too negative? Saccharine? Superficial? Insulting? Do they challenge your thinking? Disagree with you? Do they make you feel envious? Do they make references and use words you don't know? Are their voices annoying? Are they not socially or professionally useful to you? Are you afraid of the intimacy that might develop? You have your reasons. Just know what they are and whether your reasons say more about you than they do about the other person. And also know that people change, and your view of them changes, when you truly listen. It often pays to first make the effort before you decide to pull the plug.

Conclusion

You know you've arrived at the Basilica of Our Lady of San Juan del Valle when its glittery exterior mosaic depicting Jesus and Our Lady of San Juan emerges over the billboards for bail bonds and Whataburger along Interstate 2 in the border town of San Juan, Texas. The other tip-off is all the people, thousands of them, streaming into the church. They come to light candles and make offerings, but the longest lines are for the confessionals, which wind in tight S curves like security lines at the airport. Priests man the six confessional booths in constant rotation, listening in three-hour shifts for up to twelve hours a day, often extending their hours rather than turn anyone away.

Father Jorge Gómez, the young, round-faced rector at the basilica, told me the lines for confession seem to grow longer every week, even as sexual abuse scandals in the Catholic church have led many to question their faith. Father Gómez doesn't quite know what to make of the surging numbers. He doesn't think it's because we are living in a more sinful society or that people are feeling more guilty about the things they've done. In fact, many who come don't talk about sin. Some aren't even Catholic. "When the people come here, it's like they are going to a field hospital," Father Gómez said. "They so badly need to be heard, it's like a wound; they are in a critical state."

We were walking around the sanctuary as we talked, his black robe rippling with his footsteps. Originally from rural Mexico and the eldest of twelve children, he retains a sense of disbelieving wonder that he ended up at the basilica. The size of a sports arena, the church and its sprawling campus attract more than twenty thousand visitors every weekend, making it one of the most visited Catholic shrines in the United States. They come from all over—North America, Latin America, Asia, Africa, Europe, the Caribbean—but they are not tourists like many who visit, say, the Basilica of the National Shrine of the Immaculate Conception in Washington, D.C., or Saint Patrick's Cathedral in New York. The people who come to Our Lady of San Juan come to pray, and more to the point, they come to be heard.

The people waiting in line to unburden themselves on the day I visited were all ages, ethnicities, and nationalities. Multilingual priests heard confessions in four languages. Some in the queue looked as if they worked in the nearby citrus groves, while others had a Euro-hipster vibe, wearing slim-fit suits and expensive Italian shoes fastened with gold buckles. Most of them stared at their phones as they waited their turn.

"I've begun to think there is a crisis of listening in our world," Father Gómez said. "There are a lot of people who want to talk but very few who want to listen, and we are seeing people suffer from it. I just let the people talk. At the very end, they say how nice it was to talk, but I didn't talk. I think it's just making yourself available to listen to the people; that's what they are starved for."

There's very little training in Catholic seminaries on how to listen to confessions, Father Gómez told me. For him, the best preparation has been to regularly go to confession himself. "I need to sit down in front of another priest with a humble heart and confess my own sins so that it gives me the tender compassion when I'm on the other side of the screen," he said.

This kind of empathy is important for any listener. It's hard to develop the sensitivity and respect for another person's vulnerability without knowing what it's like to be vulnerable yourself. Those who stick to superficialities in their conversations or who are jokey all the time don't know what it's like to give of themselves and, therefore, have a hard time knowing how to receive.

Anyone who has shared something personal and received a thoughtless or uncomprehending response knows how it makes your soul want to crawl back in its hiding place. Whether someone is confessing a misdeed, proposing an idea, sharing a dream, revealing an anxiety, or recalling a significant event—that person is giving up a piece of him or herself. And if you don't handle it with care, the person will start to edit future conversations with you, knowing, "I can't be real with this person."

When you engage with someone, your behavior does

two things: 1) it helps or hinders your understanding, and 2) strengthens or weakens the relationship. Listening is your best bet on both counts. As discussed throughout this book, it's possible, with awareness and patience, to develop your skill as a listener and do it extremely well. But there will still be times when you lose your focus or tolerance, or both. Even Father Gómez said there are times when he zones out. Listening is like playing a sport or musical instrument in that you can get better and better with practice and persistence, but you will never achieve total mastery. Some may have more natural ability and some may have to try harder, but everyone can benefit from making the effort.

The lines at Our Lady of San Juan speak to a fundamental and urgent human need to be heard. When something wonderful or terrible happens to you, what's your first instinct? It's probably to tell someone. We will tell our troubles and triumphs to strangers, pets, and even potted plants if no one else is around. But listening is the flip side of that impulse and arguably no less critical to our well-being. We long to receive as much as we long to transmit. When we are too busy to listen, when we look at our phones, jump in too soon with our opinions, or make assumptions, we prevent others' thoughts and emotions from being genuinely expressed. And we end up hollow or emptier than we would be otherwise.

Listening heightens your awareness. It makes you feel. As you become more attuned to the thoughts and emotions of others, you become more alive to the world and it becomes more alive to you. Life otherwise can become a muted existence, with days spent cocooned in unquestioned beliefs and fixed concepts, where, even though the world and the people in it are always changing, nothing is ventured beyond the borders of what you already know or accept as true. It feels safe, but it's really just stifling.

The Swiss psychologist Jean Piaget talked about the *collective monologue* of preschoolers. Put several of them together and they jabber away to themselves rather than to one another. The parallel between the typical sandbox confab and what passes for discourse today is obvious. It would be funny if we weren't suffering the consequences politically, economically, socially, and psychologically. To engage in *collective dialogue,* which Piaget defined as listening to and being responsive to one another, is to be mature, with all the relational capacity that implies.

Henry David Thoreau wrote, "The greatest compliment that was ever paid me was when one asked me what I thought, and attended to my answer." It is flattering when someone listens to you, which is why we are drawn to those increasingly rare individuals who actually do. Listening is a courtesy and, more fundamentally, a sign of respect. It's impossible to convince someone that you respect them by telling them so. It must be demonstrated, and listening is the simplest way to do that.

But listening is no easy task. Our magnificent brains race along faster than others can speak, making us easily distracted. We overestimate what we already know and, mired in our arrogance, remain unaware of all we misunderstand. We also fear that if we listen too carefully, we might discover that our thinking is flawed or that another person's emotions might be too much to bear. And so we retreat into our own heads, talk over one another, or reach for our phones.

Technology does not so much interfere with listening as make it seem unnecessary. Our devices indulge our fear of intimacy by fooling us into thinking that we are socially connected even when we are achingly alone. We avoid the messiness and imperfections of others, retreating into the relative safety of our devices, swiping and deleting with abandon. The result is a loss of richness and nuance in our social interactions, and we suffer from a creeping sense of dissatisfaction.

Not listening reduces the level of discourse. We experience and evaluate our words differently when said aloud to an attentive listener versus when they are in our heads or tapped out in 140 characters. A listener has a reactive effect on the speaker. As a result, careful listening elevates the conversation because speakers become more responsible and aware of what they are saying.

While listening is the epitome of graciousness, it is not a courtesy you owe everyone. That isn't possible. It's to your benefit to listen to as many different people, with as much curiosity as you can muster, but you ultimately get to decide when and where to draw the line. To be a good listener does not mean you must suffer fools gladly, or indefinitely, but rather helps you more easily identify fools and makes you wise to their foolishness. And perhaps most important, listening keeps you from being the fool yourself.

Listening is often regarded as talking's meek counterpart, but it is actually the more powerful position in communication. You learn when you listen. It's how you divine truth and detect deception. And though listening requires that you let people have their say, it doesn't mean you remain forever silent. In fact, how one responds is the measure of a good listener and, arguably, the measure of a good person.

In our fast-paced and frenetic culture, listening is seen as a drag. Conversations unfold slowly and may need to be revisited. Listening takes effort. Understanding and intimacy must be earned. While people often say, "I can't talk right now," what they really mean is "I can't listen right now." And for many, it seems they never get around to it. This, despite what we all want most in life—to understand and be understood—only happens when we slow down and take the time to listen.

Gratitude

In journalism, your story is only as good as your sources, which is why I am profoundly grateful to the many people who were generous with their time and knowledge as I researched this book. None of them had to take my call, respond to my email, or meet me in person. And yet, they did. I appreciate their willingness to engage with me more than I can adequately express.

These individuals are far too numerous to list, and indeed, many of them do not wish to be identified. But every conversation was consequential and influenced what I wrote. Moreover, as I replayed recorded interviews and recalled people's voices while reading over my notes, I was always in good company even on my loneliest days writing. This book is, in many ways, my gift in return.

I also want to recognize the many developmental, behavioral, social, and neuroscience researchers whose work I cited. I am grateful to those who graciously sent me full text copies of their studies and patiently answered my questions. And I'm further indebted to those researchers who have made their papers open access and readily available online.

Similarly, I'm grateful to Project Gutenberg and the Internet Archive, which proved invaluable when I was trying to track down an obscure book or text. These two nonprofit and volunteer-supported initiatives have made millions of digitized books and texts available without charge to researchers, scholars, and the just plain curious. And I'd be remiss if I didn't mention my local Houston Public Library and Rice University's Fondren Library as well as the Perry-Castañeda Library at the University of Texas at Austin. I made extravagant use of their collections and their quiet.

Special thanks to Ghada Asfour, who tackled the tedium of fact-checking every word of this book with gusto and good humor, and also to Ben Murphy for his intelligent and intuitive indexing. Likewise, I salute Clay Smith for designing the book's cover and Elizabeth Catalano for managing the behind-the-scenes machinations of turning what was a very long, unformatted text file into an actual, physical book.

Enormous and ongoing gratitude to my U.S. publisher, Celadon Books, and to my editor, Ryan Doherty, who encouraged and reassured me with his stories. "Do you want to hear a story?" Well, yes.

Of course, this book would not be possible were it not for the privilege of working for several esteemed publications, most notably the many years I've contributed to *The New York Times*. I'm grateful to my editors there, former and current, including Trish Hall, Scott Veale, Honor Jones, Michael Mason, Patrick Farrell, Roberta Zeff, Jim Kerstetter, and Alexandra Jacobs. They let me loose on countless assignments, giving me what is essentially a license to listen.

Notes

INTRODUCTION

2 *No man ever listened* "Meeting President and Mrs. Coolidge," America's Story from America's Library, Library of Congress, http://www.americasli brary.gov/aa/keller/aa_keller_coolidge_1.html.

2 *given men one tongue* Crossley Hastings Crossley and Crossley Hastings, *The Golden Sayings of Epictetus, with the Hymns of Cleanthes* (Urbana, IL: Project Gutenberg, 2006), 256, http://www.gutenberg.org/ebooks/871.

1: THE LOST ART OF LISTENING

5 *for a short column* Kate Murphy, "Oliver Sacks," *New York Times,* July 16, 2011, https://www.nytimes.com/2011/07/17/opinion/sunday/17download.html.

5 *inability to recognize faces* Oliver Sacks, "Face-Blind," *New Yorker,* August 30, 2010, http://www.newyorker.com/magazine/2010/08/30/face-blind.

9 *increases the risk of death* Julianne Holt-Lunstad, Timothy B. Smith, and J. Bradley Laytong, "Social Relationships and Mortality Risk: A Meta-Analytic Review," *PLOS Medicine* 7, no. 7 (2010), https://doi.org/10.1371/journal.pmed .1000316; Julianne Holt-Lunstad, Timothy B. Smith, Mark Baker, Tyler Harris, and David Stephenson, "Loneliness and Social Isolation as Risk Factors for Mortality: A Meta-Analytic Review," *Perspectives on Psychological Science* 10, no. 2 (2015): 227–237, https://doi.org/10.1177/1745691614568352; Amy Novotney, "Social Isolation: It Could Kill You," *Monitor on Psychology,* 50, no. 5, (May 2019), https://www.apa.org/monitor/2019/05/ce-corner-isolation.

10 *I am lonely* "i am lonely will anyone speak to me," Lounge, July 14, 2004, https:// www.loungeforums.com/on-topic/i-am-lonely-will-anyone-speak-to-me-2420; Oliver Burkeman, "Anybody There?," *Guardian,* August 29, 2005, https:// www.theguardian.com/technology/2005/aug/30/g2.onlinesupplement; Robert Andrews, "Misery Loves (Cyber) Company," *Wired,* June, 30, 2005, https://www.wired.com/2005/06/misery-loves-cyber-company; Tori Tefler, "'I Am Lonely, Will Anyone Speak to Me': Inside the Saddest Thread on the Internet, Ten Years Later," *Salon,* November 20, 2014, https://www.salon .com/2014/11/19/i_am_lonely_will_anyone_speak_to_me_inside_the _saddest_thread_on_the_internet_ten_years_later/.

10 *survey of twenty thousand Americans* "New Cigna Study Reveals Loneliness at Epidemic Levels in America," Newsroom, Cigna Corporation, May 1, 2018, https://www.cigna.com/newsroom/news-releases/2018/new-cigna-study -reveals-loneliness-at-epidemic-levels-in-america.

10 *Compare that to the 1980s* Vivek Murthy, "The Loneliness Epidemic," *Harvard Business Review,* October 12, 2017, https://hbr.org/cover-story/2017/09/ work-and-the-loneliness-epidemic.

10 *a thirty-year high* "Vital Signs: Trends in State Suicide Rates—United States, 1999–2016 and Circumstances Contributing to Suicide—27 States, 2015," Centers for Disease Control and Prevention, June 8, 2018, https://www.cdc .gov/mmwr/volumes/67/wr/mm6722a1.htm?s_cid=mm6722a1_w; Sabrina Tavernise, "U.S. Suicide Rate Surges to a 30-Year High," *New York Times*, April 22, 2016, https://www.nytimes.com/2016/04/22/health/us-suicide-rate -surges-to-a-30-year-high.html.

10 *American life expectancy is now declining* "Life Expectancy," Centers for Disease Control and Prevention, July 26, 2018, https://www.cdc.gov/nchs/data/nvsr /nvsr67/nvsr67_05.pdf; Anne Case and Angus Deaton, "Mortality and Morbidity in the 21st Century," Brookings Papers on Economic Activity, https:// www.brookings.edu/wp-content/uploads/2017/08/casetextsp17bpea.pdf.

10 *often associated with loneliness* Ariel Stravynski and Richard Boyer, "Loneliness in Relation to Suicide Ideation and Parasuicide: A Population-Wide Study," *Suicide and Life-Threatening Behavior* 31, no. 1 (2001): 32–40; Rachel Wurzman, "How isolation fuels opioid addiction," TEDxMidAtlantic, October 29, 2018, https://www.ted.com/talks/rachel_wurzman_how _isolation_fuels_opioid_addiction/transcript?language=en; Andrew Solomon, "Suicide, a Crime of Loneliness," *New Yorker,* August 14, 2014, https:// www.newyorker.com/culture/cultural-comment/suicide-crime-loneliness.

10 *The World Health Organization reports* "Suicide: Key Facts," World Health Organization, August 24, 2018, https://www.who.int/news-room/fact-sheets/detail

/suicide; "Prevention of Suicidal Behaviours: A Task for All," World Health Organization, https://www.who.int/mental_health/prevention/suicide/background/en/.

11 *appoint a "minister of loneliness"* Ceylan Yeginsu, "U.K. Appoints a Minster for Loneliness," *New York Times,* January 17, 2018, https://www.nytimes.com/2018/01/17/world/europe/uk-britain-loneliness.html.

11 *2017 government commissioned report* "Jo Cox Commission on Loneliness," Age UK, https://www.ageuk.org.uk/globalassets/age-uk/documents/reports-and-publications/reports-and-briefings/active-communities/rb_dec17_jocox_commission_finalreport.pdf.

11 *pretend to be lonely people's friends* Family Romance, http://family-romance.com/; Roc Morin, "How to Hire Fake Friends and Family," *Atlantic,* November 7, 2017, https://www.theatlantic.com/family/archive/2017/11/paying-for-fake-friends-and-family/545060/; Elif Batuman, "Japan's Rent-a-Family Industry," *New Yorker,* April 30, 2018, https://www.newyorker.com/magazine/2018/04/30/japans-rent-a-family-industry.

11 *Loneliness does not discriminate* "New Cigna Study Reveals Loneliness at Epidemic Levels in America," Cigna Corporation, May 1, 2018; 2018 CIGNA U.S. Loneliness Index, https://www.multivu.com/players/English/8294451-cigna-us-loneliness-survey/docs/IndexReport_1524069371598-173525450.pdf.

11 *doubled since 2008* Gregory Plemmons, Matthew Hall, Stephanie Doupnik, James Gay, Charlotte Brown, Whitney Browning, Robert Casey et al. "Hospitalization for Suicide Ideation or Attempt: 2008–2015," *Pediatrics* 141, no. 6 (2018): e20172426, https://doi.org/10.1542/peds.2017-2426.

11 *Much has been written* Jean M. Twenge, "Have Smartphones Destroyed a Generation?," *Atlantic,* September 2017, https://www.theatlantic.com/magazine/archive/2017/09/has-the-smartphone-destroyed-a-generation/534198/; Jean Twenge and Heejung Park, "The Decline in Adult Activities Among US Adolescents, 1976–2016," *Child Development* 90, no. 2 (2019): 638–654, https://doi.org/10.1111/cdev.12930; Jess Williams, "Are My Generation Really as Boring as Everyone Says?," *New Statesman America,* September 19, 2014, https://www.newstatesman.com/comment/2014/09/kids-are-alright-0; Stephanie Hanes, "Becoming an Adult: Why More Adolescents Now Say 'Don't Rush Me,'" *Christian Science Monitor,* January 14, 2019, https://www.csmonitor.com/USA/Society/2019/0114/Becoming-an-adult-Why-more-adolescents-now-say-Don-t-rush-me; Tara Bahrampour, "Why Are Today's Teens Putting Off Sex, Driving, Dating and Drinking?," *Chicago Tribune,* September 19, 2017, https://www.chicagotribune.com/lifestyles/parenting/ct-teens-not-drinking-20170919-story.html.

12 *habitually play video games* Niko Männikkö, Heidi Ruotsalainen, Jouko Miettunen, Halley M. Pontes, and Maria Kääriäinen, "Problematic Gaming Behaviour and Health-Related Outcomes: A Systematic Review and Meta-Analysis," *Journal of Health Psychology,* December 1, 2017, https://doi .org/10.1177/1359105317740414.

13 *compilations on YouTube* "Sorkinisms—A Supercut," *YouTube video*, 7:21, posted by Kevin T. Porter, June 25, 2012, https://www.youtube.com/watch? v=S78RzZr3IwI.

14 *profoundly lonely and depressed people* "The Ten-Year Lunch: The Wit and Legend of the Algonquin Round Table," Vimeo video, 55:48, directed by Aviva Slesin, written by Peter Foges and Mary Jo Kaplan, aired September 28, 1987, on PBS, https://vimeo.com/100320182.

14 *three suicide attempts* Carol Kort, *A to Z of American Women Writers* (New York: Facts on File, 2007), 245.

14 *beset with self-loathing* Richard Meryman, *Mank: The Wit, World, and Life of Herman Mankiewicz* (New York: Morrow, 1978), 97.

14 *Dorothy Parker said* Aubrey Malone, *Writing Under the Influence: Alcohol and the Works of 13 American Authors* (Jefferson, NC: McFarland, 2017), 46–47.

15 *John Bercow told the BBC* "Female MPs Shunning PMQs, Says John Bercow," BBC, April 17, 2014, https://www.bbc.com/news/uk-politics -27062577.

15 *popping up on their caller ID* Dan Cassino, "How Today's Political Polling Works," *Harvard Business Review,* August 1, 2016, https://hbr.org/2016/08 /how-todays-political-polling-works.

16 *fake or bot accounts* Nicholas Confessore, Gabriel J. X. Dance, Richard Harris, and Mark Hansen, "The Follower Factory," *New York Times,* January 27, 2018, https://www.nytimes.com/interactive/2018/01/27/technology/social-media -bots.html; "A 'Dirty and Open Secret': Can Social Media Curb Fake Followers?," *Knowledge@Wharton* podcast, Wharton School of the University of Pennsylvania, February 2, 2018, http://knowledge.wharton.upenn.edu/article /twitter-and-the-bots/.

16 *do not belong to real people* Janet Burns, "How Many Social Media Users Are Real People?," *Gizmodo,* June 4, 2018, https://gizmodo.com/how-many-social -media-users-are-real-people-1826447042; Onur Varol, Emilio Ferrara, Clayton A. Davis, Filippo Menczer, and Alessandro Flammini, "Online Human-Bot Interactions: Detection, Estimation, and Characterization," *International AAAI Conference on Web and Social Media (ICWSM)*, March 27, 2017, https:// arxiv.org/abs/1703.03107; Chengcheng Shao, Pik-Mai Hui, Lei Wang, Xinwen

Jiang, Alessandro Flammini, Filippo Menczer, and Giovanni Luca Ciam-paglia, "Anatomy of an Online Misinformation Network," *PLOS One* 13, no. 4 (2018): e0196087, https://doi.org/10.1371/journal.pone.0196087.

16 *study showed 20 percent of tweets* Alessandro Bessi and Emilio Ferrara, "Social Bots Distort the 2016 U.S. Presidential Election Online Discussion," *First Monday* 21, no. 11 (2016), http://dx.doi.org/10.5210/fm.v21i11.7090.

16 *Audits of the Twitter accounts* Shea Bennet, "67% of Taylor Swift's Twitter Followers are Bots, Says Study: An Audit of the Most Popular Musical Artists on Twitter Suggests They're Mostly Followed by Non-Human Profiles," *Adweek,* February 4, 2015, https://www.adweek.com/digital/twitter-bots-problem/; "The World's Biggest Music Stars: Who's Faking It on Twitter?," *Music Business Worldwide,* January 31, 2015, https://www.musicbusinessworldwide.com /katy-perry-justin-bieber-and-lady-gaga-whos-faking-it-on-twitter/.

17 *The 1 percent rule* Trevor van Mierlo, "The 1% Rule in Four Digital Health Social Networks: An Observational Study," *Journal of Medical Internet Research* 16, no. 2 (2014), https://doi.org/10.2196/jmir.2966; Bradley Carron-Arthura, John A. Cunningham, and Kathleen M. Griffith, "Describing the Distribution of Engagement in an Internet Support Group by Post Frequency: A Comparison of the 90-9-1 Principle and Zipf's Law," *Internet Interventions* 1, no. 4 (2014): 165–168, https://doi.org/10.1016/j.invent.2014.09 .003; Ling Jiang, Kristijan Mirkovski, Jeffrey D. Wall, Christian Wagner, and Paul Benjamin Lowry, "Proposing the Core Contributor Withdrawal Theory (CCWT) to Understand Core Contributor Withdrawal from Online Peer-Production Communities," *Internet Research* 28, no. 4 (2018): 988–1028, https://doi.org/10.1108/IntR-05-2017-0215.

17 *the silent are the vast majority* Bora Zivkovic, "Commenting Threads: Good, Bad, or Not At All," *A Blog Around the Clock* (blog), *Scientific American,* January 28, 2013, https://blogs.scientificamerican.com/a-blog-around-the -clock/commenting-threads-good-bad-or-not-at-all/; Nate Cohn and Kevin Quealy, "The Democratic Electorate on Twitter Is Not the Actual Democratic Electorate," *New York Times,* April 9, 2019, https://www.nytimes.com /interactive/2019/04/08/upshot/democratic-electorate-twitter-real-life.html.

19 *New Yorker cartoon where* Tom Toro, "Behold, as I Guide Our Conversation to My Narrow Area of Expertise," *New Yorker,* March 2, 2017, https://www .newyorker.com/cartoon/a20667.

2: THAT SYNCING FEELING: THE NEUROSCIENCE OF LISTENING

21 *gave himself a "personal challenge"* Mark Zuckerberg's Facebook page, posted January 3, 2017, https://www.facebook.com/zuck/posts/10103385178272401.

21 *entourage of up to eight aides* Reid J. Epstein and Deepa Seetharaman, "Mark Zuckerberg Hits the Road to Meet Regular Folks—With a Few Conditions," *Wall Street Journal,* July 12, 2017, https://www.wsj.com/articles/mark-zuckerberg -hits-the-road-to-meet-regular-folkswith-a-few-conditions-1499873098.

22 *what makes someone a bad listener* Lynn Cooper and Trey Buchanan, "Taking Aim at Good Targets: Inter-Rater Agreement of Listening Competency," *International Journal of Listening* 17, no. 1 (2003): 88–114, https://doi.org/10 .1080/10904018.2003.10499057.

23 *alert to the human voice* Pascal Belin, Shirley Fecteau, and Catherine Bedard, "Thinking the Voice: Neural Correlates of Voice Perception," *Trends in Cognitive Sciences* 8, no. 3 (2004): 129–135, https://doi.org/10.1016/j.tics.2004.01 .008; May Gratier and Gisèle Apter-Danon, "The Improvised Musicality of Belonging: Repetition and Variation in Mother-Infant Vocal Interaction," in *Communicative Musicality: Exploring the Basis of Human Companionship,* ed. Stephen Malloch and Colwyn Trevarthen (New York: Oxford University Press, 2009), 301–327; Ana Fló, Perrine Brusini, Francesco Macagno, Marina Nespor, Jacques Mehler, and Alissa L. Ferry, "Newborns Are Sensitive to Multiple Cues for Word Segmentation in Continuous Speech," *Developmental Science* (2019): e12802, https://doi.org/10.1111/desc.12802.

23 *just sixteen weeks' gestation* Viola Marx and Emese Nagy, "Fetal Behavioural Responses to Maternal Voice and Touch," *PLOS One* 10, no. 6 (2015): e0129118, https://doi.org/10.1371/journal.pone.0129118; "Fetal Development: The 2nd Trimester," Mayo Clinic, https://www.mayoclinic.org/healthy-life style/pregnancy-week-by-week/in-depth/fetal-development/art-20046151.

23 *distinguish between language and other sounds* Eino Partanen, Teija Kujala, Risto Näätänen, Auli Liitola, Anke Sambeth, and Minna Huotilainen, "Learning-Induced Neural Plasticity of Speech Processing Before Birth," *PNAS* 110, no. 7 (2013), https://doi.org/10.1073/pnas.1302159110.

23 *startled by an angry outburst* J. P. Lecanuet, C. Granier-Deferre, and M. C. Busnel, "Fetal Cardiac and Motor Responses to Octave-Band Noises as a Function of Central Frequency, Intensity and Heart Rate Variability," *Early Human Development* 18, no. 2–3 (1988): 81–93, https://doi.org/10.1016/0378-3782(88)90045-X.

23 *senses of touch and hearing* James Hallenbeck, *Palliative Care Perspectives* (New York: Oxford University Press, 2003), 220.

24 *ability to empathize and affiliate* Anouk P. Netten, Carolien Rieffe, Stephanie C. P. M. Theunissen, Wim Soede, Evelien Dirks, Jeroen J. Briaire, and Johan H. M. Frijns, "Low Empathy in Deaf and Hard of Hearing (Pre) Adolescents Compared to Normal Hearing Controls," *PLOS One* 10, no. 4 (2015): e0124102, https://doi.org/10.1371/journal.pone.0124102.

24 *much worse misfortune* Diane Ackerman, *A Natural History of the Senses* (New York: Vintage Books, 1991), 191.

25 *Hasson looked at fMRI scans* A. Zadbood, J. Chen, Y. C. Leong, K. A. Norman, and U. Hasson, "How We Transmit Memories to Other Brains: Constructing Shared Neural Representations Via Communication," *Cerebral Cortex* 27, no. 10 (2017): 4988–5000, https://doi.org/10.1093/cercor/bhx202.

25 *A subsequent study* Carolyn Parkinson, Adam M. Kleinbaum, and Thalia Wheatley, "Similar Neural Responses Predict Friendship," *Nature Communications* 9, no. 332 (2018), https://doi.org/10.1038/s41467-017-02722-7.

26 *the synchrony that developed* Michael Lewis, *The Undoing Project* (New York: W. W. Norton, 2017).

26 *waiting for it* Ibid., 238.

26 *sharing a mind* Ibid., 182.

27 *emphasizes this more than attachment theory* Inge Bretheron, "The Origins of Attachment Theory: John Bowlby and Mary Ainsworth," *Developmental Psychology 28,* no. 5 (1992): 759–775, http://dx.doi.org/10.1037/0012-1649.28.5.759; Mary D. Salter Ainsworth, Mary C. Blehar, Everett Waters, and Sally N. Wall, *Patterns of Attachment: A Psychological Study of the Strange Situation* (New York: Psychology Press, 2015); John Bowlby, *A Secure Base: Parent-Child Attachment and Healthy Human Development* (New York: Basic Books, 1988); Kent Hoffman, Glen Cooper, Bert Powell, and Christine M. Benton, *Raising a Secure Child: How Circle of Security Parenting Can Help You Nurture Your Child's Attachment, Emotional Resilience, and Freedom to Explore* (New York: Guilford Press, 2017); Howard Steele and Miriam Steele, *Handbook of Attachment-Based Interventions* (New York: Guilford Press, 2017); Jude Cassidy, *Handbook of Attachment: Theory, Research, and Clinical Applications, 3rd ed.* (New York: Guilford Press, 2018); Amir Levine and Rachel Heller, *Attached: The New Science of Adult Attachment and How It Can Help You Find—And Keep—Love* (New York: Tarcher Perigee, 2011).

30 *validated in several published studies* Teresa Lind, Kristin Bernard, Emily Ross, and Mary Dozier, "Intervention Effects on Negative Affect of CPS-Referred Children: Results of a Randomized Clinical Trial," *Child Abuse & Neglect* 38, no. 9 (2014): 1459–1467, https://doi.org/10.1016/j.chiabu.2014.04.004; Anne P. Murphy, Howard Steele, Jordan Bate, Adella Nikitiades, Brooke Allman, Karen A. Bonuck, Paul Meissner, and Miriam Steele, "Group Attachment-Based Intervention: Trauma-Informed Care for Families with Adverse Childhood Experiences," *Family and Community Health* 38, no. 3 (2015): 268–279, https://doi.org/10.1097/FCH.0000000000000074; Kristin Bernard, Mary Dozier, Johanna Bick, Erin Lewis-Morrarty, Oliver Lindhiem, and Elizabeth

Carlson, "Enhancing Attachment Organization Among Maltreated Children: Results of a Randomized Clinical Trial," *Child Development* 83, no. 2 (2012): 623–636, https://doi.org/10.1111/j.1467-8624.2011.01712.x.

32 *makes us feel most lonely* Lesley Caldwell and Helen Taylor Robinson, eds., *The Collected Works of D. W. Winnicott,* vol. 6 (New York: Oxford University Press, 2017), 529.

34 *touching without being touched* Amir Amedi, Gilad Jacobson, Talma Hendler, Rafael Malach, and Ehud Zohary, "Convergence of Visual and Tactile Shape Processing in the Human Lateral Occipital Complex," *Cerebral Cortex* 12, no. 11 (2002): 1202–1212, https://doi.org/10.1093/cercor/12.11.1202; Gary Chapman, *The 5 Love Languages* (Chicago, IL: Northfield Publishing, 1992), 107–118; Lisbeth Lipari, *Listening, Thinking, Being: Toward an Ethics of Attunement* (University Park, PA: Pennsylvania State University Press, 2014), 9.

3: LISTENING TO YOUR CURIOSITY: WHAT WE CAN LEARN FROM TODDLERS

37 *Browse the three-volume* Charles R. Berger and Michael E. Roloff, eds., *The International Encyclopedia of Interpersonal Communication* (Malden, MA: Wiley Blackwell, 2016), https://onlinelibrary.wiley.com/browse/book/10.1002/9781118540190/title?pageSize=20&startPage=&alphabetRange=l.

37 *won't even find listening* Mark Knapp and John Daly, eds., *The SAGE Handbook of Interpersonal Communication,* 4th ed. (Thousand Oaks, CA: Sage, 2011), https://us.sagepub.com/en-us/nam/the-sage-handbook-of-interpersonal-communication/book234032.

37 *definition of listening* Debra Worthington and Graham Bodie, "Defining Listening: A Historical, Theoretical, and Pragmatic Assessment," in *The Sourcebook of Listening Research: Methodology and Measures,* ed. Debra Worthington and Graham Bodie (New York: Wiley-Blackwell, 2017), 4.

39 *more curious and open* Mario Mikulincer, "Adult Attachment Style and Information Processing: Individual Differences in Curiosity and Cognitive Closure," *Journal of Personality and Social Psychology* 72, no. 5 (1997): 1217–1230, http://dx.doi.org/10.1037/0022-3514.72.5.1217.

39 *collection of his interviews* Studs Terkel, *Working: People Talk About What They Do All Day and How They Feel About What They Do* (New York: Ballantine, 1989).

39 *real tool is curiosity Studs Terkel: Listening to America,* directed by Eric Simonson (New York: HBO Documentary Films, 2009).

40 *didn't have a vowel* Studs Terkel, *Talking to Myself: A Memoir of My Times* (New York: Pantheon Books, 1977), 32.

40 *when talking to inattentive listeners* Monisha Pasupathi and Jacob Billitteri, "Being and Becoming Through Being Heard: Listener Effects on Stories and Selves," *International Journal of Listening* 29, no. 2 (2015): 67–84, https://doi.org/10.1080/10904018.2015.1029363; Monisha Pasupathi, Lisa M. Stallworth, and Kyle Murdoch, "How What We Tell Becomes What We Know: Listener Effects on Speakers' Long-Term Memory for Events," *Discourse Processes* 26, no. 1 (1998): 1–25, https://doi.org/10.1080/01638539809545035; Monisha Pasupathi and B. Rich, "Inattentive Listening Undermines Self-Verification in Personal Storytelling," *Journal of Personality* 73, no. 4 (2005), https://doi.org/10.1111/j.1467-6494.2005.00338.x.

40 *more friends in two months* Dale Carnegie, *How to Win Friends and Influence People, rev. ed.* (New York: Simon & Schuster, 1981), 44.

41 *lived mostly in seclusion* Robert D. McFadden, "Ingvar Kamprad, Founder of IKEA and Creator of a Global Empire, Dies at 91," *New York Times,* January 28, 2018, https://www.nytimes.com/2018/01/28/obituaries/ingvar-kamprad-dies.html.

41 *serving the majority of people* Richard Heller, "The Billionaire Next Door," *Forbes,* August 7, 2000, https://www.forbes.com/global/2000/0807/0315036a.html#c9f65ef4b69d.

41 *Thinking you already know how a conversation* Todd B. Kashdan, Ryne A. Sherman, Jessica Yarbro, and David C. Funder, "How Are Curious People Viewed and How Do They Behave in Social Situations? From the Perspectives of Self, Friends, Parents, and Unacquainted Observers," *Journal of Personality* 81, no. 2 (2012), https://doi.org/10.1111/j.1467-6494.2012.00796.x.

42 *hundreds of bus and train commuters* Nicholas Epley and Juliana Schroeder, "Mistakenly Seeking Solitude," *Journal of Experimental Psychology* 143, no. 5 (2014): 1980–1999, http://dx.doi.org/10.1037/a0037323.

43 *release of a feel-good chemical* Colin G. DeYoung, "The Neuromodulator of Exploration: A Unifying Theory of the Role of Dopamine in Personality," *Frontiers in Human Neuroscience* 7, no. 762 (2013), https://doi.org/10.3389/fnhum.2013.00762.

44 *Pakistani nuclear scientist* Robert L. Grenier, *88 Days to Kandahar: A CIA Diary* (New York: Simon & Schuster, 2015), 175.

4: I Know What You're Going to Say: Assumptions as Earplugs

47 *saving seemingly hopeless marriages* Laurie Abraham, *The Husbands and Wives Club: A Year in the Life of a Couples Therapy Group* (New York: Touchstone, 2013).

48 *researchers at Williams College* Kenneth Savitsky, Boaz Keysar, Nicholas Epley, Travis Carter, and Ashley Swanson, "The Closeness-Communication Bias: Increased Egocentrism Among Friends Versus Strangers," *Journal of Experimental Social Psychology* 47, no. 1 (2011): 269–273, https://doi.org/10.1016/j.jesp.2010.09.005.

50 *The French writer André Maurois* André Maurois, *Memoirs 1885–1967* (London: Bodley Head, 1970), 218.

50 *Dunbar's Number* R. I. M. Dunbar, "Neocortex Size as a Constraint on Group Size in Primates," *Journal of Human Evolution* 22, no. 6 (1992): 469–493, https://doi.org/10.1016/0047-2484(92)90081-J.

51 *hierarchical "layers of friendship"* Kate Murphy, "Do Your Friends Actually Like You?," *New York Times,* August 6, 2016, https://www.nytimes.com/2016/08/07/opinion/sunday/do-your-friends-actually-like-you.html.

53 *In an in-depth study* Mario Luis Small, *Someone To Talk To* (New York: Oxford University Press, 2017).

55 *Every man has some reminiscences* Fyodor Dostoyevsky, *Notes from the Underground* (Urbana, IL: Project Gutenberg, 1996), 35, https://www.gutenberg.org/files/600/600-h/600-h.htm.

56 *confirmation bias* Raymond Nickerson, "Confirmation Bias: A Ubiquitous Phenomenon in Many Guises," *Review of General Psychology* 2, no. 2 (1998): 175–220, https://doi.org/10.1037/1089-2680.2.2.175.

56 *expectancy bias* María Ruz, Anna Moser, and Kristin Webster, "Social Expectations Bias Decision-Making in Uncertain Inter-Personal Situations," *PLOS One* 6, no. 2 (2011): e15762, https://doi.org/10.1371/journal.pone.0015762; Elisha Y. Babad, "Expectancy Bias in Scoring as a Function of Ability and Ethnic Labels," *Psychological Reports* 46, no. 2 (1980): 625–626, https://doi.org/10.2466/pr0.1980.46.2.625; Cindy M. Cabeleira, Shari A. Steinman, Melissa M. Burgess, Romola S. Bucks, Colin MacLeod, Wilson Melo, and Bethany A. Teachman, "Expectancy Bias in Anxious Samples," *Emotion* 14, no. 3 (2014): 588, https://doi.org/10.1037/a0035899.

56 *broad stereotypes* Perry Hinton, "Implicit Stereotypes and the Predictive Brain: Cognition and Culture in 'Biased' Person Perception," *Palgrave Communications* 3, no. 17086 (2017), https://doi.org/10.1057/palcomms.2017.86.

57 *we all harbor prejudices* David Hamilton and Tina Trolier, "Stereotypes and Stereotyping: An Overview of the Cognitive Approach," in *Prejudice, Discrimination, and Racism,* ed. J. F. Dovidio and S. L. Gaertner (San Diego: Academic Press, 1986), 127–163.

58 *social signaling theory* Brian L. Connelly, S. Trevis Certo, and R. Duane Ireland, "Signaling Theory: A Review and Assessment," *Journal of Management*

37, no. 1 (2010): 39–67, https://doi.org/10.1177/0149206310388419; Lee Cronk, "The Application of Animal Signaling Theory to Human Phenomena: Some Thoughts and Clarifications," *Social Science Information* 44, no. 4 (December 1, 2005): 603–620, https://doi.org/10.1177/0539018405058203.

58 *social identity theory* Jonah Berger and Chip Heath, "Who Drives Divergence? Identity Signaling, Outgroup Dissimilarity, and the Abandonment of Cultural Tastes," *Journal of Personality and Social Psychology* 95, no. 3 (2008): 593–607, http://dx.doi.org/10.1037/0022-3514.95.3.593; Naomi Ellemers and S. Alexander Haslam, "Social Identity Theory," in *Handbook of Theories of Social Psychology,* vol. 2, ed. Paul Van Lange, Arie Kruglanski, and Tory Higgins (Thousand Oaks, CA: Sage, 2012), 379–398; Henri Tajfel, "Social Identity and Intergroup Behaviour," *Social Science Information* 13, no. 2 (1974): 65–93, https://doi.org/10.1177/053901847401300204.

58 *clothes they wear* Rob Nelissen and Marijn Meijers, "Social Benefits of Luxury Brands as Costly Signals of Wealth and Status," *Evolution and Human Behavior* 32, no. 5 (2011): 343–355.

59 *correspondingly been losing adherents* Allen Downey, "The U.S. Is Retreating from Religion," *Observations* (blog), *Scientific American,* October 20, 2017, https://blogs.scientificamerican.com/observations/the-u-s-is-retreating-from-religion/.

59 *custom-made for signaling* Danah Boyd and Nicole Ellison, "Social Network Sites: Definition, History, and Scholarship," *Journal of Computer-Mediated Communication* 13, no. 1 (2007): 210–230, https://doi.org/10.1111/j.1083-6101.2007.00393.x.

59 *Showing that you follow* Cliff Lampe, Nicole Ellison, and Charles Steinfield, "A Familiar Face(book): Profile Elements as Signals in an Online Social Network," *Proceedings of the SIGCHI Conference on Human Factors in Computing Systems*, San Jose, CA (2007): 435–444, https://doi.org/10.1145/1240624.1240695.

59 *reluctant to give their surnames* Nicole Hong, "The New Dating No-No: Asking for a Last Name," *Wall Street Journal,* January 24, 2018, https://www.wsj.com/articles/the-new-dating-no-no-asking-for-a-last-name-1516810482.

5: THE TONE-DEAF RESPONSE: WHY PEOPLE WOULD RATHER TALK TO THEIR DOG

62 *descriptive and evaluative information* Graham Bodie, Kaitlin Cannava, and Andrea Vickery, "Supportive Communication and the Adequate Paraphrase," *Communication Research Reports* 33, no. 2 (2016): 166–172, http://dx.doi.org/10.1080/08824096.2016.1154839.

63 *I hear the words* Carl Ransom Rogers, *A Way of Being* (New York: Houghton Mifflin, 1980), 8.

65 *always has two reasons* Fred Shapiro, *The Yale Book of Quotations* (New Haven, CT: Yale University Press, 2006), 537.

66 *say a single word Bowling for Columbine,* directed by Michael Moore (Beverly Hills, CA: United Artists 2002).

67 *a desire for revenge* James Fox and Monica DeLateur, "Mass Shootings in America: Moving Beyond Newtown," *Homicide Studies* 18, no. 1 (2014): 125–145, https://doi.org/10.1177/1088767913510297.

67 *commonality among mass murderers* Alex Yablon, "What Do Most Mass Shooters Have in Common? It's Not Politics, Violent Video Games or Occult Beliefs," *Chicago Tribune,* September 18, 2017, https://www.chicagotribune.com/news/opinion/commentary/ct-perspec-mass-shootings-video-games-politics-0917-story.html.

68 *Nice to meet you* Steve Chawkins, "Dick Bass Dies at 85; Texas Oilman Was First to Scale 'Seven Summits,'" *Los Angeles Times,* July 29, 2015, https://www.latimes.com/local/obituaries/la-me-0730-richard-bass-20150730-story.html; Roger Horchow and Sally Horchow, *The Art of Friendship* (New York: St. Martin's Press, 2005), 33.

6: TALKING LIKE A TORTOISE, THINKING LIKE A HARE: THE SPEECH-THOUGHT DIFFERENTIAL

70 *Talking Like a Tortoise* Ralph Nichols and Leonard Stevens, *Are You Listening?* (New York: McGraw Hill, 1957), 82.

70 *caused by the* speech-thought differential Ralph Nichols and Leonard Stevens, "Listening to People," *Harvard Business Review,* September 1957, https://hbr.org/1957/09/listening-to-people; Clella Jaffe, *Public Speaking: Concepts and Skills for a Diverse Society* (Boston: Wadsworth Publishing, 2012), 58; Teri Kwal Gamble and Michael W. Gamble, *Interpersonal Communication: Building Connections Together* (Thousand Oaks, CA: Sage, 2014), 106.

70 *eighty-six billion brain cells* Frederico Azevedo, Ludmila Carvalho, Lea T. Grinberg, José Marcelo Farfel, Renata Ferretti, Renata Leite, Wilson Jacob Filho, et al., "Equal Numbers of Neuronal and Nonneuronal Cells Make the Human Brain an Isometrically Scaled-Up Primate Brain," *Journal of Comparative Neurology* 513, no. 5 (2009): 532–541, https://doi.org/10.1002/cne.21974.

71 *more neurotic and self-conscious* Alexander Penney, Victoria Miedema, and Dwight Mazmanian, "Intelligence and Emotional Disorders: Is the Worrying and Ruminating Mind a More Intelligent Mind?," *Personality and Individual Differences* 74 (2015): 90–93, https://doi.org/10.1016/j.paid.2014.10.005.

72 *challenging for introverts* Adam S. McHugh, "For Introverts, Listening Is an Act of Inward Hospitality," *Introvert, Dear: For Introverts and Highly Sensitive People* (blog), October 13, 2017, https://introvertdear.com/news/listen -introverts-inner-world/.

72 *Spare thinking time* Nichols and Stevens, "Listening to People."

72 *more persuasive debaters* "Listening Legend Interview, Dr. Ralph Nichols," *Listening Post,* summer 2003, https://www.listen.org/Legend-Interview.

73 *missed at least half* Nichols and Stevens, "Listening to People."

75 *self-psychology holds* Heinz Kohut, *Self Psychology and the Humanities: Reflections on a New Psychoanalytic Approach,* ed. Charles Strozier (New York: W. W. Norton, 1980).

76 *talking on a rooftop terrace Annie Hall,* directed by Woody Allen (Hollywood, CA: United Artists, 1977).

7: LISTENING TO OPPOSING VIEWS: WHY IT FEELS LIKE BEING CHASED BY A BEAR

79 *staunch political positions* Jonas T. Kaplan, Sarah I. Gimbel, and Sam Harris, "Neural Correlates of Maintaining One's Political Beliefs in the Face of Counterevidence," *Scientific Reports* 6, no. 39589 (2016), https://doi.org/10 .1038/srep39589.

79 *made them feel "unsafe"* "Free Speech Advocate on the State of College Campuses," Steve Inskeep interview with Greg Lukianoff, *Morning Edition,* NPR, May 29, 2017, https://www.npr.org/2017/05/29/530555442/free -speech-advocate-on-the-state-of-college-campuses; Conor Friedersdorf, "Middlebury Reckons with a Protest Gone Wrong," *Atlantic,* March 6, 2017, https://www.theatlantic.com/politics/archive/2017/03/middleburys-liberals -respond-to-an-protest-gone-wrong/518652/.

79 *survey of college and university students* John Villasenor, "Views Among College Students Regarding the First Amendment: Results from a New Survey," *Fixgov* (blog) Brookings Institution, September 18, 2017, https:// www.brookings.edu/blog/fixgov/2017/09/18/views-among-college-students -regarding-the-first-amendment-results-from-a-new-survey/.

80 *calling their ideas "dangerous"* Richard Felton, "Ted Cruz: Democratic Candidates Are a 'Dangerous Socialist . . . and Bernie Sanders,'" *Guardian,* September 19, 2015, https://www.theguardian.com/us-news/2015/sep/19 /ted-cruz-hillary-clinton-mackinac-republican-leadership-conference.

80 *After a particularly partisan fight* Charles Gibson, "Restoring Comity to Congress," Harvard University Shorenstein Center Discussion Paper Series, January 2011, https://shorensteincenter.org/wp-content/uploads/2012/03/d60_gibson.pdf.

80 *Old buddy, that's politics* Olivia Newman, *Liberalism in Practice: The Psychology and Pedagogy of Public Reason* (Cambridge, MA: MIT Press, 2015), 98.

80 *Social Security reform legislation* Martin Tolchin, "Social Security: Compromise at Long Last," *New York Times,* January 20, 1983, https://www.nytimes.com/1983/01/20/us/social-security-compromise-at-long-last.html.

80 *McCain wrote in an editorial* John McCain, "It's Time Congress Returns to Regular Order," *Washington Post,* August 31, 2017, https://www.washingtonpost.com/opinions/john-mccain-its-time-congress-returns-to-regular-order/2017/08/31/f62a3e0c-8cfb-11e7-8df5-c2e5cf46c1e2_story.html.

80 *"talking stick" incident* Avery Anapol, "Senator Using 'Talking Stick' Breaks Collins' Glass Elephant During Shutdown Talks," *The Hill,* January 22, 2018, https://thehill.com/homenews/senate/370163-unnamed-senator-throws-talking-stick-breaks-collins-glass-elephant-during.

81 *"alternative facts"* "Conway: Press Secretary Gave 'Alternative Facts,'" *Meet the Press,* NBC video, 3:39, January 22, 2017, https://www.nbcnews.com/meet-the-press/video/conway-press-secretary-gave-alternative-facts-860142147643.

81 *Donald Trump famously said* "Donald Trump: 'My Primary Consultant Is Myself,'" YouTube video, 3:11, posted by MSNBC, March 16, 2016, https://www.youtube.com/watch?v=W7CBp8lQ6ro.

82 *but also afraid* "Partisanship and Political Animosity in 2016," Pew Research Center, June 22, 2016, http://assets.pewresearch.org/wp-content/uploads/sites/5/2016/06/06-22-16-Partisanship-and-animosity-release.pdf.

82 *stopped talking to a friend* Jeremy Peters, "In a Divided Era, One Thing Seems to Unite: Political Anger," *New York Times,* August 17, 2018, https://www.nytimes.com/2018/08/17/us/politics/political-fights.html.

84 *activity in your amygdala* Oshin Vartanian and David R. Mandel, eds., *Neuroscience of Decision Making* (New York: Psychology Press, 2011), 89–93.

84 *inverse relationship between amygdala activity* Joseph LeDoux, *The Emotional Brain: The Mysterious Underpinnings of Emotional Life* (New York: Touchstone, 1998); Daniel Goleman, *Emotional Intelligence: Why It Can Matter More Than IQ* (New York: Bantam Books, 1995), 13–33.

85 *apt to suffer from anxiety and depression* Matthew Scult, Annchen Knodt, Spenser Radtke, Bartholomew Brigidi, and Ahmad R. Hariri, "Prefrontal Executive Control Rescues Risk for Anxiety Associated with High Threat and Low Reward Brain Function," *Cerebral Cortex* 29, no. 1 (2017): 70–76, https://doi.org/10.1093/cercor/bhx304.

85 *so-called helicopter parents* M. Justin Kim, Matthew Scult, Annchen Knodt, Spenser Radtke, Tracy d'Arbeloff, Bartholomew Brigidi, and Ahmad R. Hariri, "A Link Between Childhood Adversity and Trait Anger Reflects Relative Activity of the Amygdala and Dorsolateral Prefrontal Cortex," *Biological Psychiatry: Cognitive Neuroscience and Neuroimaging* 3, no. 7 (2018): 644–649, https://doi.org/10.1016/j.bpsc.2018.03.006.

85 *an excess of neurons* Thomas A. Avino, Nicole Barger, Martha V. Vargas, Erin L. Carlson, David G. Amaral, Melissa D. Bauman, and Cynthia M. Schumann, "Neuron Numbers Increase in the Human Amygdala from Birth to Adulthood, but Not in Autism," *Proceedings of the National Academy of Sciences* 115, no. 14 (2018): 3710–3715, https://doi.org/10.1073/pnas.1801912115.

86 *really happened in Oklahoma City* Austin Prickett, "Police: Fight Over Star Wars and Star Trek Led to Assault," KOKH Fox25, July 6, 2017, https://okcfox .com/news/local/police-fight-over-star-wars-and-star-trek-led-to-assault.

86 *what is known as learning* Carl Rogers, *On Becoming a Person: A Therapist's View of Psychotherapy* (Boston: Houghton Mifflin, 1961), 25.

87 *"negative capability"* John Keats, *Selected Letters of John Keats*, ed. Grant F. Scott (Cambridge, MA: Harvard University Press, 2002), 60.

87 *known as* cognitive complexity Jesse G. Delia, Ruth Anne Clark, and David E. Switzer, "Cognitive Complexity and Impression Formation in Informal Social Interaction," *Speech Monographs*, 41, no. 4 (1974): 299–308, https://doi.org /10.1080/03637757409375854; Claudia L. Hale and Jesse G. Delia, "Cognitive Complexity and Social Perspective-taking," *Communication Monographs*, 43, no. 3 (1976): 195–203, https://doi.org/10.1080/03637757609375932; Michael J. Beatty and Steven K. Payne, "Listening Comprehension as a Function of Cognitive Complexity: A Research Note," *Communication Monographs*, 51, no. 1 (1984): 85–89, https://doi.org/10.1080/03637758409390186.

87 *make better judgments* B. R. Burleson and J. J. Rack, "Constructivism: Explaining Individual Differences in Communication Skill," in *Engaging Theories in Interpersonal Communication*, ed. L. A. Baxter and D. O. Braithwaite (Thousand Oaks, CA: Sage, 2008), 51–63; P. M. Spengler and D. C. Strohmer, "Clinical Judgmental Biases: The Moderating Roles of Counselor Cognitive Complexity and Counselor Client Preferences," *Journal of Counseling Psychology*, 41, no. 1 (1994), 8–17, http://dx.doi.org/10.1037/0022-0167.41.1.8.

88 *standing up to him* Walter Isaacson, *Steve Jobs* (New York: Simon & Schuster, 2011), 317.

88 *Jobs berated him* Kim Scott, *Radical Candor* (New York: St. Martin's Press, 2017), 80.

8: FOCUSING ON WHAT'S IMPORTANT: LISTENING IN THE AGE OF BIG DATA

91 *hired by the United States Office* Robert K. Merton, "The Focused Interview and Focus Groups: Continuities and Discontinuities," *Public Opinion Quarterly* 51 (1987): 550–566, http://citeseerx.ist.psu.edu/viewdoc/download?doi =10.1.1.890.112&rep=rep1&type=pdf.

91 *to research propaganda* Peter Simonson, "Merton's Sociology of Rhetoric," in *Robert K. Merton: Sociology of Science and Sociology as Science*, ed. Craig Calhoun (New York: Columbia University Press, 2017), 214–252.

91 *the so-called focused interview* Liza Featherstone, *Divining Desire: Focus Groups and the Culture of Consultation* (New York: OR Books, 2017), 15–16.

92 *consumers in a focus group* Ernest Dichter, *The Strategy of Desire* (New York: Routledge, 2017); Dinitia Smith, "When Flour Power Invaded the Kitchen," *New York Times,* April 14, 2004, https://www.nytimes.com/2004/04/14/dining /when-flour-power-invaded-the-kitchen.html.

93 *people lie* Will Leitch, "Group Thinker," *New York Magazine,* June 21, 2004, https://nymag.com/nymetro/shopping/features/9299/.

95 *modernized Aunt Jemima* Jon Berry, "Marketers Reach Out to Blacks," *Chicago Tribune,* May 12, 1991, https://www.chicagotribune.com/news/ct-xpm -1991-05-12-9102110986-story.html.

96 *Joseph Henry Hairston* "Army's First Black Helicopter Pilot Honored at George Washington University," *GW Today,* November 4, 2014, https:// gwtoday.gwu.edu/army%E2%80%99s-first-black-helicopter-pilot-honored -george-washington-university; "Joining a Segregated Army," Joseph Henry Hairston interview, Digital Collections of the National WWII Museum, 2015, https://www.ww2online.org/view/joseph-hairston.

98 *half-billion-dollar brand* "P&G's Billion-Dollar Brands: Trusted, Valued, Recognized," Procter & Gamble, https://www.pg.com/en_US/downloads /media/Fact_Sheets_BB_FA.pdf; John Colapinto, "Famous Names: Does It Matter What a Product Is Called?," *New Yorker,* October 3, 2011, https:// www.newyorker.com/magazine/2011/10/03/famous-names.

98 *his book, Bit by Bit* Matthew Salganik, *Bit by Bit: Social Research in the Digital Age* (Princeton, NJ: Princeton University Press, 2017).

98 *Darwin's wide-ranging reading* "Darwin Correspondence Project," University of Cambridge, https://www.darwinproject.ac.uk/people/about-darwin /what-darwin-read/darwin-s-reading-notebooks.

98 *Amazon's algorithmic recommendations* Greg Linden, Brent Smith, and Jeremy York, "Amazon.com Recommendations Item-to-Item Collaborative Filtering,"

IEEE Internet Computing, January–February 2003, https://www.cs.umd.edu /~samir/498/Amazon-Recommendations.pdf.

9: IMPROVISATIONAL LISTENING: A FUNNY THING HAPPENED ON THE WAY TO WORK

103 *Google commissioned a study* Charles Duhigg, "What Google Learned from Its Quest to Build the Perfect Team," *New York Times,* February 25, 2016, https://www.nytimes.com/2016/02/28/magazine/what-google-learned -from-its-quest-to-build-the-perfect-team.html.

104 *the most productive teams* "Guide: Understand Team Effectiveness," *re: Work,* https://rework.withgoogle.com/guides/understanding-team-effectiveness /steps/introduction/.

104 *job growth since 1980* David Deming, "The Growing Importance of Social Skills in the Labor Market," *Quarterly Journal of Economics* 132, no. 4 (2017): 1593–1640, https://doi.org/10.1093/qje/qjx022.

105 *ballooned by 50 percent* Rob Cross, Reb Rebele, and Adam Grant, "Collaborative Overload," *Harvard Business Review,* January–February 2016, 74–79, https://hbr.org/2016/01/collaborative-overload.

105 *Many large companies* "Current and Former Clients," Business Improv, http://businessimprov.com/clientspartners/.

110 *Carl Jung, early in his career* Nelle Morton, *The Journey Is Home* (Boston, MA: Beacon Press, 1985), 209.

111 *competence and confidence* T. Bradford Bitterly, Alison Brooks, and Maurice Schweitzer, "Risky Business: When Humor Increases and Decreases Status," *Journal of Personality and Social Psychology* 112, no. 3 (2017): 431–455, https://doi.org/10.1037/pspi0000079.

112 *intimacy and security* E. De Koning and R. L. Weiss, "The Relational Humor Inventory: Functions of Humor in Close Relationships," *American Journal of Family Therapy* 30, no. 1 (2002): 1–18, https://doi.org/10.1080 /019261802753455615.

112 *feelings of connectedness* John C. Meyer, *Understanding Humor Through Communication: Why Be Funny, Anyway* (Lanham, MD: Lexington Books, 2015), 81–87.

112 *put-down or mean humor* Nathan Miczo, Joshua Averbeck, and Theresa Mariani, "Affiliative and Aggressive Humor, Attachment Dimensions, and Interaction Goals," *Communication Studies* 60, no. 5 (2009): 443–459, https:// doi.org/10.1080/10510970903260301; Meyer, *Understanding Humor Through Communication,* 88–89.

10: CONVERSATIONAL SENSITIVITY: WHAT TERRY GROSS, LBJ, AND CON MEN HAVE IN COMMON

115 *with a lump of clay* Katherine Hampsten, "How Miscommunication Happens (and How to Avoid It)," TED-Ed animation, https://ed.ted.com /lessons/how-to-avoid-miscommunication-katherine-hampsten#review.

115 *call it* conversational sensitivity John A. Daly, Anita L. Vangelisti, and Suzanne M. Daughton, "The Nature and Correlates of Conversational Sensitivity," *Human Communication Research* 14, no. 2 (1987): 167–202, https://doi.org/10 .1111/j.1468-2958.1987.tb00126.x.

116 *related to cognitive complexity* Don W. Stacks and Mary Ann Murphy, "Conversational Sensitivity: Further Validation and Extension," *Communication Reports* 6, no. 1 (1993): 18–24, https://doi.org/10.1080/08934219309367557.

116 *intuition, often called the sixth sense* Herbert Simon, "What Is An Explanation of Behavior?," *Psychological Science* 3, no. 3 (1992): 150–161, https://doi.org/10.1111 /j.1467-9280.1992.tb00017.x.

118 *personal stuff is discussed* Stacks and Murphy, "Conversational Sensitivity."

120 *a million words* "How Many Words Are There in English?," *Merriam-Webster,* https://www.merriam-webster.com/help/faq-how-many-english-words.

120 *tipping out their muck* Cyril Connolly, *The Unquiet Grave: A Word Cycle by Palinurus* (New York: Persea Books, 2005), 93.

120 *compacted composition of all* Walt Whitman, *The Portable Walt Whitman,* ed. Michael Warner (New York: Penguin Books, 2004), 557.

121 *dozens of regional dialects* Bert Vaux, Harvard Dialect Survey, 2003, http:// dialect.redlog.net/.

121 good sex Sara McClelland, "Intimate Justice: Sexual Satisfaction in Young Adults," (Ph.D. dissertation, City University of New York, 2009), https://doi .org/10.1111/j.1751-9004.2010.00293.x.

121 *are full of echoes* "The Only Surviving Recording of Virginia Woolf," BBC, March 28, 2016, http://www.bbc.com/culture/story/20160324-the-only -surviving-recording-of-virginia-woolf.

122 *Sapir-Whorf hypothesis* Konrad Koerner, "The Sapir-Whorf Hypothesis: A Preliminary History and a Bibliographical Essay," *AnthroSource,* December 1992, https://doi.org/10.1525/jlin.1992.2.2.173.

122 *demonstrated linguistic relativity* Emanuel Bylund and Panos Athanasopoulos, "The Whorfian Time Warp: Representing Duration Through the Language Hourglass," *Journal of Experimental Psychology* 146, no. 7 (2017): 911–916, https://doi.org/10.1037/xge0000314.

123 *higher degree of self-awareness* Jennifer R. Salibury and Guo-Ming Chen. "An Examination of the Relationship Between Conversation Sensitivity and Listen-

ing Styles," *Intercultural Communication Studies*, 16, no. 1 (2007): 251–262.; Daly et al., "The Nature and Correlates of Conversational Sensitivity"; Stacks and Murphy, "Conversational Sensitivity."

123 *known as* self-monitoring Daly et al., "The Nature and Correlates of Conversational Sensitivity."

123 *his 1948 book* Theodor Reik, *Listening with the Third Ear* (New York: Farrar, Straus and Giroux, 1948).

124 *People think Johnson talks* "Robert Caro on the Fall of New York, and Glenn Close on Complicated Characters," *New Yorker Radio Hour,* WNYC, May 4, 2018, https://www.newyorker.com/podcast/the-new-yorker-radio-hour/robert -caro-on-the-fall-of-new-york-and-glenn-close-on-complicated-characters.

124 *lying is often a cooperative act* Pamela Meyer, *Liespotting: Proven Techniques to Detect Deception* (New York: St. Martin's Press, 2010), 22.

125 *con artist Mel Weinberg* Robert D. McFadden, "Mel Weinberg, 93, the F.B.I.'s Lure in the Abscam Sting, Dies," *New York Times,* June 6, 2018, https:// www.nytimes.com/2018/06/06/obituaries/mel-weinberg-dead-abscam -informant.html.

125 *congressmen in the Abscam sting* "ABSCAM," *FBI,* https://www.fbi.gov /history/famous-cases/abscam.

125 *keep hopin' we're for real* Leslie Maitland, "At the Heart of the Abscam Debate," *New York Times Magazine,* July 25, 1982, https://www.nytimes .com/1982/07/25/magazine/at-the-heart-of-the-abscam-debate.html.

125 *people who are well motivated* Sasan Baleghizadeh and Amir Hossein Rahimi, "The Relationship Among Listening Performance, Metacognitive Strategy Use and Motivation from a Self-determination Theory Perspective," *Theory and Practice in Language Studies* 1, no. 1 (2011): 61–67, https:// doi.org/10.4304/tpls.1.1.61-67; Jeremy Biesanz and Lauren Human, "The Cost of Forming More Accurate Impressions: Accuracy-Motivated Perceivers See the Personality of Others More Distinctively but Less Normatively Than Perceivers Without an Explicit Goal," *Psychological Science* 21, no. 4 (2009): 589–594, https://doi.org/10.1177/0956797610364121; James Hilton and John Darley, "The Effects of Interaction Goals on Person Perception," ed. Mark P. Zanna, *Advances in Experimental Social Psychology* 24 (1991), 235–268; Daly et al., "The Nature and Correlates of Conversational Sensitivity."

127 *around 250,000 deaths* "Study Suggests Medical Errors Now Third Leading Cause of Death in the U.S.," Johns Hopkins Medicine, May 3, 2016, https:// www.hopkinsmedicine.org/news/media/releases/study_suggests_medical _errors_now_third_leading_cause_of_death_in_the_us.

127 *valuable reminders* Laura Silvestri, "The Heuristic Value of Misunderstanding," *Civilisations* 65, no. 1 (2016), 107–126, https://www.cairn.info/revue-civilisations-2016-1-page-107.htm; Amy Lee, Rhiannon D. Williams, Marta A. Shaw, and Yiyun Jie, "First-Year Students' Perspectives on Intercultural Learning," *Teaching in Higher Education* 19, no. 5 (2014): 543–554; Lipari, *Listening, Thinking, Being*, 8.

127 *In the words of Miles Davis* Paul Maher Jr. and Michael Dorr, eds., *Miles on Miles: Interviews and Encounters with Miles Davis* (Chicago: Lawrence Hill Books, 2009), 70.

11: LISTENING TO YOURSELF: THE VOLUBLE INNER VOICE

129 *do it in our heads* Jane Lidstone, Elizabeth Meins, and Charles Fernyhough, "Individual Differences in Children's Private Speech: Consistency Across Tasks, Timepoints, and Contexts," *Cognitive Development* 26, no. 3 (2011): 203–213, https://doi.org/10.1016/j.cogdev.2011.02.002.

129 *same parts of our brains* Ben Alderson-Day, Susanne Weis, Simon McCarthy-Jones, Peter Moseley, David Smailes, and Charles Fernyhough, "The Brain's Conversation with Itself: Neural Substrates of Dialogic Inner Speech." *Social Cognitive and Affective Neuroscience* 11, no. 1 (2015): 110–120, https://doi.org/10.1093/scan/nsv094; Alain Morin and Breanne Hamper, "Self-Reflection and the Inner Voice: Activation of the Left Inferior Frontal Gyrus During Perceptual and Conceptual Self-Referential Thinking," *Open Neuroimaging Journal* 6 (2012): 78–89, https://doi.org/10.2174/1874440001206010078.

129 *taking the perspective of another* Charles Fernyhough, *The Voices Within* (New York: Basic Books, 2016), 74.

130 *higher performance on cognitive tasks* Tuija Aro, Anna-Maija Poikkeus, Marja-Leena Laakso, Asko Tolvanen, and Timo Ahonen, "Associations Between Private Speech, Behavioral Self-Regulation, and Cognitive Abilities," *International Journal of Behavioral Development* 39, no. 6 (2014): 508–518, https://doi.org/10.1177/0165025414556094; Ben Alderson-Day and Charles Fernyhough, "Inner Speech: Development, Cognitive Functions, Phenomenology, and Neurobiology," *Psychological Bulletin* 141, no. 5 (2015): 931–965, http://dx.doi.org/10.1037/bul0000021.

130 *more involved parents* Douglas Behrend, Karl Rosengren, and Marion Perlmutter, "The Relation Between Private Speech and Parental Interactive Style," in *Private Speech: From Social Interaction to Self-Regulation*, ed. Rafael Diaz and Laura Berk (Hillsdale, NJ: Lawrence Erlbaum Associates, 1992), 85–100.

130 *Appalachian families* Laura Berk and Ruth Garvin, "Development of Private Speech Among Low-Income Appalachian Children," *Developmental Psychology* 20, no. 2 (1984): 271–286, http://dx.doi.org/10.1037/0012-1649.20.2.271.

130 *low-income urban families* Laura Berk, "Development of Private Speech Among Preschool Children," *Early Child Development and Care* 24, no. 1–2 (1986): 113–136, https://doi.org/10.1080/0300443860240107.

131 *rated the external sound* Xing Tian, Nai Ding, Xiangbin Teng, Fan Bai, and David Poeppel, "Imagined Speech Influences Perceived Loudness of Sound," *Nature Human Behavior* 2, no. 3 (2018): 225–234, https://doi.org/10.1038/s41562-018-0305-8.

132 *we sound out words* Marianne Abramson and Stephen D. Goldinger, "What the Reader's Eye Tells the Mind's Ear: Silent Reading Activates Inner Speech," *Perception & Psychophysics* 59, no. 7 (1997): 1059–1068, https://doi.org/10.3758/BF03205520.

132 *pace consistent with the speech* Jessica Alexander and Lynne Nygaard, "Reading Voices and Hearing Text: Talker-Specific Auditory Imagery in Reading," *Journal of Experimental Psychology: Human Perception and Performance* 34, no. 2 (2008): 446–459, http://dx.doi.org/10.1037/0096-1523.34.2.446.

132 *reading direct versus indirect speech* Bo Yao, Pascal Belin, and Christophe Scheepers, "Silent Reading of Direct versus Indirect Speech Activates Voice-selective Areas in the Auditory Cortex," *Journal of Cognitive Neuroscience* 23, no. 10 (October 2011): 3146–3152, https://doi.org/10.1162/jocn_a_00022.

132 *teamed up with The Guardian* Ben Alderson-Day, Marco Bernini, and Charles Fernyhough, "Uncharted Features and Dynamics of Reading: Voices, Characters, and Crossing of Experiences," *Consciousness and Cognition* 49 (2017): 98–109, https://doi.org/10.1016/j.concog.2017.01.003.

133 *certain pitch of excitement* Rob Couteau, "The Romance of Places: An Interview with Ray Bradbury," in *Conversations with Ray Bradbury,* ed. Steven L. Aggelis (Jackson: University Press of Mississippi, 2004), 122.

134 *self-administering shocks* Timothy Wilson, David Reinhard, Erin C. Westgate, Daniel T. Gilbert, Nicole Ellerbeck, Cheryl Hahn, and Casey L. Brown, "Just Think: The Challenges of the Disengaged Mind," *Science* 345, no. 6 (2014): 75–77, https://doi.org/10.1126/science.1250830.

135 *I argue with myself* James Gleik, *Genius: The Life and Science of Richard Feynman* (New York: Pantheon, 1992), 230.

135 *appreciating where we are* Richard Feynman, *The Pleasure of Finding Things Out,* ed. Jeffrey Robbins (Cambridge, MA: Perseus Books, 1999), 110.

12: Supporting, Not Shifting, the Conversation

136 *I was the cleverest woman* Dick Leonard, *The Great Rivalry: Gladstone and Disraeli* (London: I. B. Tauris, 2013), 202–203; "Stanley Weintraub: Disraeli: A Biography," *C-SPAN video, 58:56,* February 6, 1994, https://www.c-span .org/video/?54339-1/disraeli-biography.

137 *angel in the marble* "Angels in the Marble?," *Economist*, September 6, 2001, https://www.economist.com/united-states/2001/09/06/angels-in-the-marble.

137 *hundred informal dinner conversations* Charles Derber, *The Pursuit of Attention* (New York: Oxford University Press, 2000).

140 *like an insider* Howard Becker, *Outsiders: Studies in the Sociology of Deviance* (New York: Free Press, 2018).

140 *"Beckerisme," is required reading* Adam Gopnik, "The Outside Game," *New Yorker,* January 5, 2015, https://www.newyorker.com/magazine/2015/01/12 /outside-game.

141 *open and empathetic listeners* Leonardo Christov-Moore, Elizabeth Simpson, Gino Coudé, Kristina Grigaityte, Marco Iacobonia, and Pier Ferrari, "Empathy: Gender Effects in Brain and Behavior," *Neuroscience & Biobehavioral Reviews* 46, no. 4 (2014): 604–627, https://doi.org/10.1016/j.neubiorev.2014.09.001.

141 *women focus more on* David Geary, "Sexual Selection and Human Vulnerability," in *Evolution of Vulnerability* (San Diego: Academic Press, 2015), 11–39, https://doi.org/10.1016/B978-0-12-801562-9.09996-8; Debra Worthington and Margaret Fitch-Hauser, *Listening: Processes, Functions and Competency* (New York: Routledge, 2016), 32–34; Deborah Tannen, *You Just Don't Understand: Women and Men in Conversation* (New York: HarperCollins, 1990), 74–95.

141 *nature or nurture* Tara Chaplin and Amelia Aldao, "Gender Differences in Emotion Expression in Children: A Meta-Analytic Review," *Psychological Bulletin* 139, no. 4 (2013): 735–765, https://doi.org/10.1037/a0030737.

141 *even infant girls* Megan R. Gunnar and Margaret Donahue, "Sex Differences in Social Responsiveness Between Six Months and Twelve Months," *Child Development* (1980): 262–265, http://dx.doi.org/10.2307/1129619; Gerianne M. Alexander and Teresa Wilcox, "Sex Differences in Early Infancy," *Child Development Perspectives* 6, no. 4 (2012): 400–406, https://doi.org/10 .1111/j.1750-8606.2012.00247.x; Agneta Fischer, *Gender and Emotion: Social Psychological Perspectives* (Cambridge: Cambridge University Press, 2000).

141 *form of the male brain* Simon Baron-Cohen, Sarah Cassidy, Bonnie Auyeung, Carrie Allison, Maryam Achoukhi, Sarah Robertson, Alexa Pohl, et al., "Attenuation of Typical Sex Differences in 800 Adults with Autism vs. 3,900 Controls," *PLOS One* 9, no. 7 (2014), https://doi.org/10.1371/journal.pone.0102251.

142 *perceived as significantly louder* Mélanie Aeschlimann, Jean-François Knebel, Micah M. Murray, and Stephanie Clarke, "Emotional Pre-Eminence of Human Vocalizations," *Brain Topography* 20, no. 4 (2008): 239–248, https://doi .org/10.1007/s10548-008-0051-8.

143 *five times more upset* Andrew G. Miner, Theresa M. Glomb, and Charles Hulin, "Experience Sampling Mood and Its Correlates at Work," *Journal of Occupational and Organizational Psychology* 78 (2005): 171–193, https://doi .org/10.1348/096317905X40105.

143 *for a relationship to succeed* Kyle Benson, "The Magic Relationship Ratio, According to Science," Gottman Institute, October 4, 2017, https://www .gottman.com/blog/the-magic-relationship-ratio-according-science/.

143 *another kind of shift response* Kelsey Crowe and Emily McDowell, *There Is No Good Card for This: What To Do and Say When Life is Scary, Awful and Unfair to People You Love* (New York: HarperOne, 2017).

144 *Quaker practice of forming "clearness committees"* "Clearness Committees— What They Are and What They Do," Friends General Conference, https:// www.fgcquaker.org/resources/clearness-committees-what-they-are-and -what-they-do.

148 *when mothers just listened* Bethany Rittle-Johnson, Megan Saylor, and Kathryn E. Swygert, "Learning from Explaining: Does It Matter If Mom Is Listening?," *Journal of Experimental Child Psychology* 100, no. 3 (2008): 215–224, https://doi.org/10.1016/j.jecp.2007.10.002.

148 *more detailed solutions* Robert M. Krauss, "The Role of the Listener: Addressee Influences on Message Formulation," *Journal of Language and Social Psychology* 6, no. 2 (1987): 81–98, https://doi.org/10.1177/0261927X8700600201; Kate Loewenthal, "The Development of Codes in Public and Private Language," *Psychonomic Science* 8, no. 10 (1967): 449–450, https://doi.org/10 .3758/BF03332285.

149 *Great Conversations* "About Us," Great Conversations, https://www.greatconversations.com/about-us/.

150 *intense feelings of closeness* Arthur Aron, Edward Melinat, Elaine Aron, Robert Vallone, and Reness Bator, "The Experiental Generation of Interpersonal Closeness: A Procedure and Some Preliminary Findings," *Personality and Social Psychology Bulletin* 23, no. 4 (1997): 363–377, https://doi.org/10 .1177/0146167297234003.

150 *resurfaced in a 2015 essay* Mandy Len Catron, "To Fall in Love with Anyone, Do This," *New York Times,* January 9, 2015, https://www.nytimes.com/2015 /01/11/fashion/modern-love-to-fall-in-love-with-anyone-do-this.html.

152 *generative soul of their work* Michael Lewis, "How Tom Wolfe Became . . . Tom Wolfe," *Vanity Fair,* October 8, 2015, https://www.vanityfair.com /culture/2015/10/how-tom-wolfe-became-tom-wolfe; John McPhee, "Omission," *New Yorker,* September 7, 2015, https://www.newyorker.com/magazine /2015/09/14/omission; Neely Tucker, "How Richard Price Does It: New York Dialogue, Only Better," *Washington Post,* March 1, 2015, https://www .washingtonpost.com/lifestyle/style/how-richard-price-does-it-new-york -dialogue-only-better/2015/03/01/11ad2f04-bdec-11e4-bdfa-b8e8f594e6ee _story.html.

152 *telling you who they are* Elizabeth Strout, *The Burgess Boys* (New York: Random House, 2014), 160.

152 *people aren't listening that much* "Elizabeth Strout, 'Anything Is Possible,'" YouTube video, 55:04, posted by Politics and Prose, May 9, 2017, https:// www.youtube.com/watch?v=Y_gDvl2z4nQ&feature=youtu.be.

13: HAMMERS, ANVILS, AND STIRRUPS: TURNING SOUND WAVES INTO BRAIN WAVES

154 *can hear approaching clouds* "Elephants Can Hear the Sound of Approaching Clouds," BBC, December 11, 2015, http://www.bbc.com/earth/story /20151115-elephants-can-hear-the-sound-of-approaching-clouds; Michael Garstang, David R. Fitzjarrald, Kurt Fristrup, and Conrad Brain, "The Daily Cycle of Low-Frequency Elephant Calls and Near-Surface Atmospheric Conditions," *Earth Interactions* 9, no. 14 (2005): 1–21, https://doi.org /10.1175/EI147.1.

155 *reflexive reaction to it* Lizabeth M. Romanski and Joseph E. LeDoux, "Bilateral Destruction of Neocortical and Perirhinal Projection Targets of the Acoustic Thalamus Does Not Disrupt Auditory Fear Conditioning," *Neuroscience Letters* 142, no. 2 (1992): 228–232, https://doi.org/10.1016/0304 -3940(92)90379-L; "The Auditory Cortex" in *Neuroscience 2nd Edition*, eds. D. Purves, G. J. Augustine, D. Fitzpatrick, et al (Sunderland, MA: Sinauer Associates, 2001), https://www.ncbi.nlm.nih.gov/books/NBK10900/; Gary L. Wenk, *The Brain: What Everyone Needs To Know* (New York: Oxford University Press, 2017), 143–144.

155 *German neurologist Carl Wernicke* Judy Duchan, "Carl Wernicke 1848–1905," History of Speech-Language Pathology, University at Buffalo–SUNY, http:// www.acsu.buffalo.edu/~duchan/new_history/hist19c/subpages/wernicke .html; Gertrude H. Eggert, *Wernicke's Works on Aphasia: A Sourcebook and Review: Early Sources in Aphasia and Related Disorders, vol. 1* (The Hague: Mouton Publishers, 1977).

156 *specialized clusters of neurons* C. Tang, L. S. Hamilton, and E. F. Chang, "Intonational Speech Prosody Encoding in the Human Auditory Cortex," *Science* 357, no. 6353 (2017): 797–801, https://doi.org/10.1126/science.aam8577.

156 *musicians, whose art depends* Dana Strait, Nina Kraus, Erika Skoe, and Richard Ashley, "Musical Experience and Neural Efficiency-Effects of Training on Subcortical Processing of Vocal Expressions of Emotion," *European Journal of Neuroscience* 29 (2009): 661–668, https://doi.org/10.1111/j.1460-9568 .2009.06617.x.

156 *musicians unfamiliar with Mandarin* Chao-Yang Lee and Tsun-Hui Hung, "Identification of Mandarin Tones by English-Speaking Musicians and Nonmusicians," *The Journal of the Acoustical Society of America* 124, no. 3235 (2008), https://doi.org/10.1121/1.2990713; Céline Marie, Franco Delogu, Giulia Lampis, Marta Olivetti Belardinelli, and Mireille Besson, "Influence of Musical Expertise on Segmental and Tonal Processing in Mandarin Chinese," *Journal of Cognitive Neuroscience* 23, no. 10 (2011): 2701–2715.

156 *another intriguing fMRI experiment* Yaara Yeshurun, Stephen Swanson, Erez Simony, Janice Chen, Christina Lazaridi, Christopher J. Honey, and Uri Hasson, "Same Story, Different Story: The Neural Representation of Interpretive Frameworks," *Psychological Science* 28, no. 3 (2017): 307–319, https://doi.org/10.1177/0956797616682029.

156 *J. D. Salinger short story* J. D. Salinger, "Pretty Mouth and Green My Eyes," *New Yorker,* July 6, 1951, https://www.newyorker.com/magazine/1951/07/14 /pretty-mouth-and-green-my-eyes.

157 *right-ear advantage* M. P. Bryden, "An Overview of the Dichotic Listening Procedure and Its Relation to Cerebral Organization," in *Handbook of Dichotic Listening: Theory, Methods and Research,* ed. K. Hugdahl (Oxford, UK: John Wiley & Sons, 1988), 1–43; Gina Geffen, "The Development of the Right Ear Advantage in Dichotic Listening with Focused Attention," *Cortex* 14, no. 2 (1978): 169–177, https://doi.org/10.1016/S0010-9452(78)80042-2.

157 *emotional aspects of speech* Abdulrahman D. Alzahrani and Marwan A. Almuhammadi, "Left Ear Advantages in Detecting Emotional Tones Using Dichotic Listening Task in an Arabic Sample," *Laterality: Asymmetries of Body, Brain and Cognition* 18, no. 6 (2013): 730–747, https://doi.org/10.1080 /1357650X.2012.762373; Teow-Chong Sim and Carolyn Martinez, "Emotion words are remembered better in the left ear." *Laterality: Asymmetries of Body, Brain and Cognition* 10, no. 2 (2005): 149—159, https://doi.org/10.1080 /13576500342000365.

157 *appreciation of music* Diana Deutsch, "Dichotic Listening to Melodic Patterns and Its Relationship to Hemispheric Specialization of Function," *Music*

Perception: An Interdisciplinary Journal 3, no. 2 (1985): 127–154, https://doi .org/10.2307/40285329.

158 *wiring may be reversed* Anne L. Foundas, David M. Corey, Megan M. Hurley, and Kenneth M. Heilman, "Verbal Dichotic Listening in Right and Left-Handed Adults: Laterality Effects of Directed Attention," *Cortex* 42, no. 1 (2006): 79–86, https://doi.org/10.1016/S0010-9452(08)70324-1; Kenneth Hugdahl and Britta Andersson, "Dichotic Listening in 126 Left-Handed Children: Ear Advantages, Familial Sinistrality and Sex Differences," *Neuropsychologia* 27, no. 7 (1989): 999–1006, https://doi.org/10.1016/0028 -3932(89)90075-4.

158 *left or right side of headphones* James Jerger, "The Remarkable History of Right-Ear Advantage," *Hearing Review* 25, no. 1 (2018): 12–16, http://www .hearingreview.com/2017/12/remarkable-history-right-ear-advantage/.

158 *ingenious study by Italian researchers* Daniele Marzoli and Luca Tommasi, "Side Biases in Humans (Homo sapiens): Three Ecological Studies on Hemispheric Asymmetries," *Naturwissenschaften* 96, no. 9 (2009): 1099–1106, https://doi.org/10.1007/s00114-009-0571-4.

160 *earliest vertebrates had inner ears* Seth Horowitz, *The Universal Sense: How Hearing Shapes the Mind* (New York: Bloomsbury, 2012), 14.

160 *response to pressure* John Carey and Nivee Arnin, "Evolutionary Changes in the Cochlea and Labyrinth: Solving the Problem of Sound Transmission to the Balance Organs of the Inner Ear," *Anatomical Record Part A: Discoveries in Molecular, Cellular, and Evolutionary Biology* 288A, no. 4 (2006), https:// doi.org/10.1002/ar.a.20306.

160 *up to twenty decibels* Horowitz, *Universal Sense*, 75.

161 *feels so darn good* Cassie Shortsleeve, "Why It Feels So Damn Good to Stick a Q-tip in Your Ear," *Men's Health*, March 7, 2017, https://www.menshealth .com/health/a19542654/why-sticking-qtips-in-ear-feels-so-good/.

161 *don't call it "eargasm" for nothing* "Having an EARGASM by Cleaning Your Ears with a Q-tip," Facebook page, https://www.facebook.com/Having-an -EARGASM-by-cleaning-your-ears-with-a-Q-tip-270935093839/.

161 *Protruding from each hair cell* Chonnettia Jones and Ping Chen, "Chapter Eight Primary Cilia in Planar Cell Polarity Regulation of the Inner Ear," *Current Topics in Developmental Biology* 85 (2008): 197–224, https://doi.org /10.1016/S0070-2153(08)00808-9; William Yost, *Fundamentals of Hearing*, 5th ed. (Burlington, MA: Academic Press, 2001): 73–95.

162 *damage to those hair cells* Trevor Mcgill and Harold F. Schuknecht, "Human Cochlear Changes in Noise Induced Hearing Loss," *Laryngoscope* 86, no. 9 (1976), https://doi.org/10.1288/00005537-197609000-00001.

162 *everyday activities can damage* "Decibel Exposure Time Guidelines," Dangerous Decibels, http://dangerousdecibels.org/education/information-center /decibel-exposure-time-guidelines/; "Occupational Noise Exposure Revised Criteria 1998," Centers for Disease Control and Prevention, National Institute for Occupational Safety and Health, https://www.cdc.gov/niosh/docs /98-126/pdfs/98-126.pdf?id=10.26616/NIOSHPUB98126.

163 *1.1 billion young people* "1.1 Billion People at Risk of Hearing Loss," February 27, 2015, World Health Organization, https://www.who.int/mediacentre /news/releases/2015/ear-care/en/.

163 *48 million people* "One in Five Americans Has Hearing Loss: New nationally representative estimate shows wide scope of problem," Johns Hopkins Medicine News and Publications, November 14, 2011, https://www .hopkinsmedicine.org/news/media/releases/one_in_five_americans_has _hearing_loss; "Statistics and Facts About Hearing Loss," Center for Hearing and Communication, http://chchearing.org/facts-about-hearing -loss/.

163 *sixty-five percent are under age sixty-five* "12 Myths About Hearing Loss," AARP, https://www.aarp.org/health/conditions-treatments/info-2016/hearing -loss-myths-information-kb.html.

163 *third most common chronic physical condition* "Worker Hearing Loss," Centers for Disease Control and Prevention, https://www.cdc.gov/features/worker -hearing-loss/index.html.

164 *susceptability to auditory hallucinations* A. R. Powers, C. Mathys, and P. R. Corlett, "Pavlovian Conditioning–Induced Hallucinations Result from Overweighting of Perceptual Priors," *Science* 357, no. 6351 (2017): 596–600, https://doi.org/10.1126/science.aan3458; C. E. Seashore, "Measurements of Illusions and Hallucinations in Normal Life," *Studies from the Yale Psychological Laboratory* 3 (1895); D. G. Ellson, "Hallucinations Produced by Sensory Conditioning," *Journal of Experimental Psychology* 28, no. 1 (1941): 1–20, http://dx.doi.org/10.1037/h0054167; H. V. Helmholz, *Treatise on Physiological Optics, vol. 3* (New York: Dover, 1962).

164 *notebook of his "mishearings"* Oliver Sacks, "Mishearings," *New York Times,* June 5, 2015, https://www.nytimes.com/2015/06/07/opinion/oliver-sacks -mishearings.html.

165 *Sylvia Wright coined the term* Sylvia Wright, "The Death of Lady Mondegreen," in *Get Away from Me with Those Christmas Gifts* (New York: McGraw Hill, 1957).

165 *McGurk effect* Kaisa Tippana, "What Is the McGurk Effect?," *Frontiers in Psychology* 5, no. 725 (2014), https://doi.org/10.3389/fpsyg.2014.00725. See

also: "Try this bizarre audio illusion!" YouTube video, 3:25, posted by BBC, November 10, 2010, https://www.youtube.com/watch?v=G-lN8vWm3m0.

165 *poor emotional and social outcomes* Andrea Ciorba, Chiara Bianchini, Stefano Pelucchi, and Antonio Pastore, "The Impact of Hearing Loss on the Quality of Life of Elderly Adults," *Clinical Interventions in Aging* 7 (2017): 159–163, https://doi.org/10.2147/CIA.S26059; "Hearing Loss Impact," Cleveland Clinic, https://my.clevelandclinic.org/health/diseases/17052-hearing-loss-impact; Mary Kaland and Kate Salvatore, "The Psychology of Hearing Loss," *ASHA Leader,* March 1, 2002, https://doi.org/10.1044/leader.FTR1.07052002.4.

165 *60 percent of maximum volume* "Make Listening Safe," World Health Organization, https://www.who.int/pbd/deafness/activities/1706_PBD_leaftlet _A4_English_lowres_for_web170215.pdf.

166 *Earwax buildup* Daniel F. McCarter, Angela Courtney, Susan M Pollart, "Cerumen Impaction," *American Family Physician* 75, no. 10 (2007): 1523–1528.

166 *visual as aural enterprise* Ruth Campbell, "The Processing of Audio-Visual Speech: Empirical and Neural Bases," *Philosophical Transactions of the Royal Society B* 363, no. 1493 (2008): 1001–1010, https://doi.org/10.1098/rstb.2007 .2155.

166 *visual and auditory cortices* Paul Johns, *Clinical Neuroscience* (London: Churchill Livingston, 2014), 27–47.

166 *20 percent of your comprehension* Horst M. Müller, "Neurobiological Aspects of Meaning Constitution During Language Processing," in *Situated Communication,* eds. Gert Rickheit and Ipke Wachsmuth (New York: Mouton de Gruyter, 2006), 243; David Owen, "High-Tech Hope for the Hard of Hearing," *New Yorker,* March 27, 2017, https://www.newyorker.com /magazine/2017/04/03/high-tech-hope-for-the-hard-of-hearing.

166 *55 percent of the emotional content* Albert Mehrabian, *Silent Messages: Implicit Communication of Emotions and Attitudes* (Belmont, CA: Wadsworth Publishing, 1981), 75–80; Dilip Sundaram and Cynthia Webster, "The Role of Nonverbal Communication in Service Encounters," *Journal of Services Marketing* 14, no. 5 (2000): 378–391, https://doi.org/10.1108/08876040010341008; Cynthia Barnum and Natasha Wolniansky, "Taking Cues from Body Language," *Management Review* 78, no. 6 (1989): 59–61; Jon E. Grahe and Frank J. Bernieri, "The Importance of Nonverbal Cues in Judging Rapport," *Journal of Nonverbal Behavior* 23, no. 4 (1999): 253–269, https://doi.org/10.1023 /A:1021698725361.

166 *betrayal oozes out of him* John O'Neill, *The Domestic Economy of the Soul: Freud's Five Case Studies* (Thousand Oaks, CA: Sage, 2011), 67.

167 *involuntary pre-language* Irenaus Eibl-Eibesfeldt, *Love and Hate: A Natural History of Behavior Patterns (Foundations of Human Behavior), 1st ed.* (New York: Routledge, 2017); Charles Darwin, *The Expression of the Emotions in Man and Animals* (New York: Oxford University Press, 1998).

167 grammaticalization *of facial expressions* C. Fabian Benitez-Quiroz, Ronnie B. Wilbur, and Aleix M. Martinez, "The Not Face: A Grammaticalization of Facial Expressions of Emotion," *Cognition* 150 (2016): 77–84, https://doi.org/10.1016/j.cognition.2016.02.004.

167 *angry all the time* Alice Schermerhorn, "Associations of Child Emotion Recognition with Interparental Conflict and Shy Child Temperament Traits," *Journal of Social and Personal Relationships* (2018), https://doi.org/10.1177/0265407518762606.

167 *time looking at screens* Kyung-Seu Cho and Jae-Moo Lee, "Influence of Smartphone Addiction Proneness of Young Children on Problematic Behaviors and Emotional Intelligence: Mediating Self-Assessment Effects of Parents Using Smartphones," *Computers in Human Behavior* 66 (2017): 303–311, https://doi.org/10.1016/j.chb.2016.09.063; Elisabeth Engelberg and Lennart Sjöberg, "Internet Use, Social Skills, and Adjustment," *Cyberpsychology & Behavior* 7, no. 1 (2004): 41–47, https://doi.org/10.1089/109493104322820101.

167 *device-free outdoor camp* Yalda T. Uhls, Minas Michikyan, Jordan Morris, Debra Garcia, Gary W. Small, Eleni Zgourou, and Patricia M. Greenfield, "Five Days at Outdoor Education Camp Without Screens Improves Preteen Skills with Nonverbal Emotion Cues," *Computers in Human Behavior* 39 (2014): 387–392, https://doi.org/10.1016/j.chb.2014.05.036.

168 *superimposed the color signatures* Carlos Benitez-Quiroz, Ramprakash Srinivasan, and Aleix M. Martinez, "Facial Color Is an Efficient Mechanism to Visually Transmit Emotion," *Proceedings of the National Academy of Sciences* 115, no. 14 (2018): 3581–3586, https://doi.org/10.1073/pnas.1716084115.

170 *just 7 percent* Mehrabian, *Silent Messages*, 75–80.

171 *technological reasons* Sascha Segan, "How to Make Your Cell Phone Calls Sound Better," *PC Magazine,* April 13, 2018, https://www.pcmag.com/article/360357/how-to-make-your-cell-phone-calls-sound-better.

14: ADDICTED TO DISTRACTION

172 *device dependency* Jon E. Grant and Samuel R. Chamberlain, "Expanding the Definition of Addiction: DSM-5 vs. ICD-11," *CNS Spectrums* 21, no. 4 (2016): 300–303, https://doi.org/10.1017/S1092852916000183.

173 *losing our ability to daydream* Rebecca McMillan, Scott Barry Kaufman, and Jerome L. Singer, "Ode to Positive Constructive Daydreaming," *Frontiers in Psychology* 4 (2013): 626, https://doi.org/10.3389/fpsyg.2013.00626; Claire Zedelius and Jonathan Schooler, "The Richness of Inner Experience: Relating Styles of Daydreaming to Creative Processes," *Frontiers in Psychology* 6 (2016): 2063, https://doi.org/10.3389/fpsyg.2015.02063; Christopher R. Long and James R. Averill, "Solitude: An Exploration of Benefits of Being Alone," *Journal for the Theory of Social Behaviour* 33, no. 1 (2003): 21–44, https://doi.org/10.1111/1468 -5914.00204; Samantha Boardman, "Why Doing Nothing Is So Scary—And So Important," *Wall Street Journal,* June 20, 2016, https://blogs.wsj.com/experts /2016/06/20/why-doing-nothing-is-so-scary-and-so-important/.

173 *greatest advances in science* Ingrid Wickelgren, "Delivered in a Daydream: 7 Great Achievements That Arose from a Wandering Mind," *Scientific American,* February 17, 2011, https://www.scientificamerican.com/article /achievements-of-wandering-minds/.

173 *arts and letters* Maria Popova, "The Art of Constructive Daydreaming," *Brainpickings,* October 9, 2013, https://www.brainpickings.org/2013/10/09 /mind-wandering-and-creativity/.

173 *Research conducted by Microsoft* "Microsoft Attention Spans Research Report," Scribd, https://www.scribd.com/document/265348695/Microsoft-Attention -Spans-Research-Report.

173 *quibbled with how one measures* Simon Maybin, "Busting the Attention Span Myth," *BBC World Service,* March 10, 2017, https://www.bbc.com/news/health -38896790.

173 *advertisers and media companies are living* Shawn Lim, "'We Have to Focus on the Data': Adobe on the Industry's Short Attention Span," *The Drum,* March 8, 2019, https://www.thedrum.com/news/2019/03/08/we-have-focus -the-data-adobe-the-industrys-short-attention-span; Milana Saric, "How Brands Can Still Win Over Customers as Attention Spans Decrease on Social," *AdWeek,* November 21, 2017, https://www.adweek.com/brand -marketing/how-brands-can-still-win-over-customers-as-attention-spans -decrease-on-social/; Michelle Castillo, "Millennials Only Have a 5-Second Attention Span for Ads, Says comScore CEO," *CNBC,* July 21, 2017, https:// www.cnbc.com/2017/07/21/comscore-ceo-millennials-need-5-to-6-second -ads-to-hold-attention.html.

174 *about fifteen seconds* Chartbeat proprietary data.

174 *British advertising buyer* Louise Ridley, "People Swap Devices 21 Times an Hour, Says OMD," *Campaign,* January 3, 2014, https://www.campaignlive

.co.uk/article/people-swap-devices-21-times-hour-says-omd/1225960?src _site=brandrepublic.

174 *designed to grab and keep* Tim Wu, *The Attention Merchants: The Epic Scramble to Get Inside Our Heads* (New York: Alfred A. Knopf, 2016); Nir Eyal, *Hooked: How to Build Habit-Forming Products*, ed. Ryan Hoover (New York: Portfolio/Penguin, 2014); Henry Farrell, "It's No Accident Facebook Is So Addictive," *Washington Post,* August 6, 2018, https://www.washingtonpost.com/news/monkey-cage/wp /2018/08/06/its-no-accident-that-facebook-is-so-addictive/; "Why Can't We Put Down Our Smartphones?," *60 Minutes,* April 7, 2017, https://www.cbsnews.com /news/why-cant-we-put-down-our-smartphones-60-minutes/.

175 *sophisticated electronic exchanges* Kate Murphy, "The Ad-Blocking Wars," *The New York Times*, February 20, 2016, https://www.nytimes.com/2016/02/21 /opinion/sunday/the-ad-blocking-wars.html; George P. Slefo, "Six Leading Exchanges Sign Transparency Pact, But Fraud Concerns Remain," *AdAge*, October 18, 2018, https://adage.com/article/digital/exchanges-sign-letter -invite-fraudsters/315308; Junqi Jin, Chengru Song, Han Li, Kun Gai, Jun Wang, and Weinan Zhang, "Real-time Bidding with Multi-agent Reinforcement Learning in Display Advertising," In *Proceedings of the 27th ACM International Conference on Information and Knowledge Management*, 2193-2201, ACM, 2018, https://www.doi.org/10.1145/3269206.3272021.

175 *42 percent to 24 percent* Debra Worthington and Margaret Fitch-Hauser, *Listening: Processes, Functions and Competency* (New York: Routledge, 2016), 4–5.

175 *speed-listening* Megan Garber, "The Rise of 'Speed-Listening,'" *Atlantic,* June 24, 2015, https://www.theatlantic.com/technology/archive/2015/06/the -rise-of-speed-listening/396740/.

176 *great difficulty maintaining their attention* Judi Brownell, *Listening: Attitudes, Principles, and Skills* (New York: Routledge, 2018), 90.

176 *mere presence of a phone on the table* Andrew Przybylski and Netta Weinstein, "Can You Connect with Me Now? How the Presence of Mobile Communication Technology Influences Face-to-Face Conversation Quality," *Journal of Social and Personal Relationships* 30, no. 3 (2013): 237–246, https://doi.org /10.1177/0265407512453827.

176 *caregivers ignored their children* Amy Novotney, "Smartphone = Not-So-Smart Parenting?," *American Psychology Association* 47, no. 2 (2016), https:// www.apa.org/monitor/2016/02/smartphone; Cory A. Kildare and Wendy Middlemiss, "Impact of Parents Mobile Device Use on Parent-Child Interaction: A Literature Review," *Computers in Human Behavior* 75 (2017): 579–593.

177 *food industry research* "Noise Level in Restaurants," National Institute on Deafness and Other Communication Disorders, July 22, 2016, https://www.noisyplanet.nidcd.nih.gov/have-you-heard/noise-levels-restaurants; Tiffany Hsu, "Noisy Restaurants: Taking the Din Out of Dinner," *Los Angeles Times,* June 8, 2012, https://www.latimes.com/food/la-xpm-2012-jun-08-la-fi-restaurant-noise-20120504-story.html; Jill Lightner, "Yup, Seattle's Restaurants Have Gotten Noisier: How to Reverse This Trend? We're All Ears," *Seattle Times,* February 26, 2019, https://www.seattletimes.com/life/food-drink/your-suspicions-are-right-seattle-restaurants-are-getting-noisier-how-to-reverse-this-trend-were-all-ears/; Julia Beliuz, "Why Restaurants Became So Loud—And How to Fight Back," *Vox,* July 27, 2018, https://www.vox.com/2018/4/18/17168504/restaurants-noise-levels-loud-decibels; Kate Wagner, "How Restaurants Got So Loud," *Atlantic,* November 27, 2018, https://www.theatlantic.com/technology/archive/2018/11/how-restaurants-got-so-loud/576715/; Jonathan Kauffman, "Are San Francisco Restaurants Too Loud? A New App Helps Diners Navigate the Noise," *San Francisco Chronicle,* December 21, 2018, https://www.sfchronicle.com/restaurants/article/sf-restaurants-quietest-loud-app-soundprint-which-13475928.php.

177 *Zagat Dining Trends Survey* "Zagat Releases 2018 Dining Trends Survey," *Zagat* (blog), January 8, 2018, https://zagat.googleblog.com/2018/01/zagat-releases-2018-dining-trends-survey.html.

177 *overeat and make less healthy* Nanette Stroebele and John M. De Castro, "Effect of Ambience on Food Intake and Food Choice," *Nutrition* 20, no. 9 (2004): 821–838, https://doi.org/10.1016/j.nut.2004.05.012; Thomas Roballey, Colleen McGreevy, Richard R. Rongo, Michelle L. Schwantes, Peter J. Steger, Marie Wininger, and Elizabeth Gardner, "The Effect of Music on Eating Behavior," *Bulletin of the Psychonomic Society* 23, no. 3 (1985): 221–222, https://doi.org/10.3758/BF03329832; Dipayan Biswas, Kaisa Lund, and Courtney Szocs, "Sounds Like a Healthy Retail Atmospheric Strategy: Effects of Ambient Music and Background Noise on Food Sales," *Journal of the Academy of Marketing Science* 47, no. 1 (2019): 37–55, https://doi.org/10.1007/s11747-018-0583-8.

178 *makes customers more vulnerable* Richard Yalch and Eric Spangenberg, "Effects of Store Music on Shopping Behavior," *Journal of Consumer Marketing* 7, no. 2 (1990): 55–63, https://doi.org/10.1108/EUM0000000002577; Emily Anthes, "Outside In: It's So Loud, I Can't Hear My Budget!," *Psychology Today,* June 9, 2016, https://www.psychologytoday.com/us/articles/201009/outside-in-its-so-loud-i-cant-hear-my-budget; Charlotte Kemp, "Why are High Street shops so NOISY? As M&S Bans Muzak, Our Test Shows Other Stores Are Nearly as

Deafening as Nightclubs," *Daily Mail,* June 2, 2016, https://www.dailymail.co
.uk/femail/article-3620719/Why-High-Street-shops-NOISY-M-S-bans-Muzak
-test-shows-stores-nearly-deafening-nightclubs.html; Richard F. Yalch and Eric
Spangenberg, "Using Store Music for Retail Zoning: A Field Experiment," in
NA—Advances in Consumer Research, vol. 20, ed. Leigh McAlister and Michael
L. Rothschild (Provo, UT: Association for Consumer Research: 1993), 632–636.

178 *consistently shows that you cannot* Dominique Lamy, Liad Mudrik, and
Leon Y. Deouell, "Unconscious Auditory Information Can Prime Visual
Word Processing: A Process-Dissociation Procedure Study," *Consciousness
and Cognition* 17, no. 3 (2008): 688–698, https://doi.org/10.1016/j.concog
.2007.11.001; Christine Rosen, "The Myth of Multitasking," *New Atlantis* 20
(2008): 105–110; Loukia Loukopoulos, R. Key Dismukes, and Immanuel
Barshi, *The Multitasking Myth: Handling Complexity in Real-World Opera-
tions* (New London: Routledge, 2016).

178 *The often used phrase 'pay attention'* Daniel Kahneman, *Thinking, Fast and
Slow* (New York: Farrar, Straus and Giroux, 2011), 23.

179 *families eating together* Sharon Fruh, Jayne A. Fulkerson, Madhuri S.
Mulekar, Lee Ann J. Kendrick, and Clista Clanton, "The Surprising Benefits of the Family Meal," *Journal for Nurse Practitioners* 7, no. 1 (2011): 18–
22, https://doi.org/10.1016/j.nurpra.2010.04.017; Megan Harrison, Mark L.
Norris, Nicole Obeid, Maeghan Fu, Hannah Weinstangel, and Margaret
Sampson, "Systematic Review of the Effects of Family Meal Frequency
on Psychosocial Outcomes in Youth," *Canadian Family Physician* 61, no. 2
(2015): e96–e106; https://www.cfp.ca/content/61/2/e96; Barbara Fiese and
Marlene Schwartz, "Reclaiming the Family Table: Mealtimes and Child
Health and Wellbeing," *Social Policy Report* 22, no. 4 (2008); https://doi
.org/10.1002/j.2379-3988.1008.tb00057.x.

180 *an anthology of works* Eudora Welty and Ronald Sharp, eds., *Norton Book of
Friendship* (New York: W. W. Norton, 1991).

181 *invited protesters to join* "Dallas Police Chief Holds a News Conference,"
CNN, July 11, 2016, http://transcripts.cnn.com/TRANSCRIPTS/1607/11
/ath.02.html; "David Brown Press Conference on July 11, 2016," YouTube
video, 49:16, posted by "brimi925," July 13, 2016, https://www.youtube.com
/watch?v=p_uYQIMpIn4.

182 *Why aren't we smarter* "'Called to Rise': Dallas Police Chief on Overcom-
ing Racial Division," *All Things Considered,* NPR, June 6, 2017, https://
www.npr.org/2017/06/06/531787065/called-to-rise-dallas-police-chief-on
-overcoming-racial-division.

15: What Words Conceal and Silences Reveal

186   *researchers graphed around fifty thousand pauses* Stephen Levinson and Francisco Torreira, "Timing in Turn-Taking and Its Implications for Processing Models of Language," *Frontiers in Psychology* 6 (2015): 731, https://doi.org/10.3389/fpsyg.2015.00731.

186   *Studies of Dutch and German* Jan Peter De Ruiter, Holger Mitterer, and Nick J. Enfield, "Projecting the End of a Speaker's Turn: A Cognitive Cornerstone of Conversation," *Language* 82, no. 3 (2006): 515–535, https://doi.org/10.1353/lan.2006.0130; Carina Riest, Annett B. Jorschick, and Jan P. de Ruiter, "Anticipation in Turn-Taking: Mechanisms and Information Sources," *Frontiers in Psychology* 6 (2015): 89, https://doi.org/10.3389/fpsyg.2015.00089.

186   *People in Japan* Takie Sugiyama Lebra, "The Cultural Significance of Silence in Japanese Communication," *Multilingua: Journal of Cross-Cultural and Interlanguage Communication* 6, no. 4 (1987): 343–358, https://doi.org/10.1515/mult.1987.6.4.343.

186   *Japanese businesspeople tolerate* Haru Yamada, "Yappari, as I Thought: Listener Talk in Japanese Communication," *Global Advances in Business Communication* 4, no. 1 (2015): 3, https://commons.emich.edu/gabc/vol4/iss1/3.

186   *Doctor-patient interactions in Japan* Sachiko Ohtaki, Toshio Ohtaki, and Michael D. Fetters, "Doctor-Patient Communication: A Comparison of the USA and Japan," *Family Practice* 20, no. 3 (2003): 276–282, https://doi.org/10.1093/fampra/cmg308.

186   *The silent man is* Larry Samovar, Edwin R. McDaniel, Richard E. Porter, and Carolyn Sexton Roy, *Communication Between Cultures* (Ontario, Canada: Nelson Education, 2015), 334.

186   *Finns place greater value* Diana Petkova, "Beyond Silence: A Cross-Cultural Comparison Between Finnish 'Quietude' and Japanese 'Tranquility,'" *Eastern Academic Journal* 4 (2015): 1–14; https://www.academia.edu/19764499/Beyond_Silence._A_Cross-Cultural_Comparison_between_Finnish_Quietude_and_Japanese_Tranquility; Donal Carbaugh, Michael Berry, and Marjatta Nurmikari-Berry, "Coding Personhood Through Cultural Terms and Practices: Silence and Quietude as a Finnish 'Natural Way of Being,'" *Journal of Language and Social Psychology* 25, no. 3 (2006): 203–220, https://doi.org/10.1177/0261927X06289422.

187   *sign of a secure relationship* Namkje Koudenburg, Tom Postmes, and Ernestine H. Gordijn, "Conversational Flow Promotes Solidarity," *PLOS One* 8, no. 11 (2013): e78363, https://doi.org/10.1371/journal.pone.0078363.

187   *Higher-status people* Namkje Koudenburg, Tom Postmes, and Ernestine H. Gordijn, "Conversational Flow and Entitativity: The Role of Status." *British*

Journal of Social Psychology 53, no. 2 (2014): 350–366, https://doi.org/10.1111 /bjso.12027; Namkje Koudenburg, Tom Postmes, and Ernestine H. Gordijn. "Beyond Content of Conversation: The Role of Conversational Form in the Emergence and Regulation of Social Structure," *Personality and Social Psychology Review* 21, no. 1 (2017): 50–71, https://doi.org/10.1177/1088868315626022.

187 *interpret silences longer than* Felcia Roberts, Alexander L. Francis, and Melanie Morgan, "The Interaction of Inter-Turn Silence with Prosodic Cues in Listener Perceptions of 'Trouble' in Conversation," *Speech Communication* 48, no. 9 (2006): 1079–1093, https://doi.org/10.1016/j.specom .2006.02.001.

187 *nuance their expressed opinion* Namkje Koudenburg, Tom Postmes, and Ernestine H. Gordijn, "Resounding Silences: Subtle Norm Regulation in Everyday Interactions," *Social Psychology Quarterly* 76, no. 3 (2013): 224–241, https://doi.org/10.1177/0190272513496794.

187 *Tim Cook's propensity for silence* Kim Scott, *Radical Candor* (New York: St. Martin's Press, 2017), 83.

188 *feelings of belonging and well-being* Namkje Koudenburg, Tom Postmes, and Ernestine H. Gordijn, "Disrupting the Flow: How Brief Silences in Group Conversations Affect Social Needs," *Journal of Experimental Social Psychology* 47, no. 2 (2011): 512–515, https://doi.org/10.1016/j.jesp.2010.12.006.

188 *not to be found in the notes* "Gustav Mahler himself in the Netherlands (1903, 1904, 1906, 1909 and 1910)," Mahler Foundation Archive, https://mahler foundation.info/index.php/plaatsen/241-netherlands/amsterdam/1511-gus tav-mahler-himself-in-amsterdam.

188 *to what words conceal and silences reveal* Theodor Reik, *Listening with the Third Ear* (New York: Farrar, Straus and Giroux, 1948), 121–127.

190 *silence is a "pocket of possibility"* R. Murray Schafer, *Ear Cleaning: Notes for an Experimental Music Course* (Toronto, Canada: Clark & Cruickshank, 1967).

16: THE MORALITY OF LISTENING: WHY GOSSIP IS GOOD FOR YOU

193 *two-thirds of adult conversation* Robin Dunbar, "Gossip in Evolutionary Perspective," *Review of General Psychology* 8, no. 2 (2004): 100–110, https://doi .org/10.1037/1089-2680.8.2.100; Nicholas Emler, "Gossip, Reputation, and Social Adaptation," in *Good Gossip,* ed. R. F. Goodman and A. Ben-Ze'ev (Lawrence, KS: University Press of Kansas, 1994), 117–138. Viatcheslav Wlassoff, "This Is Your Brain on Gossip," PsychCentral, July 11, 2018, https:// psychcentral.com/blog/this-is-your-brain-on-gossip/; Freda-Marie Hartung, Constanze Krohn, and Marie Pirschtat, "Better Than Its Reputation? Gossip and the Reasons Why We and Individuals with 'Dark' Personalities Talk About

Others," *Frontiers in Psychology* 10 (2019): 1162, https://doi.org/10.3389/fpsyg
.2019.01162.

193 *Men gossip as much as women* Eyal Eckhaus and Batia Ben-Hador, "Gossip
and Gender Differences: A Content Analysis Approach," *Journal of Gender Studies* 28, no. 1 (2019): 97–108, https://doi.org/10.1080/09589236.2017
.1411789.

194 *children are adept gossipers* Jan Engelmann, Esther Herrmann, and Michael
Tomasello, "Preschoolers Affect Others' Reputations Through Prosocial
Gossip," *British Journal of Developmental Psychology* 34, no. 3 (2016): 447–460,
https://doi.org/10.1111/bjdp.12143.

194 *We all do it* Marianee Jaeger, Anne A. Skleder, Bruce Rind, and Ralph L. Rosnow, "Gossip, Gossipers, Gossipees," in *Good Gossip,* ed. R. F. Goodman and
A. Ben-Ze'ev (Lawrence, KS: University Press of Kansas, 1994); Jordan Litman and Mark V. Pezzo, "Individual Differences in Attitudes Towards Gossip," *Personality and Individual Differences* 38, no. 4 (2005): 963–980, https://doi
.org/10.1016/j.paid.2004.09.003; Francis McAndrew, Emily K. Bell, and Contitta Maria Garcia, "Who Do We Tell and Whom Do We Tell On? Gossip as a
Strategy for Status Enhancement," *Journal of Applied Social Psychology* 37, no.
7 (2007): 1562–1577, https://doi.org/10.1111/j.1559-1816.2007.00227.x.

194 *listening to positive gossip* Elena Martinescu, Onne Janssen, and Bernard A.
Nijstad, "Tell Me the Gossip: The Self-Evaluative Function of Receiving
Gossip About Others," *Personality and Social Psychology Bulletin* 40, no. 12
(2014): 1668–1680, https://doi.org/10.1177/0146167214554916.

194 *learn a lesson from it* Roy Baumeister, Liqing Zhang, and Kathleen D. Vohs,
"Gossip as Cultural Learning," *Review of General Psychology* 8, no. 2 (2004):
111–121, https://doi.org/10.1037/1089-2680.8.2.111.

194 *readily gossiped about others* Matthew Feinberg, Robb Willer, and Michael Schultz, "Gossip and Ostracism Promote Cooperation in Groups,"
Psychological Science 25, no. 3 (2014): 656–664, https://doi.org/10.1177
/0956797613510184.

194 *accurate or not so accurate* Miguel Fonseca and Kim Peters, "Will Any Gossip Do? Gossip Does Not Need to Be Perfectly Accurate to Promote Trust,"
Games and Economic Behavior 107 (2018): 253–281, https://doi.org/10.1016/j
.geb.2017.09.015.

195 *extension of observational learning* Baumeister et al., "Gossip as Cultural
Learning."

195 *only 3–4 percent of it is truly mean-spirited* Robin Dunbar, Anna Marriott,
and Neil Duncan, "Human Conversational Behavior," *Human Nature* 8, no.
3 (1997): 231–246, https://doi.org/10.1007/BF02912493.

196 *grooming behavior of apes* Robin Dunbar, *Grooming, Gossip, and the Evolution of Language* (Cambridge, MA: Harvard University Press, 1998).

197 *up to four individuals* Robin Dunbar and Daniel Nettle, "Size and Structure of Freely Forming Conversational Groups," *Human Nature* 6, no. 1 (1995): 67–78, https://doi.org/10.1007/BF02734136.

197 *gossip in economic terms* Frederico Boffa and Stefano Castriota, "The Economics of Gossip and Collective Reputation," *The Oxford Handbook of Gossip and Reputation* (2019): 401, https://www.doi.org/10.1093/oxford hb/9780190494087.013.21; Ronald Burt and Marc Knez, "Trust and Third-Party Gossip," in *Trust in Organizations: Frontiers of Theory and Research*, eds. Roderick Kramer and Tom Tyler (Thousand Oaks, CA: Sage,1996), 68–89; Ronald Burt, "Bandwidth and Echo: Trust, Information, and Gossip in Social Networks," in *Networks and Markets: Contributions from Economics and Sociology*, eds. A. Casella and J. E. Rauch (New York: Russell Sage Foundation, 2001), 30–74; Charlotte De Backer and Michael Gurven, "Whispering Down the Lane: The Economics of Vicarious Information Transfer," *Adaptive Behavior* 14, no. 3 (2006): 249–264, https://doi.org/10.1177/105971230601400303.

197 *social exchange theory* Peter Blau, *Exchange and Power in Social Life* (New York: Routledge, 2017).

198 *experiencing the "other."* Bettina Bergo, "Emmanuel Levinas," *Stanford Encyclopedia of Philosophy,* fall 2017, ed. Edward N. Zalta, https://plato.stanford.edu/archives/fall2017/entries/levinas/.

199 *informed our ideas of morality* Michael Tomasello, *A Natural History of Human Morality* (Cambridge, MA: Harvard University Press, 2016).

199 *guided only by the lantern* Pascal Bruckner, *The Temptation of Innocence: Living in the Age of Entitlement* (New York: Algora Publishing, 2000), 19.

200 *I have no idea* Deborah Solomon, "The Science of Second-Guessing," *New York Times,* December 12, 2004, https://www.nytimes.com/2004/12/12/magazine/the-science-of-secondguessing.html.

201 *more intense than nonsocial regrets* Mike Morrison, Kai Epstude, and Neal J. Roese, "Life Regrets and the Need to Belong," *Social Psychological and Personality Science* 3, no. 6 (2012): 675–681, https://doi.org/10.1177/1948550611435137.

201 *can't go back and do over* Amy Summerville, "The Rush of Regret: A Longitudinal Analysis of Naturalistic Regrets," *Social Psychological and Personality Science* 2, no. 6 (2011): 627–634, https://doi.org/10.1177/1948550611405072.

201 *regret is the second-most common* Susan Shimanoff, "Commonly Named Emotions in Everyday Conversations," *Perceptual and Motor Skills* 58, no. 2

(1984): 514, http://dx.doi.org/10.2466/pms.1984.58.2.514; Susan Shimanoff, "Expressing Emotions in Words: Verbal Patterns of Interaction," *Journal of Communication* 35, no. 3 (1985), http://dx.doi.org/10.1111/j.1460-2466.1985 .tb02445.x.

17: WHEN TO STOP LISTENING

202 *working on a story* Kate Murphy, "The Fake Laugh," *New York Times,* October 20, 2016, https://www.nytimes.com/2016/10/23/opinion/sunday/the-sci ence-of-the-fake-laugh.html.

203 *As George Eliot wrote* George Eliot, *Middlemarch* (New York: Harper & Brothers, 1873), 70.

204 *certain expectations in conversation* H. Paul Grice, *Studies in the Way of Words* (Cambridge, MA: Harvard University Press, 1991); H. Paul Grice, "Logic and Conversation," in *Speech Acts,* ed. P. Cole and J. L. Morgan (New York: Academic Press, 1975), 41–58.

204 *politeness and fairness in turn taking* Geoffrey Leech, *Principles of Pragmatics* (New York: Routledge, 2016); Penelope Brown and Stephen C. Levinson, *Politeness: Some Universals in Language Usage,* vol. 4 (Cambridge, UK: Cambridge University Press, 1987).

204 *calling tech support* Kate Murphy, "Why Tech Support Is (Purposely) Unbearable," *New York Times,* July 3, 2016, https://www.nytimes.com/2016/07/04/ technology/why-tech-support-is-purposely-unbearable.html.

206 *'Tis the good reader* Ralph Waldo Emerson, *The Collected Works of Ralph Waldo Emerson: Society and Solitude* (Cambridge, MA: Belknap Press, 2007), 150.

206 *You mirror each other's* Thomas Fuchs and Hanne De Jaegher, "Enactive Intersubjectivity: Participatory Sense-Making and Mutual Incorporation," *Phenomenology and the Cognitive Sciences* 8, no. 4 (2009): 465–486, https://doi.org /10.1007/s11097-009-9136-4; Alex Pentland, "Social Dynamics: Signals and Behavior," in *Proceedings of the Third International Conference on Developmental Learning (ICDL'04),* Salk Institute, San Diego, UCSD Institute for Neural Computation (2004): 263–267.

208 *We can readily accept* Robert Zajonc, "Feeling and Thinking: Preferences Need No Inferences," *American Psychologist* 35, no. 2 (1980): 151, http://dx .doi.org/10.1037/0003-066X.35.2.151.

213 *treatise* On Friendship Alexander Nehamas, *On Friendship* (New York: Basic Books, 2016).

213 *It may really be too hard* Amy Bloom, *Love Invents Us* (New York: Vintage, 1998), 205.

215 *communication privacy management theory* Sandra Petronio and Wesley T. Durham, "Communication Privacy Management Theory Significance for Interpersonal Communication," in *Engaging Theories in Interpersonal Communication: Multiple Perspectives,* ed. Dawn Braithwaite and Paul Schrodt (Thousand Oaks, CA: Sage, 2014), 335–347; Sandra Petronio and Jennifer Reierson, "Regulating the Privacy of Confidentiality: Grasping the Complexities Through Communication Privacy Management Theory," in *Uncertainty, Information Management, and Disclosure Decisions: Theories and Applications,* ed. T. A. Afifi and W. A. Afifi (New York: Routledge, 2009), 365–383; Lindsey Susan Aloia, "The Emotional, Behavioral, and Cognitive Experience of Boundary Turbulence," *Communication Studies* 69, no. 2 (2018): 180–195, https://doi.org/10.1080/10510974.2018.1426617.

216 *compared to other breakup strategies* Tara Collins and Omri Gillath, "Attachment, Breakup Strategies, and Associated Outcomes: The Effects of Security Enhancement on the Selection of Breakup Strategies," *Journal of Research in Personality* 46, no. 2 (2012): 210–222, https://doi.org/10.1016/j.jrp.2012.01.008.

CONCLUSION

222 *the* collective monologue *of preschoolers* Jean Piaget, *Language and Thought of the Child: Selected Works,* trans. Marjorie and Ruth Gabain (New York: Routledge, 2002), 1–30.

222 *greatest compliment* Henry David Thoreau, "Life Without Principle," American Studies Collection, University of Virginia, http://xroads.virginia.edu/~hyper2/thoreau/life.html.

Index

YOU'RE NOT LISTENING

BOOK CLUB GUIDE

DISCUSSION QUESTIONS

1. Has reading *You're Not Listening* changed how you listen? In what way?

2. What was the most surprising thing you learned about listening?

3. Do you think listening is a skill you are born with or one you develop?

4. Who do you have trouble listening to? Why?

5. Who do you enjoy listening to? Why?

6. Do you find some situations or environments more or less conducive to listening than others?

7. Who's the best/worst listener in your life? What makes that person a good/bad listener?

8. Do you recall a time when you didn't listen but wish you had?

9. Do you recall a time when you were glad you listened? Like maybe when someone gave you good advice or said something that tipped you off that the speaker was untrustworthy?

10. Are there certain topics of conversation that make you more or less likely to listen? What rivets your attention and what makes you shut down?

11. When do you think it's okay to stop listening to someone?

LISTENING DURING TRYING TIMES

In the months following the publication of *You're Not Listening,* a global pandemic profoundly changed how, and with whom, we socialize. No one knows how enduring these changes will be, or whether social distancing and face masks represent the new normal. But if months of home confinement have taught us anything, it's how much we long for the company of others. We have missed not only those whom we love, but also those whom we could love, if only allowed the opportunity.

The coronavirus strangely, if not surreally, underscored the message of the book. Countless readers have emailed me to say that having to maintain physical distance from other people has made them more aware of their emotional distance. They said the book has helped them listen better and become closer not only to those within their quarantine bubbles, but also to more distant friends and family whom they are now making a point of calling regularly. Moreover, the pandemic has resurrected the tradition of listening to one another's stories on front porches and front stoops. I've heard from people who said they are finally getting to know their neighbors after years of just waving to one another from their cars.

Home confinement and the narrowing of social circles have brought a reappraisal of relationships and the importance of everyday conversations. One reader emailed me to say that listening to his friends describe what they see outside their windows while stuck at home has led to some of the most intimate and illuminating conversations he has had in his life. I have also received emails from individuals who said learning to listen better, both to others and to themselves, has helped them realize which of their relationships were enriching and which were draining. It became a consideration when deciding with whom they were going to interact during the crisis.

Hearing from readers has been the best part of writing the book. Before the coronavirus made travel and large gatherings unthinkable, my favorite part of bookstore appearances and speaking engagements was always the Q&A period when one person after another stood up and talked about their difficulties, both listening and getting others to listen to them. Many said they thought they were good listeners until they read the book. "I thought I was an A+ but now realize I'm a D–," said one gentleman in a suit with pocket kerchief. The woman seated beside him, evidently his long-suffering wife, nodded in emphatic agreement.

One young woman memorably said that the book helped her land a job after two years' trying. She said she was "too chatty" during interviews, and reading the book made her realize she needed to focus more on listening to the questions interviewers were asking, and to ask questions herself, to find out what her potential employer was looking for. Others told me they were finally in stable relationships after years of round-robin dating. Parents said they were discovering who their children were, and vice versa.

Not a day goes by now that I don't receive an email from someone, somewhere, whose life has in some way been transformed by learning to listen better. I've heard from readers throughout the United States and Canada, as well as in the United Kingdom, France, Denmark, Germany, Norway, Taiwan, South Africa, New Zealand, and Australia. My atlas has gotten a workout, as I've often had to look up places where people said they were from, including the alpine village of Andermatt in Switzerland and Fergus Falls, the county seat of Otter Tail County, Minnesota.

A college student wrote that reading the book made him realize his phone was keeping him from making new friends: "The phone is a convenient place to hide when you walk into a room and don't know anyone." A human resources manager said that by asking non-judgmental questions, she was able to find common ground, and even develop affection for, a coworker whose political views were very different from her own. The leader of a team of product development engineers reached out to say their designs have been better and they have been cranking them out more quickly since he began inviting input from end users.

As a journalist, before I turn in a story, I always ask myself: "Is this helpful?" And I was determined that every chapter of *You're Not Listening* pass the same test. So when readers tell me the book has helped them, I consider it the best and highest form of praise. And readers, for their part, have returned the favor with their enthusiasm and insights, some of which became fodder for stories I've since written for *The New York Times*.

At a time when there is so much anxiety, unrest, and misinformation fulminating on- and offline, truly listening and giving due consideration to a range of views and opinions is getting harder to do. But I am optimistic. The overwhelming response to the book has shown me people want to listen. They want to understand, even if they don't agree. They want to connect and find solutions. And they are discovering that when they listen, others are more likely to listen to them. In this way, listening is a movement that can only gain momentum.

LISTENING TO LITERATURE

As *You're Not Listening* makes clear, listening is a skill that requires practice to do well. But it's also instructive to read the work of great writers and journalists who, practiced listeners themselves, can show you how it's done.

Reading well-written dialogue and descriptions of characters' mannerisms and behaviors is like listening once removed, or listening by proxy. As the story unfolds, you begin to understand complicated emotions and motivations, and perceive when there is a mismatch between thoughts, words, and deeds.

And unlike conversations in real life, you can go back and read over exactly what the characters said and did that foretold what came to pass. The following are some of my favorite books for vicarious listening:

WAR AND PEACE by Leo Tolstoy

While it recounts in fascinating detail Napoleon's ill-fated invasion of Russia in 1812, this expansive novel is virtuosic in its examination of human psychology, and of the psychology of crowds and of nations, all tipped one way or another by how well, and to whom, they listened. In the following passage, what is left unsaid is nevertheless clearly conveyed.

"Why are you going away? Why are you so upset?" Natasha asked Pierre, looking challengingly into his face.

"Because I love you!" he wanted to say, but he did not, and only blushed till the tears came, and lowered his eyes.

"Because it is better for me to come less often . . . because . . . No, simply I have business. . . ."

"Why? No, tell me!" Natasha began resolutely and suddenly stopped.

They looked at each other with dismayed and embarrassed faces. He tried to smile but could not: his smile expressed suffering, and he silently kissed her hand and went out.

THE RAZOR'S EDGE by W. Somerset Maugham

Maugham is masterful in the way he incisively yet compassionately calls out human frailty and hypocrisy. Here he describes socialites clinging with white knuckles to their younger selves and talking to fill an emptiness within.

They had the same heavily mascaraed eyelashes, the same brightly painted lips, the same rouged cheeks, the same slim figures, maintained at the cost of extreme mortification, the same clear, sharp features, the same hungry restless eyes; and you could not but be conscious that their lives were a desperate struggle to maintain their fading charms. They talked with inanity in a loud, metallic voice without a moment's pause, as though afraid that if they were silent for an instant the machine would run down and the artificial construction which was all they were would fall to pieces.

THE RIGHT STUFF by Tom Wolfe

This classic of literary journalism has colorful descriptions of the elite corps of test pilots who were the first to break the sound barrier and travel into outer space. In this excerpt, Wolfe captures astronaut Gordon Cooper's studied nonchalance when the NASA space capsule that was hurtling him around the earth seriously malfunctioned, requiring him to take over the controls to execute a safe reentry and splash down rather than rely on autopilot, which were his strict orders.

"Well . . . things are beginning to stack up a little," said Gordo. It was the same old sod-hut drawl. He sounded like the airline pilot who, having just slipped two seemingly certain mid-air collisions and finding himself in the midst of a radar fuse-out and control-tower dysarthria, says over the intercom: "Well, ladies and gentlemen, we'll be busy up here in the cockpit making our final approach into Pittsburgh, and so we want to take this opportunity to thank you for flying American and we hope we'll see you again real soon." It was second-generation Yeager, now coming from earth orbit. Cooper was having a good time. He knew everybody was in a sweat down below. But this was what he and the boys had wanted all along, wasn't it?

MIDDLEMARCH by George Eliot

A delightful nineteenth-century novel that takes you into the drawing rooms and hearts of the citizens of a small provincial town in the
English Midlands. This insightful passage demonstrates how pride
and shame can turn conversations into exercises in inauthenticity,
where both parties perceive the truth yet keep up an uncomfortable
pretense.

*Mr. Farebrother thought he could account for this speech, in striking
contrast with Lydgate's former way of talking, as the perversity which will
often spring from the moodiness of a man ill at ease in his affairs. He
answered in a tone of good-humored admission—*

*"Ah, there's enormous patience wanted with the way of the world. But
it is the easier for a man to wait patiently when he has friends who love
him, and ask for nothing better than to help him through, so far as it lies
in their power."*

*"Oh yes," said Lydgate, in a careless tone, changing his attitude and
looking at his watch. "People make much more of their difficulties than
they need to do."*

*He knew as distinctly as possible that this was an offer of help to
himself from Mr. Farebrother, and he could not bear it. So strangely
determined are we mortals, that, after having been long gratified with
the sense that he had privately done the Vicar a service, the suggestion
that the Vicar discerned his need of a service in return made him shrink
into unconquerable reticence. Besides, behind all making of such offers
what else must come?—that he should "mention his case," imply that he
wanted specific things. At that moment, suicide seemed easier.*

*Mr. Farebrother was too keen a man not to know the meaning of that
reply, and there was a certain massiveness in Lydgate's manner and tone,
corresponding with his physique, which if he repelled your advances in
the first instance seemed to put persuasive devices out of question.*

*"What time are you?" said the Vicar, devouring his wounded
feeling.*

"After eleven," said Lydgate. And they went into the drawing-room.

FAHRENHEIT 451 by Ray Bradbury

A dystopian novel that is eerie in its foreshadowing of today's digital distraction. Characters can't take their eyes off their "walls," or screens, on which play the equivalent of reality shows and jabbering social media. In the following exchange, the protagonist describes how technology is making him feel lonely, while his listener helps him dig deeper to discover the true source of his discontent.

"Nobody listens anymore. I can't talk to the walls because they're yelling at me. I can't talk to my wife; she listens to the walls. I just want someone to hear what I have to say . . ."

Faber examined Montag's thin, blue-jowled face. "How did you get shaken up? What knocked the torch out of your hands?"

"I don't know. We have everything we need to be happy, but we aren't happy. Something's missing. I looked around. The only thing I positively knew was gone was the books I'd burned in ten or twelve years. So I thought books might help."

"You're a hopeless romantic," said Faber. "It's not books you need, it's some of the things that once were in books . . . the magic is only in what books say, how they stitched the patches of the universe together into one garment for us."

KATE MURPHY is a Houston, Texas–based journalist who has written for *The New York Times, The Wall Street Journal, The Economist,* Agence France-Presse, and *Texas Monthly.*

CELADON
BOOKS

Founded in 2017, Celadon Books, a division of
Macmillan Publishers, publishes a highly curated
list of twenty to twenty-five new titles a year. The
list of both fiction and nonfiction is eclectic and
focuses on publishing commercial and literary
books and discovering and nurturing talent.